BLOND TODAY BALD TOMORROW

living life with alopecia

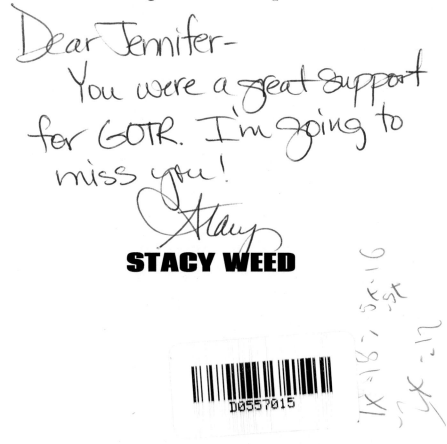

Dear Jennifer—
You were a great support for GOTR. I'm going to miss you!

Stacy

STACY WEED

Printed in the United States of America

First Printing, 2012

ISBN 978-0615721859

For additional copies contact the publisher:
blondtodaybaldtomorrow@gmail.com
www.blondtodaybaldtomorrow.com

ACKNOWLEDGEMENTS

First and foremost, I'd like to thank my daughter, Stephanie Weed, for facing a difficult and challenging situation with more poise and grace than I believed possible. Her courage and spirit are a constant source of inspiration to me. I'm grateful for the opportunity to share her story.

I could not have completed this task without the love and encouragement of my other two daughters, Lindsay and Valerie. Their enthusiastic support kept me motivated on even the darkest days. A very special thanks goes to my sister, Vicki, who was always a phone call away when I needed advice, and to my editor, Beth Bruno, who's attention to detail proved invaluable.

Lastly, my sincere gratitude goes to my husband of 28 years for supporting me wholeheartedly, asking the tough questions, steering me in the right direction, and keeping the dream alive.

One

THE GAME

After navigating our way through the Northern California high school campus, we walked into the gym and quickly made our way to the top of the bleachers. As we watched both teams warming up, the Notre Dame high school basketball team from Belmont was impressive, but didn't seem too much for our San Jose girls to handle. Warm-ups could be deceiving, however. Honestly, I didn't really care about the outcome of the game; I was just concerned about my daughter, Stephanie. Would her plan work? Was it worth the risk? I hoped and prayed that it was. There was a lot on the line. She looked pretty relaxed out on the court—most of her shots were going in. That was a good sign.

Before long, warm-ups were over and the announcer introduced the starting players. As Stephanie's name was called and she ran out in front of the crowd, I was encouraged. She seemed confident and looked great. With the formalities over and the crowd cheering, the game began. Leigh's 6'2" center, Katie Werner, got the tip on the jump ball, but unfortunately it went right to a Notre Dame player who dribbled down the court and scored. On the return, Stephanie dribbled past half court and hit Beatrice Conejero—Leigh's leading scorer—with a bounce pass just outside the key and Bea drove in for a lay-up and scored. Cheers erupted from the crowd. Both teams were off to a good start. As the quarter progressed, however, Leigh's defense faltered and their offense stalled. Time after time, Notre Dame drove down the court and in for the score. The Tigers went on a 15-2 scoring run and Leigh's chances of winning were looking grim. They needed to tighten up their defense if they were going to have any shot at coming out on top.

Once again, the guard from Notre Dame powered down the court. Stephanie had had enough. She stepped in the path of the oncoming player, set her feet and took the charge. Never one to shy away from physical contact, Stephanie didn't back down and was knocked off her feet. Tragically, when she hit the ground, her wig flopped back off the top of her head and hung there, exposing her nearly bald head.

A collective gasp could be heard throughout the gym followed by complete silence. All eyes were focused on Stephanie and the wig that was now hanging from the back of her head. For a few excruciatingly long seconds all the players on the court stood frozen in place. Moments before the gym had been full of sound, and now everything was eerily quiet. Sitting at the top of the bleachers, unable to help, my breath caught in my chest and the tears rolled down my face. Stephanie was lying on the court, her baldness tragically exposed.

Two

ALOPECIA

M aybe she's pulling it out in her sleep," the pediatrician offered.

Since the middle of sixth grade, the hairs in my left eyebrow had been disappearing. Initially it started with a tiny spot about the size of a grain of rice—barely noticeable. The spot remained fairly insignificant for awhile, but as the months went by, more and more hairs disappeared. By eighth grade, half of my eyebrow was completely gone. Every time I looked in the mirror I couldn't help staring. As much as I tried to ignore it, my eyes were always drawn to the small patch of bare skin.

I'd been penciling the spot in all along, hoping that eventually it would fill back in. Unfortunately it just kept getting worse. I could disguise the spot fairly well with a pencil, so I tried not to worry about it. However, sweat tended to make the pencil disappear. I belonged to three basketball teams and a soccer team, so I spent a lot of time sweating. Some days it seemed like I was in constant fear of my eyebrow disappearing. Small things like taking off a hooded sweatshirt or wiping sweat out of my eyes could be disastrous. Most of the time I kept a spare make-up pencil with me, but once in a while I'd get caught unprepared. Then my only option was to let my hair hang over the left side of my face and hope no one noticed the stripe above my left eye.

When we realized my eyebrow wasn't going to grow back, Mom scheduled an appointment with our family pediatrician, who suggested that I might be pulling the hairs out at night. Obviously he had never plucked his eyebrows or he'd know how hard it is to get those tiny little hairs out with tweezers, let alone with fingers. My eyebrow patch was completely bare. There was absolutely no way I could have done that in my sleep even if I wanted to. He referred us to a dermatologist.

As I walked into the dermatologist's office, I noticed the plush surroundings—marble flooring, granite counter-tops, overstuffed chairs and elegant furniture. Being more accustomed to the juvenile wallpaper and colorful toys in the pediatrician's office, I felt a little out of place surrounded by the adult décor.

"Hello. We're here for an eleven o'clock appointment," Mom informed the receptionist when we got to the counter.

"Great! What's the patient's name?"

"Stephanie Weed."

"Okay, if you could have a seat and fill out these forms, we'll be right with you." She handed Mom the obligatory clipboard. While she returned to her conversation on the phone, we sat down on the huge couches and glanced at the magazines.

I had just about decided on one when I heard, "Stephanie?"

Reluctant to leave my choice behind before I caught up on the latest celebrity gossip, I got up from the couch, magazine in hand. We followed the young assistant in stylish scrubs down the hall. Along the walls there were gold frames displaying photos of old Roman ruins. Complicated looking instruments filled the rooms we walked by. It was a hushed, serene environment—with no screaming babies.

After being directed into a room, I took a seat on the exam table and heard the familiar crunch of crinkling paper as I shifted around to get comfortable. Mom sat down in the available armchair.

"So what are you being seen for today, Stephanie?" the assistant asked.

"The hair in my left eyebrow is falling out," I answered.

After making the appropriate notations in my chart, she stepped closer toward me to get a better look.

"So you fill it in with an eye pencil?"

"Yes."

"You do a great job. I didn't notice anything until I got up close," she said as she made more notations in my chart.

"Thanks," I replied and smiled. Initially I thought it would be embarrassing having someone look so closely at my face, but strangely she made me feel at ease.

"Okay, the doctor will be in to see you in just a few minutes," she announced as she left and closed the door behind her.

For a long half hour, Mom and I sat looking at magazines and listening to the mumbled conversations coming through the walls. Finally someone stopped outside our door. After a few seconds, the doorknob turned and an older gentleman with thinning dark brown hair, glasses and a kind smile entered the room.

"Hello. You must be Stephanie," the doctor said as he extended his hand. "And you must be Mom," he guessed and shook my mom's hand also.

"I see from your chart that you have a bare spot in your left eyebrow. I can't see any problem from this distance so let's take a closer look."

He examined my eyebrow from just inches away with the aid of a mobile magnifying lamp.

"Can I get you to wipe off the eye pencil with this?" he asked and handed me an alcohol soaked gauze pad. Quickly I rubbed off the makeup, and immediately felt vulnerable with my camouflage gone, although the doctor's quiet manner did much to calm my nerves. After examining the area a second time, he turned off the light and pushed it back out of the way. I anxiously waited for his response.

"I can tell you exactly what you have. It's a skin disease called alopecia areata. It's an auto immune disease that causes the body to attack its own hair follicles and suppresses or stops hair growth and causes the hair to fall out. It's actually quite common—nearly 2% of people in this country will develop alopecia in their lifetime. That's about four to five million people."

I was stunned. There was an actual name for my condition *and* lots of other people had it—amazing. Thinking this was going to be another one of those appointments where the doctor thinks what you have is interesting but has no idea what it is or how to deal with it, I was shocked. He knew what was wrong with me! More importantly, other people had what I had. It wasn't just me. I'm not quite sure why that made me feel better—to know that other people were dealing with the same awkward problem—but it definitely did. Strange.

"Can you spell that for me?" Mom asked as she got a pen and scrap of paper out of her purse.

"A-L-O-P-E-C-I-A A-R-E-A-T-A," he replied slowly, so she could write it down. "We don't know why or how people get alopecia. We do know that it's not contagious. However, there is evidence that it is hereditary. Has anyone else in the family had hair loss like this?"

"No one that I'm aware of," Mom answered.

"Now you're probably going to go home and get on the Internet and you'll read some pretty scary things and see some disturbing pictures, but don't worry. I can tell you you're not going to lose all of your hair. People that lose all of their hair—that's called alopecia totalis—lose it within a month or two. You said you've been losing your eyebrow since sixth grade, right?"

"Yeah, that's when I first noticed a little spot."

"And you're in eighth grade now?"

"Yes."

"So that's two years and it looks like your other eyebrow isn't affected at all. Do you have any bare patches in your scalp?"

"Um, not that I've noticed," I answered a little nervously.

"Do you mind if I take a look?" he asked.

"No. That's fine," I answered, although I was apprehensive about what he was going to find. Were there patches on my head that I hadn't noticed? What I had just learned was starting to sink in. Some people lose all their hair. How do you deal with that? Having one eyebrow almost gone was bad enough. Thank goodness my long blond hair was still all there. However, the bare spot was getting harder to hide. When I would accidentally rub the makeup off, I tried not to panic. Fortunately, I didn't think anyone had noticed yet. I wasn't ready for anyone to know.

After the doctor finished examining my scalp, I looked up at him. I was afraid to hear what he had found.

"Well, I don't see any patches in your scalp. That's good news. I'm also pretty confident that we can get your eyebrow to grow back."

"Really?" Mom and I asked at the same time. I could see the look of surprise on her face and knew I looked the same way. Going to the dermatologist and finding out there was a name for my condition—that I wasn't just weird—had already made me feel better. Knowing I wasn't the only one was a relief. Now the doctor was saying he could actually get my eyebrow to grow back. Could this ordeal really be over soon? I couldn't help but wonder why we hadn't seen him months ago.

"I can inject the area that is affected with a steroid solution. The hair won't grow back immediately. It will take a while, but in a couple of weeks, you should see a small amount of hair growth."

Seriously? A couple of weeks was nothing. My nightmare might be coming to an end. That was more than I had ever hoped for.

"When the hair grows back in, is there a chance it will fall out again?" my mom asked.

Way to kill the mood, Mom, I thought.

"You never know," he answered thoughtfully. "Sometimes this happens just once and the hair grows back and never falls out again. If the hair does fall out again, we can inject that area a second time in about four weeks and hopefully keep the eyebrow full. Before I start the injections do you have any other questions?"

He wasn't rushing us at all. It was comforting to be able to talk to someone who had treated other people like me. He seemed to be genuinely concerned about what I was thinking. Mom asked lots of questions. I half listened to his answers, but half dreamed about having two full eyebrows again. You wouldn't think that eyebrows were that important—hardly even noticeable. I had never paid much attention to them except when I started losing mine. I had no idea what purpose they served, other than balancing out your face, but to me they had become quite an issue.

Before he gave me the injections, I laid back and took a deep breath hoping this was the beginning of the end of my troubles. Closing my eyes, I braced myself and waited for the treatment to be over. About a dozen times he drove the needle in just under the skin around my bare spot and injected the steroid solution. I'm not going to lie; it was painful.

To avoid infection, the doctor told me not to pencil the eyebrow back in for a couple hours, so to my horror I had to leave the office with my eyebrow wiped off. We made a return appointment on the way out. It's a good thing I could hide my eyebrow with my bangs. I kept my head down when we left so no one would notice, and soon I was back in the safety of my own home, where I didn't worry about who was looking at my face. Although the redness around the injection sites was starting to disappear, the spot was still pretty sore. Thankfully my appointment had been in the afternoon. There was no way I would go back to school without my eyebrow on.

Curiosity was eating at me and I couldn't wait to get on the computer and research this "condition" I had. My older sister, Lindsay, was on the computer when I walked in the family room.

"You need to get off the computer, Linz," I said as I crossed over to the desk where the communal computer was.

"Set the timer," Lindsay replied, annoyed. "You know the rules. I'll be off in half an hour."

I didn't budge, but stood there glaring at her. Computer time was always a battle in our house and Mom had finally established the thirty minutes on/thirty minutes off system. This was law unless you had homework to do on the web—that took priority over all. I could see Lindsay was on Facebook and wasn't doing homework and I didn't want to wait thirty minutes to Google "alopecia". Fortunately, Mom came to the rescue.

"Linz, Steph needs to get on the computer, and I need to talk to you in the kitchen," she said with such authority that Lindsay didn't argue.

Lindsay exited Facebook and headed for the kitchen. I assumed Mom was going to talk to her about what we had found out, which was great for me—I didn't want to take the time to explain everything to her right then. Although I usually loved finding out what my older sister, a high school senior, thought about everything, at that point there was only one thing on my mind. I typed A-L-O-P-E-C-I-A in the search window and hit enter.

Three

CONFRONTATION

By November, the trees around our San Jose neighborhood usually erupt in splashes of color, and this November morning was no different. Dragging my body out of bed at 6:30 am, I twisted open the blinds that were almost always shut; I loved my privacy. Instantly I was rewarded. The sky was breathtaking. The first rays of sunlight started at the horizon and stretched up as far as I could see through numerous layers of cotton candy clouds. The earth was waking up with me.

The sound of the neighbor's truck roaring to life broke the silence and the mood, so I backed away from the window and headed over to the tri-fold mirror on my dresser. The plan was that some morning soon I would wake up and see tiny hairs growing back in, but I knew better than to expect results overnight, if at all. Even so, I had to look. As I leaned in, I could tell, as the doctor had predicted, there wasn't any new hair growth in the bare spot, but I was optimistic that there would be soon. Fortunately, the injection sights weren't sore anymore.

Walking down the stairs to the kitchen, I could hear the newspaper rattle and wasn't surprised to see Dad occupying his normal spot at the kitchen table, busy working on the daily Sudoku. Mom was sipping coffee and reading the paper at the other end of the table and my younger sister Valerie was eating her cereal. Armed with information from the dermatologist and all the facts I had downloaded from the web, I started the day feeling like nothing could get me down, not even Valerie, who scowled at me from behind the cereal box.

As the doctor had forewarned, I had read some scary information on the Internet. However, there were some hopeful facts, too, and I chose to focus on those. At top of the list for me was the fact that in 90% of alopecia areata cases, the hair grows back. For 50% of patients, the hair regrows without any treatment whatsoever. That was all good. But, I had also read that the longer the period of hair loss, the less likelihood that it would grow back. I didn't dwell on that piece of information. Just knowing my condition had a name was still new and comforting to me. As I headed off to school that day my confidence and optimism were high.

At Dartmouth Middle School, the first part of the day passed uneventfully. Since the unit we were covering in P.E. was basketball, I was actually looking forward to P.E. for a change. Basketball was my sport and I loved playing against the boys and showing them up if I could. Being taller than many of them gave me a distinct advantage, but I knew that advantage would soon be gone. Mr. Lipscomb lined us up and picked two of us to be team captains. Chosen as one of the captains, I saw a rare opportunity and took it. For my first pick, to everyone's surprise, I picked Doug. Doug was an overweight kid who wasn't very coordinated and always got picked dead last. When he heard me call his name, he looked confused.

"Doug! Get over here!" I yelled.

After it registered that someone had actually chosen him and not been forced to accept him reluctantly, his face lit up. He jogged over to stand behind me, grinning from ear to ear, and even though I knew he was going to be a liability to my team I also knew that I had just made his day and that made me smile. When the teams were complete, we ran onto the court to start the game.

"Why did you have to pick Doug?" John, a stellar athlete, complained with a look of disbelief on his face.

"Just shut up and play!" I said, hoping that Doug wasn't close enough to hear the derogatory comment. John was clueless. I like to win just as much as anyone else, but sometimes you need to look at the big picture.

We played our games and managed to not get killed. Doug even scored a few points with assists from John and me. Doug didn't turn into Michael Jordan just because he got picked first, but the ego boost did make him run a little faster and try a little harder.

After stuffing my sweat soaked P.E. clothes into my locker and grabbing my lunch, I hurried out to meet Jamie. Jamie and I had met in second grade when I first moved to California, and became best friends.

Jamie was someone I could trust with my life and consequently was the only one besides my family that knew about my disappearing eyebrow.

The inner quad was full of activity that day. As was typical, the lunch line extended out the cafeteria door. I couldn't understand why anyone would wait in line for greasy fries and even greasier pizza. Enjoying the chance to be outside, everyone that wasn't in line was sitting at picnic tables or the benches surrounding the quad chowing down and catching up on the latest news. Anxious to burn off some energy, there was lots of joking, shouting, laughing and general mayhem going on. Diehard athletic types were gobbling their food down so they could get out to the basketball courts or soccer fields as soon as possible. Mr. Lipscomb, one of the gym teachers, rode by on his pink scooter, making his way to the faculty room, being careful to avoid crashing into anyone that wasn't looking. His watchful eye helped keep mischief to a minimum. Conversations were full of typical middle school drama—

"She said …"

"No!"

"Then he said…"

"No!"

"And you wouldn't believe…"

Jamie and I never paid much attention to the latest gossip—it changed by the hour anyway. We were honest with each other and had each other's back, and that was all that mattered—at least to the two of us.

We were sitting on the benches, minding our own business, having fun laughing about some of the weird things we used to do back at Guadalupe Elementary School, when Chris and a couple of his friends made an appearance. Chris was a well-built, gorgeous looking eighth grader with closely cropped brown hair and caramel eyes (not that I spent much time looking). He was the quintessential jock—always had a new girl on his arm. Because he lived around the corner from me, we hung out sometimes, but had never been more than friends. I knew better than to get tangled up with a player. Assuming he was coming over to see if I would give him a rematch on the basketball court, I quickly swallowed the wad of power bar that was in my mouth. At the end of our last duel, Chris had come up short and suffered endless ribbing from the guys. Just as much as he wanted redemption, I wanted to keep my winning record and the prospect of another game didn't scare me in the least.

To my absolute horror, when he got to within five feet of me, he pointed his finger at my left eyebrow and shouted, "Hey, did you shave off one of your eyebrows?" His voice was so loud, I was sure that anyone within fifty feet had heard. When everyone stopped what they were doing and it got real quiet I knew they all had. Suddenly all eyes were on me.

How was I supposed to answer that? Should I just grab Jamie and run? All those months of diligently hiding my secret were wiped out with a few ill chosen words bellowed by Mr. Big Man. Feelings of humiliation hung ominously close. I wasn't ready to explain my condition to any of my peers, especially when I hadn't had time to process it myself.

A funny thing happened as I heard his friends snickering in back of him. Remembering all I had found out the day before—that there were more people like me out there and probably some right at Dartmouth Middle School—I put aside my feelings of fear and shame and faced the attack head on. The tears I could have shed never fell but hardened into a glare of intense anger. How dare he embarrass me in front of all these people? He had no right.

"No, I have a skin condition called alopecia, and my eyebrow has fallen out," I spat back, answering his rude question, acting as if he was an ass to ask. My back was straight, my head held high. Daggers flashed in my eyes just daring him to take things any further.

I watched his face change from a look of superiority to a flush of embarrassment as he realized he'd hit below the belt. The rest of his crowd got real serious looking too. He dropped his head and as he backed away offered a weak, "Oh, uh, sorry."

"Yeah, get out of here, Chris!" yelled Jamie as she threw an orange peel in his direction. We both shared a good laugh when it was a direct hit between the eyes. I could always count on Jamie to keep me laughing even when the chips were down.

As quickly as the silence had settled on the rowdy crowd, it was gone in a flash. Everyone went back to their lunches and conversations as the chaos gratefully resumed. Inside, my heart was racing, but on the outside I held it together. It was going to take a lot more than that to embarrass me. Bring it on.

In a way, I guess I should've been grateful to Chris for not having to hide anymore. News traveled fast in our middle school, especially information as sensational as a missing eyebrow, and I knew by the end of the afternoon there wouldn't be one student who hadn't heard about my predicament. The great thing was, I didn't care.

Four

THE PATCH

L ater that semester, Stephanie took a six-day trip to Washington D.C. with her eighth grade class. They toured the city, experienced government and politics in action, roamed the Smithsonian, and visited numerous monuments and memorials. Sending my thirteen year old across the country on a plane with over a hundred other students made me a little apprehensive, even though I knew she was in capable hands. But she stayed in touch with glowing reports, so the week flew by.

Waiting at the airport for her flight was both frustrating and entertaining. The sheer variety of people making their way down the institutional walkways was amazing. On any given day the gamut could run from businessmen in suits with an inordinate amount of carry-on luggage, down to the dreadlocked hippie, sporting a tie-dyed Grateful Dead t-shirt on a one-way ticket to an unknown adventure. Then there were the mothers with an infant on their back, oversized diaper bag on their right shoulder, car-seat balanced precariously in front and a toddler holding their left hand—an engineering marvel that I had experienced first-hand. There was always the chance I might catch a glimpse of some famous celebrity—you just never knew who or what you might see.

After what seemed like an interminable wait, the arrival of United Airlines flight 223 from Washington Dulles was announced over the loud speaker. As I watched the parade of passengers disembarking I couldn't wait to get a glimpse of the blond that belonged to me. Person after person came through the gate, none young enough to be part of the Dartmouth group. Finally, familiar faces began to appear and not long after, Stephanie materialized out of the mass of humanity. Of course right next to her was Jamie. Looking no worse for wear, she had her comfy sweats on with her red backpack slung over her shoulder. Waving enthusiastically, I caught Steph's attention. Like any typical middle school student she rolled her eyes. To most thirteen year olds, parents were just down right embarrassing, so I didn't take it personally. However, I saw a reluctant smile creep across her face and I knew she was happy to see me.

As soon as she got within reach I grabbed her and welcomed her home with a heart-felt hug. Extremely grateful she had made it back safe and sound, I was soon to find out that my joy would be short-lived.

"I have a bare patch on my scalp," Steph whispered when I had my arms around her.

I glanced at her with a questioning look of concern, but knew that this was neither the time nor place to inquire further. I smiled and tried to convey with my eyes what I couldn't say out loud with everyone around. Yes, I was devastated to hear this ominous new development in her alopecia saga, but I was confident that she shouldn't worry. I put a reassuring arm around her shoulder.

Grateful for all the commotion and the distraction of other friends and parents as we headed down to baggage claim, the gravity of the news began to set in along with numerous questions. How did she find the spot? How big was it? Had anyone else noticed? A dozen questions flashed through my mind. They would have to wait.

At the bottom of the escalator, we were surrounded by a sea of tired students and excited parents all reuniting after spending a week apart. As per usual, the airport was a mass of chaos. People were rushing in all directions, loaded down with luggage. Packed in like groupies at a concert, we waited to grab Steph's luggage off the carousel. The cacophony all around as the eager teenagers began recounting the events of their D.C. tour was deafening. There was so much to tell— the White House, Ford's Theatre, U.S. Capitol Building, Supreme Court, Library of Congress, National Archives, Arlington National Cemetery, Washington Monument, Mount Vernon, and The Smithsonian. The list went on. What better way to keep a mass of teenagers out of trouble than to keep them busy and tired? Having crammed an amazing amount of history into a few days the kids were eager to relate their fabulous adventures. As the excitement over being home waned and exhaustion set in, the crowd was getting restless and impatient until the alarm beeped and the carousel started making its revolutions. All eyes were on the first bag to make it to the top of the ramp and come sliding down.

Thus began the endless procession of mostly black suitcases and duffle bags that looked too much like each other coming down the ramp. Most belongings were snatched up before they could make a full revolution around the track. People crammed in even closer to occupy an opportune spot to make their grab. You would think life depended on retrieving one's luggage before it made a full turn around the carousel, when in reality it was just a difference of about thirty seconds. Before long, Steph's bag came sliding down the ramp and in a flash we were out the automatic sliding doors and entering the lower floor of short term parking at San Jose International Airport. Lucky to have secured a close parking spot upon arrival, it wasn't long before the van was loaded up and we were inside.

"Steph, I'm so sorry," I sympathized as I squeezed her hand once we were in the privacy of our own car. "The patch isn't very big, is it?" I asked, being optimistic.

"I don't think so—maybe about as wide as my finger. It's right here," she said as she pointed to a spot to the right of her ear that was completely covered by her long hair. As she sighed and slumped down in the passenger seat, I could tell that the hectic pace of the trip had taken its toll.

"That's not too bad," I said, knowing that it was far too easy for me to say, but wanting to sound optimistic. "I'll call The doctor's office tomorrow and schedule an appointment as soon as possible. Since your eyebrow responded so well to the injections, I bet that spot will fill back in too."

"Hopefully, but remember he said the more patches someone had, the more likely it was for them to keep happening?"

"True, but your hair is so long, no one will ever notice a tiny spot like that. It's a good thing the patch is down on the bottom half of your head. It's really easy to hide there. When did you notice it?"

"I was sitting on the plane this morning with my elbow on the armrest and my head resting on my hand while running my fingers through my hair when I noticed this smooth spot. I was pretty sure nothing could've gotten into my hair and as I felt the area a little more I realized there was no hair—that's why it felt smooth—it was bare skin."

"So you noticed just a little while ago?" I asked, appreciating the fact that she had gone through the whole tour without this complication on her mind.

"Yeah. Jamie was sitting next to me on the plane, so I told her," Steph answered as she looked out the window.

Traffic was light so the miles sailed swiftly by as we headed down Highway 87 towards Almaden Valley. We sat in silence—both of us were lost in thought. Would this be just another little nuisance or the start of something much worse? We were both hoping and praying for the former. I didn't even want to think about the latter. At that point in time, compared to her eyebrow, this spot seemed miniscule. It was completely hidden. Knowing a positive attitude would only help matters, I kept my eyes on the road and a smile on my face. Determined that Stephanie would not see the apprehension invading my thoughts, I tried to keep my mind focused on the positive. The task wasn't too difficult—I was truly happy to have her back in San Jose, safe and sound.

Stephanie dozed off in the passenger seat.

"That long beautiful blond hair," I thought as I glanced over at her. I was curious to see what the patch looked like and was very thankful it wasn't obvious at all. I relaxed for the rest of the drive home, willing myself to keep my mind in check and not let it wander to places it shouldn't.

Stephanie stirred when she heard the garage door go up. I pulled in, being careful to not hit all the dirt bikes on the right side, but far enough over so we could wheel her suitcase on the left and not be blocked by the workbench.

"I can't wait see your pictures!" I exclaimed after we had dragged all her luggage inside.

"Mom, I'm so tired. I just want to go to bed. We hardly got any sleep all week. Can't I show you later? All I want to do is take a nap," she answered with one foot already up the stairs to her bedroom.

"If you just tell me where the camera is, I can download the pictures while you're sleeping," I offered.

Stephanie gave me the eye roll, but marched back to the table. As if it was an extreme inconvenience, she fished the digital camera out of her backpack and handed it to me. Eighth graders are so dramatic.

"There. I'm going to bed and I don't want anyone to wake me up." By the tone in her voice I could tell it would be best to let her sleep—at least I knew *I* wasn't going to wake her up.

"Enjoy sleeping in your own bed," I called cheerfully up the stairs after her. "Love you and I'm so glad you're back!"

"Me, too," she groaned and I heard her door shut.

The following Tuesday we were back in the doctor's office, waiting for his prognosis.

"I see you wore your nice jeans today," The doctor joked as he walked into the exam room. Stephanie had on a pair of stone-washed, ripped jeans, complete with holes at the knees. Everyone who was anyone had holes in their jeans. We shared a conspiratorial glance, agreeing in silence that the aging doctor didn't know teen fashion.

"So, let's see this spot," the doctor remarked as he pulled the magnifying lamp over to her head and flipped the magnifying exam glasses down over his eyes. "Just tip your head a little more that way," he instructed. I waited, holding my breath as he examined the area, hoping the news would be favorable.

"That's definitely another alopecia spot," he remarked as he swung the arm to the lamp out of the way and flipped the glasses back up on his head. "What we're going to do is inject the border around the spot to stop the immune system from attacking those hair follicles and hopefully the spot won't get any larger. After awhile the area in the middle should start to fill back in. Also, I want you to get some Rogaine—the kind for men—and rub it into the area twice a day. Don't worry about it being for males—it's just a stronger form of the medication."

The doctor made the series of injections and then commented, "I have the patch measured at a little over 1 cm right now. Keep an eye on it and periodically measure it so you can tell if it's getting any bigger. Again, don't worry. People get patches like this all the time. Come back again in four weeks and we'll see how you're doing. Are you looking forward to graduating this spring?"

"Yeah, I can't wait to get into high school," Stephanie answered.

"What high school are you going to?"

"I'll be going to Leigh."

"I know some students there," the doctor added. "Will you be playing any sports?" he inquired.

"Basketball." That subject brought a smile to her face.

"We've already talked to the varsity coach over there and he seems very interested in her," I commented as I picked up my purse and we followed the doctor out the door.

"Wow! Well, good luck with that." We shook hands and he headed down the hall to see another patient.

The doctor didn't seem alarmed at all with this new development in Stephanie's case, which helped calm my anxious nerves. Hopefully, as he predicted, this would be just a small period of inconvenience in her life. I certainly wanted to believe him. With all his medical degrees hanging on the wall, he seemed more than qualified to make an accurate prediction.

Five

THE GRAND CANYON

After discovering the bare patch on my scalp on the way home from Washington, I tried to forget about my hair. Some days that was easier than others. In March of my eighth grade year, planning a Rim to Rim hike in the Grand Canyon became a much needed distraction from the issue. Ever since fifth grade, when Mom had returned home from her first Rim to Rim adventure, I knew that someday I too would complete a Rim to Rim hike of my own. That year, Mom, along with my Aunt Margaret and another one of Aunt Margaret's friends walked from the South Rim of the Grand Canyon to the North Rim in one day. Hiking down Bright Angel Trail to the Colorado River, they crossed the river on the silver suspension bridge just above Phantom Ranch, headed along the canyon for about eight miles and up the North Kaibab Trail to the lodge at the North Rim. Covering a distance of 26 miles from lodge to lodge, which involved a 5500 ft. change in elevation by the end of the day, was tough. Despite many warnings on the park service website against attempting such a task in a single day, after that first successful trip, Mom was hooked.

The Grand Canyon National Park Service cautions:

"Over 250 people are rescued from the canyon each year. The difference between a great adventure in Grand Canyon and a trip to the hospital (or worse) is up to YOU. Under no circumstances should you attempt to hike from the rim to the river and back in one day!"

Finally, after waiting three years, I was going to get a chance to break the rules of the National Park Service. Having been impressed when I first visited the Grand Canyon at age five, I was excited for a return trip to one of the seven natural wonders of the world. Mom took training for the hike seriously and had been insistent about me preparing for it. Being able to run six miles without stopping (or complaining—the hardest part) was a requirement before she would consider taking me along. Running six miles non-stop was no longer a big deal for me, so I knew I was ready.

Our plan was to fly to Phoenix on Thursday, then drive the two hours to Tucson and spend the night with my aunt, uncle and six cousins. Friday morning we'd drive to the South Rim of the Grand Canyon. Saturday we'd complete the hike. Sunday we'd take the five-hour shuttle ride back to the South Rim followed by the five-hour drive back to Phoenix and fly back home.

Thursday May 25th we boarded our flight from San Jose to Phoenix. Getting an early start on Memorial Day weekend was great.

Having an extra day off of school was even better. Before long we were sitting in the cramped seats of the crowded plane waiting to take off from San Jose, ready for our adventure to begin. Anxious to escape the stress and worries of my growing alopecia, I knew if the Grand Canyon couldn't take my mind off my troubles, nothing could. My patch had grown from the size of a dime to the size of a quarter. Over the past couple months the spot had increased in size slowly but relentlessly. Even though I had received injections three separate times, there was no sign of any new hair growth in the middle. Although it was still easy enough to hide, the bare spot was always a nagging concern. When was it going to stop? Were the injections ever going to work?

Watching the tarmac whiz by as the plane defied gravity and lifted off, I was filled with anticipation and excitement. As the plane banked to the right we rose higher and higher. I made a pact with myself. Alopecia was staying in San Jose. Once permitted, I reclined my seat, closed my eyes and enjoyed the smooth ride to Arizona.

After a quick stop in Los Angeles, four hours later we arrived in Phoenix. Within a few feet of exiting the plane on the portable Jetway, I felt the stifling dry heat in the enclosed tunnel. With each inhale my lungs filled with the superheated air, and when I exhaled, the air seemed to stall in place. Instantaneously, every muscle in my body slowed in an attempt to adapt to the baking heat. Was I really going to hike for over ten hours in conditions like this?

"So it's like 100 degrees all year and Aunt Margaret likes that?" I asked Mom as we rolled our carry-on bags up the ramp and followed the flow of disembarking passengers back inside the air conditioned terminal to baggage claim.

"That's what she says," Mom answered. I could tell she was relieved to have the initial part of our journey over. "I don't know how Uncle Ted survives. He always hated being hot when we were younger, but he's lasted about fifteen years here now, so I guess he's adapted. I can't wait to see all of them!"

Half an hour later beads of sweat collected on my upper lip as we stood on the blacktop in the rental car lot, experiencing the full brunt of the desert heat. I found it hard to believe that anyone would choose to live in such a hot climate, much less visit for more than a week. While we waited, Mom informed me that Phoenix had the hottest climate of any major city in the United States, with temperatures over one hundred for almost five months of the year. With a population of over a million, obviously there were many hot blooded individuals that were not bothered by the oppressive heat—or maybe it was the price of real estate. Whatever the reason, I knew right then it wasn't a place I would ever choose to call home.

Much to my delight, we drove out of the airport in a maroon PT Cruiser. Mom kept complaining that she felt like she was looking through goggles to drive, but I didn't mind it. With the AC set to max we were soon on the freeway heading to Tucson.

Scenery along the two-hour drive from Phoenix to Tucson was pretty boring except for the occasional saguaro cactus and the Palo Verde trees. Adding a little green to the otherwise brown and seemingly bland landscape, the saguaro cacti, with the characteristic "L" shaped arms, looked like soldiers guarding the desert. Some were over 30 feet tall. My favorites were the crusty old weather-beaten saguaros that had several arms. Among the many scars on their trunks were holes where woodpeckers had set up camp. Towering over all the other vegetation, saguaros were definitely kings of the Sonora Desert.

The Palo Verde trees—official state tree of Arizona—caught my interest too. Spanish for "green stick" the appropriately named Palo Verde trees had no leaves. Consisting of a green trunk and green branches, the trees were green from top to bottom, but strangely without leaves. A photosynthesizing trunk was one way to handle the heat.

As the miles dragged on, my initial interest in whatever lived outside the car window waned. Due to the lack of anything else to look at, I pulled out my I-pod, plugged in my earphones and reclined the seat. Surely the miles would go by faster with music.

"Wake me up when we're getting close, okay?" I asked Mom, who was concentrating on the road.

"No problem," Mom responded and I closed my eyes.

A couple hours later we exited I-10 and found our way to my uncle's neighborhood in suburban Tucson. There were no two-story houses, which made sense. A second story bedroom would not be top on my list when it was 100+ degrees outside. Instead, the ranch style houses almost disappeared behind the various types of cacti, adobe walls, dry creek beds and orange, dirt colored boulders that covered the front yards.

As we pulled into the semicircular driveway I could see three of my cousins peering over the couch; they were looking out the front picture window. As soon as they recognized our faces, they bolted from the couch to go get the others. Thankful to be out of the car at last, we were just about to ring the bell when Aunt Margaret opened the front door and welcomed us.

The Trouard household was a beehive of activity. Six of my twenty-two cousins lived in Tucson, ranging in age from thirteen to two. With two boys and four girls there were Legos, Polly Pockets, markers, books, and all kinds of homework spread around, plus their two dogs. Once the sun went down, I was looking forward to spending some time on the trampoline out back. Even though their house was full to begin with, they were all excited to welcome two more. My uncle spent his days at the University of Arizona as a professor in biomedical engineering and my aunt worked part time as a pediatrician on the nearby Indian reservation and occasionally took night shifts in the ER. I was sure Mom had talked to Aunt Margaret about my alopecia. As they welcomed us I watched to see if Aunt Margaret stared at my eyebrow. She didn't appear to take more than a slight interest in my face and none of my cousins did either.

Incredible BBQ pork chops were served for dinner along with an amazing fruit salad and bread from their favorite bakery. After pounding down four more glasses of water—I must have drunk at least 2 gallons that day—we headed off to bed. Mom said the most important job for Thursday and Friday was to hydrate for the hike. By Thursday evening I was so sick of water I didn't want to look at another glass, but Mom kept on me and I kept drinking.

Friday morning, the kids were all off to school by the time we woke up except for two-year-old Rose. Aunt Margaret baked some incredible berry scones that we devoured for breakfast along with a couple of glasses of water. Understandably I was way more excited about the scones than I was about the water.

We packed up the car and got ready for the five-hour drive to the canyon.

"Let's make a Rose sandwich," my mom teased as we hugged the precocious two-year-old from both sides.

Rose backed away from us and with a serious face said, "That's okay. I'm not hungry. I had cereal."

It took us a second to understand, but then we busted up laughing.

After one last hug from Uncle Ted and Aunt Margaret, we were on our way. For the next two days I wasn't going to have to worry about my eyebrow at all. I'd be around Mom, but everyone else we came across, I wouldn't ever see again. So what if I drew my eyebrow in a little crooked or it looked a little too dark compared to my other one? I didn't even care if I accidentally rubbed it off. I'd waited three years to hike the canyon and I wasn't going to let something so simple as an eyebrow ruin my day.

Not even an hour down the road, we had to stop to pee and Mom loaded up on more water bottles—ugh!

"Do we really have to drink more?" I complained.

"Once we reach the North Rim tomorrow you won't have to drink any more water for the rest of the trip, but until then you're drinking," she commanded and looked at me with eyes that said, *Don't even think about messing with me.*

"But…"

"No buts. Drink!" she said. I could tell she was dead serious, so I popped the top and took another swig.

Hours and several bathroom stops later, we arrived at the South Rim of the Grand Canyon. I was in awe. The beauty was breathtaking. Almost a mile below the rim and out of sight, I knew the Colorado River was roaring and carving the canyon walls even deeper into the earth. Standing on the edge of the drop-off, the canyon wilderness was overwhelming. Floored by how incredible a collection of rocks in a giant hole could be, I stood and stared.

Looking down into the canyon from the observation deck at Bright Angel Lodge, Mom pointed out the trail we would be following the next day. She pointed across to the other side where she thought the lodge at the North Rim was. Glancing down and across it looked impossible to cross at all, much less trying to do it in a day. Even though I knew Mom had done it, it looked as though no one could cover that much ground in a day. I started to think that maybe this hike wasn't such a good idea, especially after reading the pamphlet the ranger gave us at the park entrance. Explaining the effects of heat exhaustion, heat stroke, hypothermia and hyponatremia, the guide instructed in bold letters "*under no circumstances attempt to hike from the rim to the river and back in a day*". Thinking there must be a very good reason to have the same warning plastered everywhere, I began to wonder how wise our plans were. Reassuring myself, I reasoned that if my 40+ year old mom had done it three times, then it was definitely doable for me.

As we stood staring at the canyon, a crowd started forming on the rock wall to the right of us. Sliding over to see what they were looking at, we saw two giant California Condors gliding about 100 feet down the cliff face just below us. With a wingspan of just under 9 feet, the condors were enormous but soared on the thermals with ease. Even against the tall canyon walls they looked big. One landed just underneath us, but the other kept gliding in lazy circles, entertaining the visitors above. Hesitant to leave the sight, we finally left and headed to the Bright Angle Lodge Café for our pre-hike dinner.

Following dinner, we prepared our camelbacks, backpacks and fanny packs. One bag of trail mix each, several pouches of dry Gatorade to mix with the canyon water, pretzels, Cliff bars, two apples and a change of socks for the bottom were distributed throughout our gear. With that all important job done, we watched a little TV, turned out the lights and tried to get some sleep.

Neither of us slept much that night—we were filled with too much nervous energy. Before the crack of dawn, at 5am, it was finally time for the main event. Any of the anxiety I had felt the day before was gone and I was raring to go.

We started down the Bright Angel Trail and could barely see where to step in the darkness. Because of heavy mule traffic, the trail was gouged and rough, so we had to be careful where we placed our feet. Knowing the trouble Mom had with heights, it was probably a good thing that we couldn't see the sheer drop off on the edge of the trail. With just a light jacket on, the 45 degree temperature was making my teeth chatter. Whatever we started the morning with was going to be carried all the way across, so neither of us opted for a warm bulky sweatshirt. Better to be uncomfortable for a short amount of time in the beginning than to carry extra weight later in the day when the going was tough. As the minutes went by, the sky began to lighten and the trail became easier to follow. Within the first hour, we were treated to the most beautiful sunrise I'd ever seen. At first there was the slightest hint of light coming from the east, and then as the minutes passed the light grew stronger and the colors intensified. What started as a faint glow changed to an incredible array of rose and lavender that absolutely took my breath away.

Even though it was only about fifty degrees, we had already peeled off our windbreakers. Hustling down the trail I could feel the sweat forming underneath my camelback. Skipping up and over the large rocks that littered the trail, I wanted to run but I had to slow down for Mom.

"Come on, Mom," I teased as I waited for her on one of the switchbacks. Making use of the break, I took a few pictures.

"Sorry. I really hate the downhill part. Just you wait. I bet I'll be waiting for *you* when we start climbing up the other side!" Mom declared as she carefully stepped over a large rock in the trail.

"Nah, I don't think so," I shot back as she caught up and I started hiking again.

"Are you drinking?" she asked from behind.

"Yes, Mom!" I replied and showed her the half empty bottle of Gatorade in my hand.

After hiking about four and a half miles, we hit Indian Gardens, the first of the three campgrounds we would pass. The sun was just about up and it was a comfortable seventy degrees. We made a pit stop at the outhouses—our second of the morning—then filled our bottles with Gatorade powder and water again. Most of the campers were still sleeping, so the campground was quiet. Wildlife was out in abundance. Right next to the trail we saw a couple of bighorn sheep. Passing by cautiously, I kept a close eye on the massive curled horns on either side of their heads, but they only seemed interested in munching the dry grass around them. Several deer wandered within a few feet of us and I got a great picture.

Trucking along, munching on trail mix, we finally spied the Colorado River and I knew we had almost reached the bottom.

"It's clear and green!" Mom exclaimed. "Every time I've been down here, the river has been a swirling mass of mud. That made me wonder why anyone would ever want to raft down it, although there are always one or two rafts in the river. Today, I can see the draw. It's beautiful. Wait till we walk across that bridge down there." She pointed to a silver bridge not too far in the distance. "You'll be able to see how dangerous the river is when we're down there."

Crossing the silver suspension bridge over the Colorado was a little unnerving. Through the open metal grillwork of the bridge I got a bird's eye view of the powerful currents below. When the suspension bridge started swaying slightly from side to side I quickly ran to the safety of the other side.

After crossing the river, it was a short walk to the Phantom Ranch Lodge and flushing toilets. Taking a short break we ate our lunch (Cliff bar, trail mix and an apple), changed into fresh socks, and made more Gatorade. We ducked into the Phantom Ranch Canteen, bought a cup of cold lemonade, and enjoyed the A/C for a few minutes. Next we headed out on the fairly flat eight-mile stretch across the bottom of the canyon. Mom warned me that this was the most boring part of the hike, and she was right. There was a whole lot of nothing for hours.

Just before the climb up the north side started, we took a half-mile detour down a side trail to a place called Ribbon Falls. This pit stop contained an irresistibly beautiful two-tiered waterfall. Because of the dome-like walls surrounding the falls, the echo of the water hitting bottom and bouncing off was loud enough to drown out sounds from any of the other visitors. It felt like our own personal oasis. Such a welcome change from the canyon bottom, it was nice to sit and relax in the shade and enjoy the sight and sound of the waterfalls. After a short break, we climbed approximately 40 feet to the top of the lower falls on a trail up the left side. Walking out onto the rocks where the upper falls poured down, I was completely soaked in seconds.

Reluctantly, we left Ribbon Falls and started the long hot climb up the North Kaibab Trail. After seven hours on the trail, we were about to see what we were made of. From the Colorado at the bottom to the top of the North Rim there is a change in elevation of roughly 5,500 feet—over a mile straight up. That meant that in the next three hours we would not only be hiking eight miles end to end, but battling against gravity to gain a mile in height up the steep trail—all on tired legs. Glancing up the steep canyon walls at the distant rim it looked impossible for someone to have carved out a trail on the sheer sides of the canyon. However, around every corner the trail continued winding up and up the limestone walls.

For the first half hour I was feeling tired but great. What was the big deal? What were all the warnings for? It wasn't that tough. I didn't think that I'd even be that tired when we got to the top.

All too soon, I was huffing and puffing and asking Mom if we could rest. The tables had turned and now Mom was waiting for me as I took frequent breaks. About half way up the climb, the wind started to really pick up. It was blowing at us from all directions—right, left, above and below. When you have just a three foot path between you and falling to your death, sudden powerful gusts of wind are more than terrifying. Several times we stopped and held on to the canyon wall. One gust blew Mom's clip-on sunglasses right off her face. Thinking the wind was my biggest worry, I suddenly realized how wrong I was when around a sharp corner at about waist height in the rocks, just a foot away from my shorts, a pink rattlesnake quickly wiggled by rattling its tail. Twelve inches was all there was between me and that rattler. I screamed and ran past as fast as I could, my heart nearly beating out of my chest. As long as I live I will never forget the sound of those rattles.

"Hold on. I'm going back to take a picture," Mom said once she rounded the corner.

"Are you kidding?" I screamed at her. "What are you going to do if he strikes, jump off the trail?" I thought Mom had seriously lost her mind. "You're not going back there!"

"Fine," she reluctantly agreed. "You know it's probably more afraid of us than we are of it." She slid her camera back in her fanny pack and we resumed hiking. No longer able to hang onto the mountain when the wind blew for fear of encountering another snake, I was more scared than ever and couldn't wait to be off the canyon walls.

An hour of uphill later, I didn't care about the wind anymore. I was so exhausted from nine hours of hiking I felt like I couldn't take another step. My legs felt like stumps of cement. I could feel my muscles fighting the pull of gravity with each step. The constant uphill was really taking its toll and I got to the point where I didn't think I could go on. We sat down to rest and Mom tried to get me to eat something. Eating was the last thing I wanted to do because nausea was quickly becoming an added problem. Mom insisted that it would make me feel better, but I disagreed. Somehow I didn't think throwing up all that Gatorade would make me feel better, so I refused and we started up again. My pace was so sluggish it seemed like I wasn't making any progress. Just minutes after our last rest stop, I needed to stop again.

"You have to eat something, Steph. I can't carry you out!" Mom insisted as she put some peanuts and raisins in my hand. Too tired to argue, I tossed some of the trail mix in my mouth and mechanically began to chew. My stomach started to revolt, but I managed to get it down.

"Here's some more," she thrust at me, staring like an angry drill sergeant. Convinced that she wasn't going to move unless I ate that next handful, I chucked the raisins and nuts into my mouth, certain that the second handful had no chance of staying down. I couldn't believe Mom was forcing me to eat when I felt so nauseous.

As we started up again, I was grateful that at least she wasn't harping about the water anymore. Having seen the canyon for the past nine hours I was no longer interested in scenic viewpoints or snapping pictures. I just wanted to get out of the canyon and stop hiking. By four o'clock we were getting close to the summit. We had almost reached the trees at the top, but the switchbacks were long and endless. Couldn't we just climb over the ridge instead of following this endless back and forth that was getting us nowhere? At the end of my rope, I was close to giving up.

Miraculously, about half an hour after eating I started feeling a bit better. My legs didn't seem quite so heavy, and I didn't feel like I had to rest after every few steps—I guess I needed those carbohydrates. I started to think I'd make it out of the canyon without being rescued after all.

Finally, ten and a half hours after we started and with lots of encouragement from Mom, we reached the North Kaibab trailhead. I never thought I'd be so excited to see a little brown rectangular sign.

"You did it, Steph!" Mom shouted as I responded weakly to her high five.

"Yay!" I answered with as much enthusiasm as I could. We took pictures of each other. After all the training, hydrating, dangerous encounters and physical challenges, I couldn't believe I had finally finished the hike. I was a Rim-to-Rim survivor! Now I understood why the National Park Service issued so many warnings against attempting what we had just done.

My enthusiasm was short-lived when I found out that having reached the trailhead, we still had a mile and a half walk to the lodge.

"Mom, you're kidding," I said with as much sarcasm as I could muster after she told me the tragic news. After ten hours of hiking I couldn't believe we still had another mile and a half to reach the lodge. If that wasn't bad enough, glancing in the direction we had to go, I could see that the trail was slightly uphill. My adrenaline was gone. I was completely spent.

"Isn't there some kind of bus we can take to the lodge?" I pleaded.

"No. Come on. Let's get it over with. Before you know it, we'll be sitting in those rockers on the porch and sipping hot chocolate. I know you can do it," Mom said.

Having no other choice, I trudged on with my stiff exhausted muscles and blistered feet. We looked pretty pitiful as we hobbled that last mile and a half in our sweat stained clothes and dirt covered legs. Mom was limping with curled toes because of blisters on the bottoms of them and I was waddling with my legs apart because of severely chaffed thighs. We were so tired that everything seemed funny so we spent the last few yards laughing at what a sight we were. Finally the rustic lodge with its rock pillars and green roof came into view. After checking in at the main desk, it wasn't long before we were showered and relaxing in the rocking chairs on the front porch of our rim-view cabin. My body hurt everywhere, but it was a good hurt.

Less populated than the South Rim, the North Rim was not only beautiful but peaceful. Covered with aspen and tall pine trees the forest surroundings were quite a contrast to the desert we had spent most of the day hiking in. Sitting on the porch of our cabin and drinking hot chocolate, I was completely at peace. I was looking forward to a delicious dinner in the Grand Canyon Lodge—guilt free eating that day for sure—although I was dreading the short walk to get there. After hiking for ten and a half hours over large rocks and up steep slopes, walking down stairs was particularly painful.

All-in-all, I didn't care how much I hurt or how long and exhausting the journey had been—I felt like I had accomplished something huge in my life and was satisfied. It also occurred to me as I sipped my hot chocolate while enjoying the soothing back and forth motion of the rocking chair that I hadn't thought once about my eyebrow or bare patch of scalp all day.

Six

GRADUATION

June arrived and along with it came my graduation from middle school. I thought back to seeing Lindsay four years earlier in her hot pink dress with her hair in a glamorous up-do surrounded by all her friends and thought that graduation would never come for me. It seemed like a lifetime away. My time had finally arrived.

After searching through many stores and racks of dresses, Mom and I finally found a dress at Cache in San Francisco. It was a strapless, aqua-marine sheath and fit me perfectly. Several days later we found rhinestone sandals at a discount store for $5. Everything was coming together except for my hair. Although parts of my right eyebrow had started to fall out, the injections were helping and penciling both eyebrows in was working okay. However, the small bare patch I had noticed back in February on my scalp had grown alarmingly large. It was now about 5 cm across and the injections that were working on my eyebrows had no effect on my scalp. No new bare patches had appeared, but paranoia was setting in.

Along with every other girl graduating from Dartmouth Middle School that spring, I wanted to have my hair in an up-do for the celebration, which posed a problem. Having my hair done by a stylist would mean exposing the bare spot to a complete stranger. Was I ready for that? Once the hair stylist noticed it—which was inevitable—would she question me about it in front of the other clients and would she be able to hide it? Knowing these "what ifs" could be avoided if I just did my hair myself, I was torn. Having done up-dos for my friends several times in the past, I knew I could do it, but it would be difficult working on my own hair. In the end, my desire to have my hair done won, so I made an appointment at a popular local salon.

My stomach was in knots as I walked through the door. Thoughts of leaving went through my mind as I checked in at the desk and took a seat in the waiting area. Graduation was a time of celebration and I didn't want to ruin it with my insecurities so instead of walking out, I stayed.

"Stephanie?" a short Asian stylist called. She looked cute with her edgy hair cut. I followed the stylist to her station, which fortunately was towards the back of the salon, and sat down in the hydraulic chair. My nerves finally settled down once I was seated.

"So what would you like me to do?" the stylist asked.

"I'd like my hair partly pulled up in curls with side bangs," I replied.

"Sounds great," she answered with confidence. She covered me with a black shiny drape and got to work. The place was packed. Everywhere I looked there was something going on. Blow dryers were buzzing, accented by the scent of hairspray and nail polish—I was beginning to enjoy myself. Even if my stylist did happen to say something about my hair, I was reasonably sure that no one would notice over the general commotion.

After combing out my hair, my stylist expertly pinned up the side portions and began the process of curling my hair in the back. Knowing it would take her awhile, I made myself as comfortable as possible. While she curled the back I sat perfectly still and enjoyed the sensation of someone else working on my uncooperative hair. Being pampered in a salon does wonders for a girl. There's not much else that can make you feel prettier. How ironic—I had come in that day not wanting to stay and at that moment I never wanted to leave. That feeling didn't last long, however. As the stylist worked her way around to the left side of my head I could feel my body start to tense. I knew at any minute she would uncover my bare spot.

I felt the strokes of her comb slow as she discovered it. For a few seconds, she paused and studied the area. Bracing myself for her reaction, I wasn't sure how to handle it. The moment I dreaded had arrived. Glancing to my right and left I noticed the other clients were preoccupied with their own transformations and thankfully weren't paying any attention to me. Holding my breath, I waited.

As it turned out, my fears were unnecessary. Other than the slight pause in her combing, no one would ever have known that she found something odd. Continuing on with getting my long hair curled she seemed to be unfazed by the sight of my bald spot. Breathing a sigh of relief, I sat back and enjoyed the rest of the appointment. After a little over an hour, she announced that her job was done. With a mirror in my hand she spun me around so I could see the finished product.

"So what do you think?" she asked after a few seconds.

Looking in the mirror, I was excited to see that my hair looked just like I hoped it would.

"It's great. Thanks for everything," I answered with a smile. Somehow I wanted to tell her how grateful I was that she hadn't called attention to my problem, but a simple thank you was going to have to do.

Graduation went off without a hitch. One of my good friends, Fiona, who had an incredible voice, sang the national anthem to start things off and the crowd roared with excitement. We all knew that we would see her on the big screen someday. Various awards were given— I got the female athlete and language arts awards. The English award was quite a shocker. Blah, blah, blah and finally it was over and time for the party to begin. We made the customary lap around the quad so parents could take pictures, then it was off to the graduation dance.

Mom had worked for weeks on the decorations inside the cafeteria. After walking down the red carpet to the entrance, complete with fake paparazzi and red velvet ropes, we walked into "Fabulous Las Vegas" right on our school grounds. Stretched across the stage was a giant banner with "DARTMOUTH 2006" on it. Illuminated by thousands of tiny lights, the cafeteria was transformed. Palm trees and red fabric lined the side walls. Banners for the Bellagio, Mandalay Bay, MGM, the Venetian and many high-end hotels were scattered around the room. A luau buffet waited for us outside, not that any of us girls were going to eat much in our clingy, skin-tight dresses. The band room had been transformed into a casino where we could gamble non-stop.

Jamie, Fiona, Maiko and I danced the night away. At the end of the night we would be leaving the comfort of middle school and heading our separate ways. Fiona got into Lincoln High School—a performing arts magnet school for the area. We knew she belonged there. Maiko and I were going to Leigh High School, for its good athletic programs, and Jamie was going to a private high school—Valley Christian.

Before the night was over we made plans and promises to see each other over the summer and keep our foursome strong. Long before any of us were ready, the music stopped and our life as Dartmouth students was officially over. With nostalgia we walked out of "Las Vegas" into the dark summer night and said our goodbyes. I smiled to myself as Dad sped down Blossom Hill Road away from Dartmouth for the last time. My mind replayed the events of the night as I watched each streetlight come into view and then fade away. I leaned my head against the window and nodded off.

Seven

THE BEGINNING

My heart aches for Stephanie. There are more bare patches in her scalp now, many more. For a long time she had just the one above her ear, which was fairly easy to hide. The spot had grown to roughly two inches in diameter, but there was only one. Even though the injections didn't seem to be effective, we were keeping up the protocol and hoping. A couple weeks after the start of high school, a few new patches appeared on the top of her head near the part line. For awhile she could cover the cluster of small spots by parting her hair on the other side, but as the number of patches increased that disguise was getting more and more difficult. Each time she noticed a new one I was diligent about getting her in to the dermatologist for more steroid injections. Having long hair to start out with was a blessing. It was amazing how much bare scalp she could cover with the remaining hair she had. Each morning, Steph would put her hair up in a ponytail, carefully covering all the spots. Before we got in the car and headed off to school, I would check the back and make sure no telltale patches were visible. Neither of us wanted to think of the enormity of what was happening. With more spots appearing every day the future for her hair was looking bleak. Instead of dwelling on unfortunate scenarios, however, Steph took one day at a time and did the best she could. Looking back on her childhood, I could see that all the traits that made her challenging and exasperating as a young child were going to be invaluable down the path that lay ahead.

This story was set in motion twenty-three years ago, in 1982, when I met Tracy, a graduate student in the Chemistry department at the University of California, Riverside. Having grown up in Northern California, I opted to stay in-state for college and made the 400-mile drive from San Jose to Riverside each fall to pursue a degree in chemistry. Coming from the east coast with a master's degree in chemistry from UConn, Tracy chose the Ph.D. program at Riverside because of its close proximity to Riverside International Raceway, where he could race his motorcycle while working on his degree.

"This is Tracy. He works for Dr. Rettig. Tracy, this is Stacy. She's helping out with my research," Steve announced as he introduced me to the attractive guy eating lunch with several chemistry grad students—some of whom I knew. As I stood there in my striped mini-dress and heels, my curiosity was certainly piqued. Having been a chemistry major at UC Riverside for the previous three years, I thought I had seen all the chemistry grad students at some point, but somehow I had missed this one.

"Nice to meet you," I replied as we shook hands, smiling. There was no denying the sparks that flew.

"See you tomorrow, Steve," I said as I waved goodbye to them both and continued on towards my next class.

It's strange how one short moment can change the course of your life. Within two weeks I had broken off my engagement with my long-time boyfriend and was dating Tracy, who turned out to be the teaching assistant for my Inorganic Chemistry class that semester.

We fell madly in love, and after a year and a half got married and moved to Vermont, where Tracy started his career as a Ph.D. scientist at IBM, Burlington. Fortunately I was able to find work as an organic chemist for an environmental services firm in Shelburne—just a few miles away. Moving from Silicon Valley to rural Vermont was quite a culture shock. Burlington, home to the original Ben and Jerry's Ice Cream Shop, which opened in 1978 in a renovated gas station downtown, was a small cosmopolitan New England city located on the eastern shore of Lake Champlain. Relatively speaking, shopping was almost non-existent in the areas surrounding Burlington in the mid '80s compared to the numerous mega-malls in the San Jose area. However, I found the scenic beauty in Vermont was more than worth giving up some of the shopping conveniences in California.

Much to the consternation of many of my family and friends, I—a California native who spent 23 years in a mild climate with no snow—loved living in the rural, snowy state of Vermont where barns were plentiful and cows outnumbered people. Nestled between the Adirondack Mountains of New York and the Green Mountains of

Vermont, Burlington was covered in snow nearly six months of the year. For non-skiers like myself, the winters still had their charm and the summer months were relaxing and picturesque. Thunder showers were a real treat. For Tracy, who had spent his childhood in upstate New York, life was pretty much back to the status quo—just a little more rural and significantly colder in the winter months.

Situated one mile off Route 128 on a dirt road, the first house we rented was a quaint Cape Code style, complete with vegetable garden out back and perennial garden out front in the town of Westford, population 2083. Driving through the village of Westford, it took just seconds to pass the Westford market, library, post office, school, garage, and firehouse. Literally, if you blinked, you missed it. Surrounded by open farm land, our house was in the middle of a small development consisting of about twenty houses. We were in the country, but at least we had neighbors. On the way home from work each day, it wasn't unusual to encounter a herd of cows in the road. One evening we came home to find a lost cow tied to the shed in our yard. Fortunately the farmer came and picked up his rogue livestock before nightfall. Life doesn't get much more rural than that.

Residing in the country—eleven miles to the nearest major grocery store, eighteen miles to the nearest mall and absolutely no pizza delivery—was new to both of us, but perhaps the biggest major change was heating our house with wood. Instead of simply turning the knob on a thermostat to generate heat from a hidden source somewhere in the bowels of the house, Tracy diligently kept the house warm via a fire burning in a wood stove situated in the center of the main floor. Even on brutally cold winter nights (-18 degrees F—add 49 degrees to that and water is still frozen), if he stocked the Vermont Castings wood stove chock full before going to bed, in the morning we would wake up a little chilled, but not uncomfortable. Quickly, Tracy would put fresh logs on top of the hot coals that smoldered in the stove from the night before and we'd be warm again in minutes.

Once when Tracy was gathering wood from our stash in the garage, which probably stayed at about -10 F, on the underside of one of the logs a frozen mouse was stuck to the bottom. Looking like a perfect taxidermy specimen, the mouse was frozen solid. Wherever the mouse came from, it had ended its days frozen to death just inches away from the life-sustaining warmth inside the house. Winter in Vermont was beautiful, but it could be deadly.

Heating with wood not only required diligence but also some degree of fitness. After stacking four cords of wood into neat rows in the front yard, we both could vouch for the old saying, "Wood burns twice, you know." The proof was in the sweat dripping off our faces despite the cold weather, and the stiff, sore muscles we woke up to the next day. Making good use of our gym memberships after work every day, we were both in good athletic condition, but there was no training at the gym for stacking wood.

Freezing temperatures and roaring fires had a tendency to suck all the moisture out of the air, so along with running a humidifier, we kept a cast iron kettle full of water on top of the stove that gently released a constant stream of steam into the air. Humidifying the dry air was a constant battle and we did what we could. Even with our efforts, we were in for unexpected shocks when we touched just about anything on those sub-freezing days—static electricity at work.

Yes, winters were brutal in Vermont, but sitting by a warm crackling fire with a hot cup of coffee in hand while looking out at the moon shining off the icy glaze on a pristine bed of snow in the yard did have its charm. As newlyweds with no kids yet to tie us down, we enjoyed cross-country skiing in the winter and riding Tracy's motorcycle through the windy path over Smuggler's Notch in the summer.

Because our homemade pizza never measured up and I craved more of the city life I was accustomed to, we left the country after a year and built a house in suburban Essex Junction. Essex didn't have a mall, but it did have two large grocery stores, Aubuchon's Hardware, Ben Franklins Arts and Crafts, McDonalds and pizza delivery! Tracy's commute to IBM, Burlington was just a mile. I, however, still had a ten-mile drive to work in Shelburne. The house, another Cape Cod style, with white vinyl siding, blue shutters and a gray door—a New England classic—originally had just the main floor finished, which included a kitchen, bathroom, dining room, living room and den. No bedrooms. Over the next year we spent all our spare time completing the upstairs, finishing the basement and landscaping the half-acre lot, learning many useful skills in the process. Once finished, our 1500 square foot home was the perfect spot to raise a growing family. Three years later, Lindsay, our first child, was born and I opted for early retirement.

Subzero temperatures were the norm for mid-January in Burlington, and 1992 was no exception. After having Lindsay without much difficulty, but then miscarrying six subsequent pregnancies, I couldn't believe that on January 4, 1992, my prayers were finally going to be answered. Close to four years after my initial visit to the labor and delivery ward at the Medical Center Hospital of Vermont, I was back, 39 weeks pregnant and ready to deliver our second girl, Stephanie.

After rousing my friend Carrie at 4am to watch three-year-old Lindsay, Tracy and I anxiously headed to the hospital. Fortunately there was no snow on the road—unusual for January in Vermont—so we arrived at the hospital in record time. Once it was officially determined that my water had broken, the staff didn't send me back home, even though my contractions got progressively weaker and more spaced out. Within 24 hours the baby needed to be delivered to avoid risk of infection so induction was a possibility. Walking many laps around the cardiac care unit pushing an IV pole did nothing to speed things along and the contractions ultimately stopped. Hoping to get things rolling again, the doctor started a pitocin drip. Still, I sat in the birthing room making absolutely no progress. Tracy and the doctor were down the hall watching the Washington Redskins trounce the Atlanta Falcons in the NFC football playoffs—at least someone was busy.

Although my room on the labor and delivery ward was quiet and uneventful, that couldn't be said about the rest of the floor—it was noisy and chaotic with nurses dashing from room to room trying to stay on top of things. Sitting in bed listening to women scream at the top of their lungs for what seemed like hours, I was understandably getting frustrated. Abruptly, a long session of screaming would end, followed by the compelling noise of a baby's first cry and I knew that someone's ordeal was over and the miracle of birth had happened. The lull wouldn't last for long, though. Soon I would hear screams from another room and the cycle started all over again. When was it going to be my turn?

"Don't these women believe in drugs?" I asked the nurse the next time she came in to check on me.

"Oh, they wanted drugs alright, but the anesthesiologist has been really busy and he wasn't able to get to them," she said. She quickly checked my vitals and was out the door in a flash.

Instant panic. I had been through childbirth before and knew there was absolutely no way I could make it through labor without pain killers. After all, it was the twenty-first century. Why should anybody in America have to go through the barbaric process of childbirth without them? It was beyond comprehension. I knew there were those diehards who wanted to do everything naturally and wouldn't dream of taking drugs, but they were delusional. If I hadn't been sweating at that point, I began dripping buckets after hearing the disastrous news. The possibility of a woman in labor in the hospital wanting drugs and not getting them had never crossed my mind. I knew that no amount of special breathing, hypnosis or visualization would get me through the excruciating pain I was going to feel.

"God, you can't do this to me. I need that anesthesiologist," I prayed. "I promise I won't miss another Sunday service no matter how icy, snowy or cold it is, if you just get me those drugs!"

How long did it take pitocin to work anyway? Drop by drop I watched the clear liquid fill the drip chamber and travel down the tubing that was attached directly to one of my veins with no apparent result. A couple of hours passed and I felt absolutely no change. Unable to pass the time reading because I couldn't concentrate, I was bored and getting impatient.

In an instant, that all changed. Even though I had been waiting hours for my labor to progress, I was not prepared for the breath stopping pain when the first strong contraction came over me quickly, and the process began. Silent tears were running down my cheeks the next time Tracy came back to check on me. After taking one look at me he alerted the staff and they all manned their stations ready for the main event. Football was forgotten for the day.

Hallelujah, I got my epidural, and within a couple hours Stephanie was born. She came into the world with her eyes wide open, ready for anything. Tracy and I, the proud, unsuspecting parents, had no idea what had just hit us. Lindsay, aside from the occasional tantrum, was such an easy child. She liked to follow the rules, was cautious when she should be, didn't like to get messy, was very dainty and even put herself down for naps. We would soon find out how different parenting Stephanie would be.

In the beginning of August, 1993, when Lindsay was four and Stephanie was six months old, we relocated from our Essex Junction, Vermont home to Fishkill, New York. Tracy took a job transfer with IBM and we were thrilled to be living ten minutes away from his family. Opting for a new, medium sized subdivision and wanting to avoid another move, we once again built a house with two of three floors unfinished. This house did have three completed bedrooms, however, along with living and dining rooms, kitchen and a finished loft upstairs that would serve as our family room until the basement was completed. Each house in the sprawling neighborhood sat on an acre of land. Upon completion the development would include approximately seventy single family homes, which would satisfy my need for neighbors quite nicely.

"Stephanie, get down from there!" was my constant mantra. Stephanie was an athletic toddler who climbed up everything and had no fear. Walking just wasn't exciting enough—she had to be climbing.

On a typical morning I would cook breakfast in our new, beautifully appointed kitchen while Lindsay watched Barney on the small TV on the kitchen counter. Gated to the confines of the kitchen, Stephanie was happy to motor around the tile floor and play with whatever toys she happened to find. One particular morning I was standing at the stove making scrambled eggs, when out of the corner of my eye I noticed some commotion in the corner. I turned to see Stephanie seated in her highchair, ready to eat. Knowing full well that I didn't put her in the highchair, I was puzzled. Trying to convince myself that she hadn't just climbed into her highchair—that would be impossible—I reasoned that Lindsay must have put her there, but I turned to see that Lindsay was sitting at the kitchen island, focused on the TV and nowhere near Stephanie. Even though I knew she had an insatiable desire to climb, I still couldn't understand how she managed to get into the highchair without tipping it over. This was a 1980 Fisher Price model highchair—not like its predecessors with the extremely wide bases. I was convinced that Lindsay must've somehow lifted Stephanie up and I just didn't notice. For curiosity's sake, I took Steph out and put her back down on the floor.

"Okay, get back in," I directed.

To my amazement, she climbed right over the front part of the tray, somehow carefully counterbalancing her weight so the highchair didn't tip over. Once safely over the tray she turned around and sat down, pushing her legs under the tray, and sat eagerly waiting for her breakfast. With no fear of the tile floor beneath, Steph had climbed the front of the highchair, which included a horizontal hang at one point. Her lack of fear wasn't from ignorance. Her insane drive to climb had landed her flat on the hard tile floor many times. Numerous smacks on the tile did nothing to hinder her need to climb; consequently, I was wiping blood from somewhere on her face, almost daily. Fortunately she still had all her teeth and there were no stitches at that point. For safety's sake, I tried as much as possible to lift her into the highchair myself or at least remove the tray before she started to climb, but many times she was just too quick.

A few nights after the highchair incident, Donald, Tracy's father who lived a few miles away, joined us for dinner. The previous year, Marlene—Tracy's mother, had been diagnosed with dermatomyositis and, unfortunately, had been in the hospital ever since. Donald spent his days watching out for Marlene in the hospital and several times a week would join us for dinner on his way home. One big plus in relocating to New York was that we were able to help out with Marlene and keep Pop company. He loved being around the grandkids—sharing a meal and bottle of wine with us—especially if I made dessert. Grandpa affectionately nicknamed Stephanie "little itch" because she was always on the move. After dinner he read *The Little Engine That Could* to Lindsay (Stephanie wouldn't stay on his lap); then Tracy went to give the girls a bath and put them to bed. After brushing their teeth and tucking the girls in he called for me to give the girls a kiss. I did, and then joined the two men back in the kitchen to relax and discuss the winter storm that was due to hit the next day. Not much later we heard rapid footsteps and saw Steph come running down the hallway in her Care Bear footed pajamas with a big smile on her face.

"What's Little Itch doing out here?" Grandpa asked with a smile.

"Hm, maybe I forgot to put the side up on the crib. I'll be right back. Give Grandpa and Daddy another kiss," I told her and Steph planted big slobbery kisses on both their faces. I carried her down the hall, and as I walked into her room I saw the side was up on the crib.

Ah…this is not good, I thought to myself, but I put her back in the crib anyway.

"Good night, cutie! Sleep tight. Don't let the bedbugs bite," I whispered. Knowing chances were slim to none that she would stay in the crib, I walked away nonetheless. After only a few steps down the hallway I heard giggling and little feet behind me. I turned around and saw the blond haired little rascal following me with a mischievous look on her face.

"Trace, we have a problem…" I shouted towards the kitchen. *What are we going to do now?* I wondered. Counting on the safety of her crib was how I got many tasks accomplished that would otherwise remain undone. I took my shower while she was in the crib, and loaded the dishwasher, and . . . . The crib was a necessity.

Well before turning two and way before I was ready to relinquish it, we were leaving the side of her crib down so she wouldn't have to climb over it and potentially hurt herself. Initially we put a tall gate in the doorway of her room to keep her contained. That didn't stop her for long. Soon, she figured out that if she piled up enough stuff—books, blankets, toys—by the gate she could climb up and get her leg over the top and be out of her room once again.

Landing on the wood floor in the hallway didn't bother her. A little bump was a small price to pay for freedom. Not to be outdone, we then put another gate on top of the tall gate in her doorway. A total of fifty-six vertical inches finally kept Stephanie captive in her room. Every night she fell asleep lying on the carpet, her cheek pressed against the bars of the gate. Wrapped in her crocheted orange, pink and yellow blanket with her binkie in her mouth, she was probably dreaming of her next escape.

Climbing did have its advantages—we never had to lift her onto the changing table for a diaper change. She could climb up and roll over, no problem. However, her lack of fear made the job of parenting extremely nerve-wracking.

Shortly after Stephanie mastered the crib escape, Tracy and I decided it was time to move the double bed we had stored in the attic down to her room. She seemed so small to be sleeping in a big double bed—she was barely longer than the pillow—but at that point, the crib posed more of a danger than the bed did. Once the bed was in place, we started to dismantle the crib. Taking off all the crib toys that we'd heard her banging on and playing with at night, I got a little nostalgic thinking the baby faze was leaving our family for good, or at least until grandkids appeared, and that was decades away. We lifted the crib mattress out and before we knew what was going on, Steph scaled the tall end of the crib and dove in, landing face first on the spring frame, not noticing that we'd removed the mattress. Thankfully, she survived without stitches.

As Stephanie grew so did her interests and climbing was no longer the only thing she lived for. By the age of three she spent hours drawing pictures of people, flowers, dogs, etc. The shelves in her room were loaded with piles of her artwork, whether it was coloring pages of her favorite Disney princesses or her own creations. Family portraits were the subjects in many of her drawings. Curiously she always drew herself larger than her older sister Lindsay and liked to pretend that she was six and Lindsay was only three—always a dreamer.

With time we were able to remove the gates from her door and allow her to wander around the house on her own. Each night Tracy and I would relax in the finished basement to watch TV after putting the kids to bed. Steph never needed as much sleep as Lindsay, so we allowed her to draw/color in her room until she got tired as long as she was quiet and didn't disturb her sister. One particular night while Tracy and I were lounging on the couch downstairs, we heard the sound of footsteps running down the hall upstairs into the kitchen and back down the hall again. Certain it was Stephanie, we turned the volume down on the television. After listening for a minute or two, we heard nothing further from the main floor, so we readjusted the volume and continued watching our favorite show. Just before the end of the episode, we heard footsteps again. Once more, we muted the TV, but heard nothing. For the rest of the evening, things stayed quiet upstairs.

Just after eleven I headed upstairs to check on the kids and go to bed myself. One of the favorite parts of my day was looking at the girls asleep in their beds. Perfectly relaxed after a day full of adventure they looked so angelic, lying peacefully on their pillows.

As I entered Steph's room I was met with a peculiar sight. All around the room, at a height of about three feet, page after page of her artwork was hanging; each picture was held in place by a nail. Nails! Stephanie had decorated her own room. My mind flashed back to the footsteps we had heard earlier in the evening. Racing down to the kitchen, I pulled open Tracy's tool drawer and there sat the hammer on top with a bottle of finishing nails right next to it. *At least she put everything away*, I thought. How Stephanie managed to hold the pictures up and hammer in the nails was beyond me. Top on my list for the next day was going to be installing a child lock on the tool drawer, but I couldn't help admiring the ingenuity of our three year old.

When our mischief maker turned four, life got a little easier around the Weed household. Lindsay was in school all day, which gave Stephanie and me hours together. Learning quickly that there were never any negative repercussions for making things out of 'treasures' she found in the trash, Steph regularly assembled masterpieces out of sewing scraps, recycled paper and used containers. Her drive to climb had been replaced by a desire to create.

Before long, Steph was off to school, and I was expecting our third and final girl. Brinckerhoff Elementary school survived the addition of Stephanie to its ranks and by spring, Valerie was born. Within a year Tracy was recruited by a start-up software company in Santa Clara, California. With most of my family still residing in the San Francisco Bay Area, I was thrilled at the possibility of moving back home. After several negotiations and successful house hunting trips, Tracy decided to take the job in Silicon Valley and in August of 1999 we moved back to California where our life together had begun. The girls transitioned well and there were no major problems until alopecia entered our life five years later.

Eight

SWIMMING

Stephanie's high school years started out with a bang. Making it as a starter on the girls varsity basketball team gave her self-esteem a huge boost. She loved the exciting social aspects of high school life. However, not all developments that fall were good. Towards the end of September, Stephanie began to notice several more bare spots on her scalp. Unfortunately they were on top of her head and followed her part line. Even though the appearance of more spots was not a good sign, she tried not to dwell on that. She did her best to cover the bare areas by wearing her hair in a ponytail, pulling the existing hair over any bare spots and hoping it all stayed in place.

A couple months into freshman year came the swim unit of P.E. Swimming during school wasn't any girl's idea of fun—redoing hair and makeup was a pain in the neck—but for Steph it was going to be challenging. After getting her hair perfectly positioned in the morning—

not an easy task—she was going to have to jump in the water and swim, hoping that her hair would stay in place. The rushing water was sure to uncover some of the spots she had painstakingly hidden. She would then have to get dressed and to her next class within ten minutes. Each morning it took her ten minutes just to get all the patches covered. I had no idea how she was going to manage it with so little time.

The day swimming started I was a nervous wreck. Steph was excited to wear her bikini and work on her tan during school, but I was worried sick about her hair. All day I imagined horror after horror, with me at home unable to help. Most days time flew by and before I knew it I was racing back to Leigh along with hundreds of other parents to pick up their kids, but that day the hands on the clock seemed frozen in place. None of my daily chores were enough of a distraction to keep my mind from obsessing and my stomach filled with acid.

Finally it was two o'clock and I was back in the parking lot, waiting for Stephanie to appear. With the windows down, I couldn't help but enjoy the gorgeous fall day. Warm against my skin, the afternoon sun felt good. Blowing in from the coast, a nice breeze helped settle my nerves a bit, but I was still on edge. While halfheartedly perusing the latest edition of *Better Homes and Gardens*, I heard the final bell ring. Students began pouring out of various hallways, chatting away, excited to be out of their classrooms. Goths, skaters, jocks, cheerleaders—no matter who they were they all had one thing in common; school was out for the day. Searching the sea of students for a familiar blond head, I strained to locate Stephanie. Hundreds of students passed by and I hadn't caught sight of her. Finally there she was. Walking out with Maiko, from a distance it looked like she was smiling. Her hair looked like it was up in a bun, but I couldn't see any more than that from the car. I watched her wave to Maiko as they parted ways at the curb and then she headed through the rows of parked cars. Her shoulders were back and her head was up—both good signs—and yes, she was smiling. I was relieved.

Seconds later she was in the car. As inconspicuously as possible I glanced at her wet hair, looking for bare spots and thankfully saw none. Her hair looked perfectly normal—the patches were completely hidden. I started the car and rolled up the windows ready to exit the parking lot.

"Steph, your hair looks great! How did you get all the places covered up after P.E.? You did a great job. I can't see anything!" I was feeling a little foolish about all the worrying I did that day. With her messy-bun hair style she looked just like half the female population at Leigh.

"Abby is in my class and she helped me cover the spots when we were getting ready in the locker room. Can we stop by Starbucks on the way home?" she asked with a hopeful smile.

"Okay, sure," I responded and put the car in reverse. With effort I held back tears and kept my emotions in check. My anxiety was gone. Stephanie had been bold enough to ask for help. Abby was a friend from Dartmouth, but had not been one of her really close friends. The fact that Abby didn't know about Stephanie's scalp condition, but Steph felt comfortable enough to ask her for help, was a big step for Steph and a comfort to me. I was proud of her for trusting someone enough to ask for help. I didn't try to convince myself that her battle with alopecia was close to being over, but I knew she had cleared an important hurdle that day.

Nine

HATS

D oes this really look okay?" Stephanie asked as she flipped down the sunshade on the passenger side of the car and leaned back to get a better view in the mirror. She adjusted the stone-washed chocolate brown cap we had found at a trendy store in the mall, sliding the brim slightly to the side. We were stopped in the passenger loading zone at Leigh High School. Cars were pouring into the parking lot and forming a long line of traffic out on Leigh Ave. Rushing to get their kids out of the car and hopefully to class on time, everyone under a time crunch.

"You look very stylish, and I'm not just saying that because I'm your mom!" I answered with a wry smile. It truly was a good style for her—the long straight blond hair looked nice topped by the weathered brown hat worn slightly askew.

"Yeah, right, Mom," she replied as she rolled her eyes and gathered up her backpack, lunch and gym bag and exited the car in her short jean skirt with all her gear.

"Have a good day!" I called out before she closed the door.

"You, too. Love you," she replied as she shut the door. She smiled and hurried away in a wave of students. Headed to her health class, which was on the opposite side of the sprawling campus, I hoped she'd make it on time.

As I drove home I prayed that the hat would stay on her head and not get knocked off by some joker or an unpredictable gust of wind.

When it got to the point that Stephanie couldn't hide her growing number of bare patches by putting her hair in a ponytail, I contacted the school administration and asked permission for her to wear a hat to class. Wearing a hat was against dress code, but I was reasonably certain they would make an exception. As I had hoped, the staff was very understanding. Several of her teachers emailed, letting me know they were willing to do whatever they could to help us out. I knew Stephanie felt both relieved and vulnerable with this new development. It was nice knowing the staff was in the loop, but there was no guarantee that they would keep her secret safe. She knew that none of the teachers would question her about wearing a hat, but what would the other kids think? Some of her guy friends loved to kid around. She could picture them trying to grab her hat as a joke. P.E. was constantly an issue. Having always been competitive, she knew it would be hard to hold back just to keep her cap on. Playing anything involving a ball was dangerous—the ball could catch the rim of the hat and knock it off. Wind was a factor every Wednesday when they ran their timed mile on the track. Even doing sit-ups was a problem.

In general Stephanie was coping well with her increasing hair loss. Most days she powered through as if nothing was wrong, but there were times when the tears flowed.

"It's so not fair," Steph complained between sobs, her face full of pain. "Most girls my age are worrying about what color highlights they're going to get. Every morning I wake up and have to deal with how much more of my hair is gone. I can't take it any more!" She buried her head in her bed pillows.

Wishing there was more I could do than simply hug her and offer my sympathy, I too felt helpless. Stephanie was absolutely right. As a freshman in high school her biggest worry should have been how her clothes fit or if the cute guy in Spanish class knew she existed--not when and if she would become totally bald. I could only imagine how devastating it must be to wake up each morning and see more hair on her pillow. Fortunately those cracks in her normally positive disposition rarely occurred, but when they did there was not much I could say.

Although playing sports was the main source of difficulty in dealing with alopecia, it also gave Stephanie the greatest joy. One of her biggest goals in life was to play basketball in college, and it looked like she was well on her way. She got along great with the older girls on the team—they treated her like an equal and appreciated her skills on the court. She couldn't wear a hat during practice or games, so she hid the bald spots as best she could with her hair pulled into a ponytail. A thick terry headband covered a lot, too. With every day that passed, her hair was getting thinner and thinner on top and the bald spots were becoming more obvious. Her love for basketball far outweighed any fear she felt about exposing her head, so she kept on playing. Once a basketball was in her hands, all thoughts of alopecia disappeared.

Ten

ACUPUNCTURE

I was becoming desperate to save what was left of my hair and ready to try anything. Mom found a local acupuncturist who accepted our health insurance and boasted great results with hair re-growth. The field of acupuncture was new to us, so the Chinese doctor patiently explained the theory of acupuncture at my first visit. I was amazed to hear that it originated in China more than 2000 years ago, and was the oldest and most commonly used medicine in the world. She explained that acupuncture treated the overall well-being of the patient rather than just symptoms. I learned about "chi," which is a person's life force. Acupuncture points lie along lines in the body where chi flows. According to the Chinese, health depends on a person's chi being able to move in a smooth and balanced way through those imaginary lines under the skin. When a person's chi becomes unbalanced, health problems occur. Acupuncturists stick long skinny needles under the skin in specific areas to get the chi flowing correctly. Once the chi is back in balance, the body's natural healing mechanisms can take over.

When Mom first suggested going to an acupuncturist, I thought the whole idea was crazy, but after hearing the doctor explain the theory behind it, I was ready to give it a try. Besides, needles didn't bother me and I had nothing to lose.

Three times a week I went for treatment. After the doctor inserted dozens of needles under my skin, she would cover me with a warm blanket, put on a soothing CD, turn out the lights and leave the room. Within minutes I was asleep—completely relaxed. Occasionally if I shifted positions, the blanket brushed up against the needles in my legs or arms, which hurt and woke me up, but for the most part acupuncture was a nice break from my hectic schedule.

"Steph, Coach Ernie called me today. While we were talking, I told him about your alopecia," Mom told me when she picked me up after school.

"What?!" I screamed back. "Why would you do that? There's no reason he has to know." I was fuming. With my arms folded tightly across my chest I stared out the window as we sat across from each other in the front seat of the car. *Way to ruin an otherwise pretty stellar day, Mom,* I thought. As if my life wasn't complicated enough. What was she thinking? It was bad enough that the teachers had to know, but my coaches didn't. I had planned on asking if we could stop by Starbucks on the way home, but I didn't want to go ANYWHERE with her after hearing that news.

"Steph, with all the acupuncture and dermatology appointments, I wanted them to know there was a good reason for you being late to practice. Ernie was very supportive and asked if he could do anything to help," Mom explained.

"Yeah, and I'm sure he's going to tell Gary too and when I go to practice tonight they're both going to be staring at my head. Thanks a lot, Mom! I can't believe you told them without asking me first." I was pissed. This was my problem and I wanted to deal with it my way. So what if I was late to practice a few times and didn't ride on the team bus to a couple of games? She had no right to tell them.

"I didn't think you would mind and since Ernie happened to call me I thought I would explain why you had been late to practice so much. Since all your teachers knew, I thought it wouldn't be a big deal if the coaches knew too. But I really am sorry and I promise I'll ask you before I tell anyone else. Promise! You're right that it should be up to you who finds out and when. Can you forgive me?" she pleaded.

I could tell she genuinely felt bad, but no way was I going to cut her any slack. "I don't know," I answered out of closed lips. Ugh! I knew when I walked into practice that night that Ernie and Gary were going to stare at me. Of course they would try to make it look like they weren't staring, but I would know.

As soon as we pulled into the garage, I got out of the car, stomped up to my room and slammed the door. Putting as much distance as physically possible between Mom and me, I lay on my bed and stared at the ceiling. I was in the big bedroom upstairs now, since Lindsay had left for college. Two months ago, right before all my bald spots started appearing, we had moved Lindsay down to the dorms in Cal Poly, San Luis Obispo. Sure, I was jealous—she had started a new phase in her life: no parents, no curfews, making her own schedule and cute guys everywhere. To top it off, the campus was about ten minutes from Avila Beach and students got to ride the city bus there for free. The day we got back from moving Lindsay into the dorms I bought two gallons of paint and started redecorating her old room. Mom wouldn't buy me a new bed set, so I was stuck with the red and pink Hawaiian floral comforter that was Lindsay's originally, so I worked around it. To mix things up, I painted the top half of the room a lime green color and the bottom half tan. The red and pink comforter really popped against the bright green. A couple of lime throw pillows, along with my hot pink shag blanket and pillow made the bed look pretty good. I found a tall jeweled candle holder for the desk and a pink crystal chandelier to hang in the middle of the room to pull the whole look together. At that moment I would've given anything to be down in SLO with Lindsay instead of stuck in my new room with Mom downstairs.

Lying there on my bed, I wondered if my life could get any worse. Within minutes I heard a soft tap on the door.

"What is it?" I barked.

"It's Mom," she said cautiously through the door. "We need to do your treatment if we're going to get it done before you go to practice."

Even though I could tell from the tone in her voice that she definitely felt bad, I was still mad. She should feel bad. Maybe that would keep her from blabbing to anyone else. She just didn't understand the looks I got from people that knew about the alopecia.

They tried not to stare, but they couldn't help themselves and invariably did stare.

"Fine," I sighed. "I'll be down in a minute."

Nothing happened after the first couple weeks of acupuncture, so the doctor added two more treatments. One involved Mom tapping the bare patches on my scalp with a tool shaped like a very small hammer with a group of seven short needles on the head—called a seven star needle. The idea was that pricking my skin hundreds of times with the hammer would make the blood flow, which would also make my chi flow better. There were hundreds of red dots on my scalp after the treatment, so we knew blood was flowing. That process took about twenty minutes. After that was over we did moxibustion. For this treatment, moxa—the mugwort herb—was used to warm my scalp. Mom held a lit moxa stick, which looked like a large cigar, with the smoldering end about 1/2" away from the areas where my hair was gone. The heat along with chemicals in the moxa stick were also supposed to increase the flow of chi. To prevent my head from burning and to enhance the effect of the moxa, Mom held a thin slice of fresh ginger in place between my scalp and the moxa stick, letting the warmth from the burning stick penetrate my scalp for as long as I could stand it. When it got too hot she would move onto another area.

Still miffed at Mom, I didn't say much when I got downstairs ready to begin. Everything was set out on the kitchen table and I plopped down in the black kitchen chair without making eye contact. Sitting with a rigid posture, I made it clear that I wasn't in the mood to talk and took off my cap. I just wanted to get the treatment over with. Always good at reading my moods, Mom didn't say anything and began wiping the bare patches on my scalp with alcohol. The coolness of the alcohol felt good against my scalp and started to make my anger fade. My determination to hold a grudge faltered and I closed my eyes and began to surrender. Before long, the needle pricks were over.

"Okay, Steph. Let's go out back and try this cigar thing," Mom said once she got my skin wiped off and the supplies put away.

"Can I watch?" Valerie asked eagerly.

I shot her a glare that could kill.

"No," Mom answered. "You stay in here and watch TV. Stephanie doesn't need an audience for this. We'll be right outside. If there's an emergency, you can come get me; otherwise you stay inside. If anyone calls, take a message please."

Wow, Mom was actually considering my feelings. That was nice for a change. Realizing that maybe I was being a little unfair, I still was not willing to admit it and kept my cold shoulder directed her way.

We walked through the side bathroom door out onto the patio surrounding our pool. It was strange being out back by the pool in November with the leaves turning. In the summer I spent hours in the backyard, floating in the pool, tanning, swinging in the hammock, listening to the radio, gazing at the palm trees next door, but once the cooler weather arrived it was like the backyard didn't exist. Nonetheless, there we were surrounded by the telltale signs of fall.

I sat on the ground and leaned back against Mom's legs while she sat in one of the lounge chairs. Neither of us had done the moxa stick treatment before, so we weren't really sure what to expect. Mom had a little trouble getting the stick lit, but finally after both of us blew on it till we were about to pass out, it stayed lit. You could feel the heat from the glowing end.

"Are you ready?" Mom asked with a doubtful smile as she looked at the burning stick and then my head.

"Sure. Go for it," I answered as I turned around and leaned back against her chair. Immediately I felt the cold wet piece of ginger against my scalp.

"Can you feel that?" Mom asked after a few seconds.

"What..." I questioned, but as soon as the word was out of my mouth I felt a warming sensation against my scalp. For a while it felt soothing—the warm ginger soaking into my skin—but then it began to get too hot, so she moved to a new area. We were so intent on what we were doing that at first neither of us noticed the strange smell.

"Sniff, sniff," I heard Mom inhale. Then again, "Sniff, sniff," coming from behind me. Then I heard her laugh.

"What is it, Mom?" I asked turning around, and then I inhaled too.

"You know what this smells like, don't you?" Mom asked with a raised eyebrow.

At first I couldn't place the smell. It was vaguely familiar, but I couldn't figure it out. The neurons fired away in my memory and finally I remembered a group of kids lying in the grass at the park by our house smoking a joint.

"Are you thinking what I'm thinking?" I asked, not wanting to admit to anything.

"It smells just like pot!" she shouted, astonished. "Did the doctor tell us what was in this stick?"

I shrugged because I honestly couldn't remember. We had learned a lot in the past two weeks about acupuncture and I couldn't keep it all straight. Obviously, Mom couldn't either.

"I can see it now. The neighbors are going to call the cops because it smells like a big weed party is going on in our backyard. This thing reeks!" she shouted as she held it as far away as possible, laughing.

Surrendering to and joining in with her laughter, I added, "Yeah, that's just what we both need right now is the cops showing up while you hold a burning stick to my bald head."

As we laughed together, silently we acknowledged a truce. As always, I just couldn't stay mad at Mom for any length of time, no matter how hard I tried or how determined I was. We continued with the treatment for the next half hour. Thankfully we never heard a siren.

Eleven

THE NEW LOOK

"Mom, I think I'm ready to get a wig," Stephanie announced when she came down for breakfast. She looked rather somber.

In the midst of the typical morning chaos, I stopped. Days had gone by with more and more hair disappearing from the top of Stephanie's head. New patches appeared daily, even though we were consistent with the acupuncture and cortisone shots. It seemed we were powerless to stop the loss. Daily I wished it was my hair instead of hers. I was 45 years old, happily married with three beautiful girls—I didn't need hair. If someone had to lose their hair, why couldn't it be mine? As every parent knows, it's hard to see your child suffer. I prayed for a miracle.

As with many other times in my life, my plan wasn't God's plan and Stephanie's hair loss continued. Wearing a hat still disguised her problem, but I knew it wasn't going to for much longer. I was certain she would need a wig soon, but didn't want to push her into something

మmother౸౸౸   82

she wasn't ready for. At that point, if her hat had come off...well, I didn't even want to think about it.

I dropped the turkey sandwich I was preparing, walked over and wrapped my arms around her. "Are you sure?" I asked, knowing it was the right time, but also knowing this was a monumental decision.

"Yep," she answered as she pushed away and busied herself getting a bowl of Special K to eat. I could tell that getting all mushy was the last thing she needed, so I let her be and continued with my normal routine, stuffing lunch bags.

"Just make the appointment so I don't have to miss basketball," she said with a mouthful of milk and cereal as she read the comics.

"Would you rather miss school?" I asked. I had no idea how booked up the salons would be.

"No," she replied. "Just try to make it after school but before practice."

Hoping I could find just such an appointment, I scurried through the rest of the morning, impatient to begin my search in the yellow pages once I got the girls to school.

Driving home from dropping the girls off, it seemed there was a conspiracy against me—all the lights were red and I had to wait for pedestrians in three different crosswalks. The traffic light cycles were seriously messed up. Anxious to start my research, I dropped my purse on the kitchen table as soon as I walked in the door and grabbed the phone book out of the desk. One ad in particular caught my eye—The New Look Institute.

Hoping I had made the right choice, I dialed their number and was greeted by a friendly female voice on the other end.

"The New Look Institute, how can I help you?"

"My fourteen year old daughter has alopecia and needs to be fitted for a wig," I replied.

"No problem. Can you hold for just a moment?" she asked.

"Sure."

While on hold I was plagued with thoughts of uncertainty. I had no experience with wigs. I wasn't sure what to ask or what to look for. I was completely out of my element, but was determined to find exactly what Stephanie needed.

"Hello, this is Sima. I understand your daughter has alopecia and needs to be fitted for a wig."

"Yes, she's been wearing a hat, but her hair loss has worsened to the point where that's not going to work much longer, so I'd like to get her in as soon as possible."

"Sure. Let me ask you, does she know you're making an appointment for her?" Sima inquired.

"Yes," I assured her. "She asked me to make the appointment this morning." I realized that my instincts had been correct to wait for Stephanie to ask about making an appointment, and I felt a little relieved.

"Can you come in at 5 o'clock tonight?"

After checking Steph's basketball schedule and noting that practice didn't start until seven, I took the available appointment and hung up the phone.

"That went well," I uttered to our fat black cat, Tibby, and walked upstairs to gather up the laundry.

Neither of us said much that evening on the way to Stephanie's appointment. I was grateful that I was able to drop Valerie off at my sister's house—just a mile from ours—so all my attention could be focused on what Sima had to say. Eventually we found the suite of office buildings and after parking, walked up the stairs to the office. We opened the door to a brightly lit, tastefully decorated lobby.

"Can I help you?" the young receptionist asked from behind the marble counter surrounding her desk.

"Yes," I answered quickly so Stephanie didn't have to talk. "We have a five o'clock appointment."

She checked her appointment book and smiled directly at Stephanie. "You must be Stephanie. Come right this way."

She led us to a private waiting area and motioned for us to sit on the black leather couches. After we assured her that we didn't need anything to drink, she asked us to relax and enjoy the magazines.

"Sima will be with you shortly," she said and left, shutting the door behind her.

We were grateful for the privacy. Stephanie perked up a bit when she saw several of her favorite magazines resting on the speckled granite coffee table in front of us and wasted no time diving into the latest issue of *People*. Taking into account what I had seen of the office up to that point, I was feeling pretty confident that I had made a good choice. After a few minutes a professionally dressed, middle-aged women with short chestnut hair opened the door and introduced herself.

"Hi, I'm Sima. It's very nice to meet you," she said with a slight European accent that I couldn't quite place.

"I'm Stacy, and this is my daughter Stephanie," I responded, while shaking her extended hand.

"Great, Stephanie. It's nice to meet you. Let's move over across the hall to my office. There's a lot more room in there. Are you busy getting ready for the holidays?"

"I'm starting. My oldest daughter is coming home from college for Thanksgiving next Wednesday, so we're all looking forward to that," I replied, enjoying her friendly manner.

As we walked into the spacious office, with a large round black table in the middle, the first thing that caught my eye was a tower of what looked like hundreds of sample hair colors on the back counter. Looking at what I presumed were all the possible hair color choices for Stephanie lifted my spirits a bit.

"Have a seat, please." She motioned to the chairs on the other side of the table and sat down herself. "Stephanie, you're a very beautiful girl and you have gorgeous hair."

"Thanks," Stephanie said tentatively. She seemed slightly embarrassed but was starting to relax.

"I understand you have alopecia. When did you first notice any hair loss?" Sima asked.

Between the two of us, we gave her a brief synopsis of the past two years. She was a sympathetic listener. I could tell she genuinely felt compassion for Stephanie and the hardships Stephanie had been through.

"Well, let's see what we can do about this," she said with an air of confidence as she rose from her chair. "Come sit over here." She motioned for Stephanie to sit in a swivel chair that faced a large mirror on the side of the room. "May I take your hat off?" she asked hesitantly, knowing that it was going to be tough emotionally for Stephanie to expose her head to a stranger.

Slowly, Stephanie removed her cap. With the cap on, Steph looked just like any other teenage girl with long straight blond hair—you wouldn't know she had a care in the world, but once the cap was off her secret was there for all to see. The fluorescent lighting unkindly reflected off the bare patches in her scalp. At that point she had lost close to a third of her hair on top. I watched this scene unfold with a heavy heart. Again, I wished that I could take her place in that chair, but knew that wasn't going to happen. Feeling the tears come dangerously close to the surface, I pulled myself together. Stephanie didn't need a distraught mom; she needed someone strong and reassuring to help her through this process. So I took a deep breath and told myself I couldn't let my emotions get the best of me.

"Stephanie, I'm so sorry," Sima said when she saw the extent of the hair loss. "This year must've been difficult, starting high school and having to deal with this, but I do know that I can help you. We have many different wigs that all look very natural. Partial hair pieces can be glued in place or you can opt for a full wig."

"We wouldn't be interested in a partial hairpiece," I interjected quickly, "and probably nothing that is glued on. She plays basketball over at Leigh High School and it gets pretty rough on the court. I would be afraid her skin might come off along with the hair if it is glued." I shuddered at the thought of that. "What are your feelings about human hair wigs versus acrylic?" I asked, having pretty much decided before even stepping in the office that human hair had to look more natural and would be better overall.

"That's a very good question," she answered. "Like with most things, there are advantages and disadvantages to both. Human hair looks more natural, but it is much heavier than acrylic. A big advantage for human hair is you can use styling tools on it—curling irons, straighteners, blow-dryers—so you have the option of many different looks with human hair. Acrylic wigs can't take any heat or they will frizz and melt, so you can't change the style; however, after you wash them the style is permanent, so you just let them air dry and they bounce right back to their original shape. Human hair wigs need to be styled each time they are washed and they need to be washed more often. Once a week is what we recommend for human hair, but the acrylics can go about a month between washings. Human hair has a more natural feel, and it also has more breathability so your scalp doesn't get as hot. Also, the longevity of human hair wigs is greater than synthetic, but they do cost quite a bit more."

"We're definitely interested in human hair," I volunteered. The closer we could get to Stephanie's original hair, the better, even if it did cost more.

"Let me ask you, Stephanie, would you be willing to trim this?" Sima asked as she held the meager amount of what was left of Stephanie's hair in her hands. Immediately a fearful look swept across Stephanie's face.

"You don't have too," Sima assured her when she saw the apprehension. "If you did trim it short, a wig would fit much better, but I assure you we can get a good fit without trimming anything." With that pronouncement, Stephanie relaxed again. Losing her hair piece by piece over the past few months had been traumatic enough. To lose what was left in one day would be too much.

"Do you have any human hair wigs that she can try on?" I asked, curious to see exactly what they looked like.

"Of course! I will be right back with some samples you can try on," she replied. "I will bring out several different lengths and colors."

As soon as she left, Stephanie and I got up simultaneously from our seats and dashed around the table to the myriad of hair samples on the black credenza against the back wall. What looked to be about ten large bangle-sized rings dangled from a dark metal stand. Each ring held approximately fifty hair samples, so we were gazing at over 500 hair colors. What incredible choices there were—Harvest Gold, Strawberry Swirl, Caramel Cream, Butterscotch, Vanilla Lush, Gold Blond. So many possibilities.

"Look, Steph. 'Spring Honey' matches your hair color perfectly!" I exclaimed, holding the sample next to her hair, amazed the shade was dead on.

"I don't know…I think 'Vanilla Lush' is closer to the color my hair used to be on top. My hair always was a little darker underneath. I like 'Spring Honey' though. What do you think about 'Gold Blond'?" she asked holding the sample against her cheek and beside her eyes.

"Hmm…"

Before I could respond, the door opened and Sima rushed in with several wigs in her arms. Caught red-handed messing with her supplies, we dropped the hair color rings and walked guiltily back to our seats. I could feel the color rising in my face.

"Sorry," I apologized, "we were just looking at all the colors. There are so many," I explained, hoping she wasn't too bothered.

"Oh, be my guest," she gestured with a wave of her hand to all the samples. "You are more than welcome to look at the color rings."

"Let's try this one on," suggested Sima as she held up a mid-length, layered, light blond wig. Stephanie sat in the chair facing the mirror as Sima placed the wig on her head. Once Sima got it situated, Steph looked in the mirror, mildly pleased, turning her head right and left to get a full view. "Take a look at the back," Sima said, offering her a large hand-held mirror. "What do you think? I think it looks very attractive on you."

"It's not bad," Stephanie answered, still getting used to the look, running her fingers through the strands and brushing some to the side. "Do you have anything a little longer?" she asked. Having always worn her hair below her shoulders, this shorter cut made her look older and not quite like herself.

"I think I might have one longer style in the back. You know the longer the hair is, the more the wig is going to cost," Sima cautioned.

"Yes, that makes sense," I replied, "but I think the longer length might look more natural on her, although this does look surprisingly good."

"Sure," Sima acknowledged. "Before I get the longer style, I want you to humor me and try on this dark short wig, just for kicks." She smiled and handed Stephanie the dark hair.

Knowing that Steph had always been a natural blond I was convinced the dark espresso color would look completely wrong. That is until she put the wig on. She looked gorgeous with her face framed by the dark color. Never in a million years would I have picked dark brown for her. True, the cut wasn't right—it was much too short—but the effect the color had on her blue eyes and light complexion was amazing.

"Steph, that color looks great!" I blurted out with enthusiasm. "I know it's too short, but I can't believe how good you look in dark hair."

"Mom, I'm NOT getting a brown wig!" Stephanie adamantly replied, while still checking herself out in the mirror. I could tell she thought the color was interesting, but it definitely did not win her over.

"I always recommend trying different colors. That's one advantage to wearing wigs—it's so easy to change your look. I'll be right back with the long blond one," Sima said.

As soon as the door shut I remarked, "Steph, I know you don't want to get a dark wig, but I just can't get over how good it looked on you. It really enhances your blue eyes. It makes them look gigantic."

"Thanks," she answered, "but for now, I still want to be a blond." She finished with a conspiratorial smile. All-in-all the appointment was going much better than I thought it would. We were almost having fun.

The door opened again and Sima came in with a long, straight, blond wig that looked amazingly like Stephanie's own hair.

"I think this might be the one," Sima asserted as she placed the wig in just the right position on Steph's head. If I hadn't known it was a wig, I would never have guessed it wasn't Stephanie's own hair. I could tell by the look of satisfaction in Steph's eyes that she liked it too. A few long wispy bangs framed her face, but the rest of the hair hung straight down to about the middle of her back—pretty much identical to the way she had always worn her hair.

"What do you think, Steph?" I asked.

"Yeah, I like this one the best," she replied.

Relief flooded my entire body. I didn't think we would find the perfect wig for Stephanie at the first place we looked, but we had. I had never dreamed it would be that easy.

"So, now the important question: How much does a wig like that cost?" I asked, knowing it wasn't going to be cheap.

"Let me see," Sima said as she pulled a calculator out of one of the drawers and began to add things up. "I can order this one for $1600. I would need a deposit of $800 to place the order and then the balance when it comes in. It would cost somewhat less if the hair was say, three inches shorter," she offered, but I knew we had to go with the longer length.

Yikes! I knew it was going to be pricey, but I wasn't quite prepared for that figure.

"I saw in your add something about health insurance. Are wigs covered?" I asked.

"Some policies cover them and others don't. It depends on what kind of insurance you have. If you purchase a wig from us, you can send the receipt to your insurance company. Make sure you list it as a hair prosthesis."

"We have United Health Care. Do you have any experience with them?" I asked.

"I'm not familiar with that company, but as I said, if you decide to place an order, you would just submit your receipt to your insurance company."

Yes, it was a large sum of money, but at that point Stephanie needed help, and I believed I didn't have a choice.

"So how soon could we have it?" I asked.

"You mean if you ordered it tonight?" she asked. I could tell she was surprised I wasn't deterred by the price.

"Yes, I'd like to order it tonight," I assured her. "You do take VISA, I assume?"

"Yes, of course! Let's see." She checked her calendar and did a few mental calculations. "I could have it here by next Wednesday, which would work out well with the long Thanksgiving weekend coming up. That way, Stephanie, you would have a few days to get comfortable wearing your wig before you went back to school," she wisely recommended.

"Great. Let's place the order. Here's my card," I said with a smile as I handed over my VISA.

Twelve

THE WIG

Gazing into my dresser mirror, I could hear Mom calling from downstairs, but I didn't answer. Too intent on brushing my hair, I ignored the persistent pleas directed up the stairs.

"Steph, come on. It's time to go right now!" Mom insisted. I could hear the keys jingling in her hand as she walked through the foyer to grab her coat from the hall closet.

Not terribly bothered by her impatience, I called back down, "Be there in a few..." and continued to comb my hair, ignoring the urgency in her voice, determined not to hurry. Liking what I saw while I gazed in the mirror, I could tell it was going to be a great day. Something seemed different about that morning. After applying concealer and bronzer to my face, I brushed two shades of eye shadow on my lids and then finished with eye liner and mascara. Satisfied with what I saw, I ducked into the bathroom to brush my teeth.

"I'll be out in the car, Steph. Make it quick!" Mom yelled, obviously exasperated. I heard her muttering something as she raced through the kitchen and out the garage door before letting it slam shut. Every morning it was the same story. Always underestimating how long it took me to get ready, I habitually lagged behind. Mom would nag me to move faster, but it never worked. No matter what I tried, I just couldn't seem to get my act together in the morning.

Opening the top drawer in the bathroom I saw the cute wide white leather headband I had bought the previous week and knew that it would look great with my long-sleeved, dark blue t-shirt. Even though I heard the garage door go up, I took a few extra seconds to touch up my hair.

"Wow! I look really good," I thought to myself as I brushed out my hair. Something was different, but I just couldn't put my finger on it. I continued to brush as I stared into the mirror. Curious about how everything had fallen into place so easily that morning, I continued looking at my reflection, brushing my hair, and ignoring the fact that time was ticking away. One stroke after another, I kept brushing, knowing that despite her threats, Mom was not going to leave without me. All of a sudden, I panicked. I realized that I'd been absentmindedly brushing my hair pretty fast and hard. Cautiously, I took a look at the brush to see what I'd lost. Lately I'd been so careful brushing my hair— more came out with every stroke so I tried to be as gentle as possible and brush only when absolutely necessary. To my surprise, I looked at the brush and it had very little hair in it. I couldn't believe it. Normally there were handfuls of hair in the brush. Taking a look in the mirror I suddenly realized that I couldn't see any bare spots on the top of my head. Stepping in closer so I could get a good look all around my head, frantically I fingered through my scalp, knowing the patches had to be there somewhere. Inch after inch I examined and couldn't find anything except healthy long, gorgeous hair. Did I really have a full head of hair? After still more checking, I couldn't find a single bare spot. I couldn't figure out how it had happened, but my hair was back, and it looked great. After dealing for so long with my thinning hair, it was a relief to have nothing to hide. So what if I was late to class?

"Stephanie, it's time to get up!" I heard as I felt Mom shaking my arm. "Steph, get up now!"

Abruptly, I opened my eyes and realized it was all a dream. Utterly depressed, I lifted my head off the pillow and saw more strands of hair that I'd lost through the night. I felt like I couldn't go on. I'd been trying so hard to not let things get to me, but sometimes the sadness overwhelmed me. My dream felt so real, it was cruel. Why did I ever have to wake up? Day after day hoping the worst was over and then waking up to the grim reality of more hair being gone was heartbreaking. When watching the hair pile up in the shower drain I felt like life's possibilities were slipping away along with my hair. Why couldn't I be like all my other friends and have a simple thing that they all took for granted—hair?

For a split second, I wanted to dive under the covers and never come out again. Somehow, I willed myself to get out of bed.

This is not going to beat me! I thought as I looked in the mirror. Quitting was not an option. Staring at my reflection, I tried not to focus on the ugly bare patches, which made the long strands of hair I still had look pitifully inadequate. Looking in my eyes, I knew that I was the same girl inside that I always had been. Nothing about me had changed; I was just missing some hair. I was a beautiful, worthwhile person who still had a lot of living left to do.

In that moment I realized that in dealing with life it wasn't necessarily the big battles that were the hardest. Sometimes just walking out the door was huge. With every day came a chance of failure, but also came the chance to succeed. Each day that I walked out our front door, patches and all, I was winning. Somehow, I was going to win the war.

Wednesday morning dawned, and I gradually opened my eyes and saw that it was already ten o'clock. Snuggling in the warmth of my comforter hours later than I normally did was such a luxury. Life just didn't get much better than that. Feeling rested and relaxed, I reveled in the fact that for the next five days, there would be no alarm clocks, no classes to rush off too, and no new homework assignments. It was Thanksgiving break.

Lying in bed, enjoying being lazy, I suddenly remembered my wig appointment, an appointment that was coming not a moment too soon. The day before, Dad had asked me to straighten up and vacuum my room. Always the comedian, he warned me to watch out for any animals that might be living under my bed. Normally Mom and Dad didn't bother me too much about my room on weekdays—they knew I was busy—but Lindsay was coming home from college for Thanksgiving and Mom wanted the house to be presentable. After Dad insisted that I get busy on my room or I would lose my phone for the night, I grumbled a few times and got started. Losing my phone was a punishment I wasn't willing to endure. After picking up my clothes off the floor, I got the vacuum cleaner from Valerie's room. For the first few passes, vacuuming was going well. It looked like I would be done in no time. I couldn't help thinking that vacuuming was a big waste of time, but to keep possession of my phone I was willing to do just about anything. Unfortunately, I was half done with the job when I heard the vacuum start making a high-pitched whining noise and smelled the pungent scent of burning rubber. Great. Couldn't the vacuum keep working for a few more minutes?

"Dad!" I yelled down the stairs. "Something's wrong with the vacuum cleaner." I waited and heard no response. "Dad!" I yelled louder.

"I'm coming, Steph. Just hang on a minute," Dad called from his office downstairs. Sitting on my bed, impatient to get the pointless task done, I was getting increasingly annoyed. A couple minutes later I heard him coming up the stairs.

"What's the problem?" he asked as he took the vacuum cleaner out of my hands and turned the power on. Immediately we both witnessed the horrible high-pitched whine of the motor and were overwhelmed by the harsh smell coming from the machine.

"Whoa, okay. That's not good," Dad remarked as he cut the power. "Let's see what the problem is." With that, Dad unplugged the vacuum and unzipped the compartment that held the bag in place and started to remove the bag. As he disconnected the bag from the intake pipe and pulled it away, we both stared with disbelief at an enormous wad of hair that remained lodged in the opening—long, blond hair. My hair. The volume of hair was so great and was jammed in so tight, that no air was getting through. Slowly he began pulling on the obstruction and eventually it loosened and dislodged. That was the tip of the iceberg. As he pulled, more and more hair appeared from the clogged line. Compacted into a dense mass, my hair filled the entire length of the pipe. Staring mournfully at the mess, I looked at the massive amount of hair that I had painstakingly tried to save. Most people pull hair out of their brushes daily, never thinking twice about it, because new hair follicles are always working to replace the loss. For me, when the hair came out, it was gone permanently. End of story. Looking at the large pile of hair on the floor that had come from my head was depressing. It wasn't coming back and I knew it. Once Dad got that part of the vacuum cleared, he turned the machine upside down to look at the roller. We weren't saying much at that point. Crushed by the reality of what I was witnessing, I couldn't speak. Hundreds more strands of long blond hair were wound so tight around the roller that it couldn't budge. When Dad finally got the roller cleared and moving freely and the vacuum back in commission, he set it down and walked over to me and hugged me.

"I'm sorry, Steph," he said and left the room. He knew I needed to be alone.

Once again I shook off the forces that threatened to drag me down into a spiral of despair, realizing that within hours I was going to be on my way to pick up the answer to my problems—my wig. Fortunately, Lindsay would be home and was going with me to the styling appointment. That was a relief. I knew she would help me decide what would look good and I trusted her sense of style completely. After all, we had been fighting over each other's clothes for the past five years. What she liked, I liked and vice versa, which made for much arguing concerning our wardrobes when she was living at home. Today, the fact that we had such similar tastes was going to come in handy.

When we arrived at the building in South San Jose, Mom dropped Lindsay and me off and took Valerie with her to get something to eat while we headed in for the appointment. The last thing I needed was an audience. As Lindsay and I walked up the stairs in the inner courtyard to the office, my nerves got the best of me. Mom and Dad had spent so much money on this wig, what if I didn't like it? What if they cut it wrong? What if the color was bad? Sima had warned us the wigs couldn't be returned once they were ordered. At $1600, it was a stretch to order this one and I knew ordering a replacement was not feasible.

"Lindsay," I said as I grabbed her arm at the top of the stairs, before we opened the door, "you tell them what I want. I'm so nervous I feel like I'm going to barf and I don't want to talk."

"Sure, no problem," she agreed, "but, what kind of style do you want?" She was very sympathetic and I knew she would do anything I asked.

"I don't know…" I couldn't even think straight. The nerves were just too much. We both were lost in thought for a moment, standing out on the cement walkway just outside the office door. Part of me wanted to run and never look back, but I knew I had no choice.

"What about big round curls like Jessica Simpson's?" Lindsay suggested, excited about her idea.

"Okay, that sounds good," I agreed. That was all I needed to get me in the door.

We walked in and Lindsay introduced herself. She told the receptionist that I was there for an appointment. The receptionist, who was about Lindsay's age, smiled back and asked us to follow her as she led us down a different hallway than I had seen at my previous visit. With her ever-present smile, she opened the door into a small private room that had a salon chair in the middle. The room was a bit smaller than a dentist's exam room, but there was enough space for the salon chair, a second chair for Lindsay, and a cabinet full of styling tools. Curiously, there was no large mirror on the wall in front of the chair.

A few moments later, a young Asian girl, who looked to be in her mid-twenties, entered the room and introduced herself as my stylist. In her hands, she carried a black shiny cardboard box about the size of a shoe box that I thought probably contained my wig. The anticipation built as I waited for her to open the box. I didn't have to wait long. Within seconds, she had taken the long brownish-blond hairpiece out of the box and draped it over her left hand.

"What do you think?" the girl asked as she shook the hair so it hung naturally.

Fear does amazing things to the body. I knew I needed to answer her question, but my mouth would not open. My tongue felt thick and my lips wouldn't move. Disappointment overwhelmed me. The color was all wrong—it was way too dark. To me it looked nothing like the bright blond hair sample that we had chosen; it was more like a murky dirty blond. That's not what worried me most. My biggest concern was the volume of hair. There was so much hair—enough hair for my whole basketball team. At that point, I mentally checked out. Hope for a future looking like everyone else was slipping from me. Devastated, I reasoned that if $1600 could not buy natural looking hair, there was no hope.

"Can you thin it out a little?" I heard Lindsay ask.

"Sure. Stephanie, could you take off your hat? I'll put the wig on you. Then I can get started," the stylist said.

Mechanically, I complied with her request, and sat frozen in place, emotionless. Frequently I felt the tug of a razor as she cut away some of the thickness from underneath. It didn't take her long to realize that I wouldn't be answering any of her questions, so she directed all her queries to Lindsay. Grateful for the absence of a mirror, I sat, counting the minutes till I could escape what was becoming a living hell. Finally, after close to an hour, the trimming and thinning was done and the stylist started with the curling iron. I heard Lindsay say something about large curls, but was doubtful that my hair would end up looking anything like I wanted. Certain that the barrel of the curling iron she was using was way too small, I still could not speak. It was hopeless. As the stylist continued with the curling iron, I could hear tapping and eventually realized it was Lindsay texting someone on her phone. I suspected she was texting Mom.

Somehow I managed to hold myself together during the hour and a half long process of thinning and styling the dreadful wig. Relief swept over me when she removed the drape and shook off the loose hair. My torturous session was over and I couldn't wait to leave. Any relief I felt abruptly vanished when she put a large mirror in my hand. With nothing else to do but look, I did. The vision staring back at me was far worse than I imagined. Did she think I was heading for the Country Western Music Awards? Just as I suspected, the curls were extremely tight and there were millions of them. And if that wasn't bad enough, my bangs were curled under, making my forehead look way too big. Maybe in Nashville this hair style would take the prize, but it certainly wasn't right for a teenager in Silicon Valley. Feeling that I couldn't hold the tears back much longer, I wanted to grab my purse and run.

To my complete horror, when I left the room, five members of the staff were anxiously waiting outside the door to see the results. Sima, camera in hand, asked if she could take a picture.

"It looks beautiful, Stephanie!" she exclaimed.

Somehow I managed half a smile, then turned to Mom. "Let's go," I mumbled.

Finally, in the privacy of our car, the tears came.

Mom tried to comfort me. "Steph, it looks good," she offered, rubbing my arm. Quickly I pulled away from her as if her touch burned. We both knew she was saying that for my benefit only. It simply was not true and I didn't want her sympathy. I looked like a poodle and I couldn't wait to get home and take the ghastly wig off. Slumping as far down in the front seat as I could, I told Mom through my tears that I didn't want to talk about it, and asked her to get me home.

Later, at home in my bedroom, after having a good long cry, I started to pull myself together.

There had to be a way to fix my hair. I made my way over to the stool that I sat on every morning. Gazing into the large mirror on my dresser, I took a deep breath. As opposed to the fluorescent lighting at the shop, the natural light in my bedroom made the color of the wig look a little better, which lifted my spirits a bit. Also, I reminded myself that one advantage to having a human hair wig was that I could dye it. Color was only a temporary problem. But what was I going to do with all those curls? I plugged in my straightener and got to work ironing out all the ridiculous looking curls. After I got one side of the wig done and thought that it looked decent, I was cautiously optimistic that my life might not be ruined after all. Forty minutes later I was finished. With a critical eye, I sat staring at my reflection and was actually almost pleased.

The only flaw remaining was that the wig was a little puffy around the top of my head. Other than that it looked pretty good. Was that actually a smile creeping onto my face?

One of my stretchy headbands took care of the puffiness on top and the transformation was complete. Sitting there approving the sleek modifications I had just made, I realized that having a wig was monumental. It no longer mattered how much hair I lost each day. I could brush as much and scrub as hard as I wanted and it wouldn't make a difference. I wouldn't have to dodge questions about my hat or fear that someone would grab it—I didn't have to wear a hat anymore. Full of excitement, I rushed downstairs, anxious to show off my new look.

When I rounded the corner into the kitchen, Mom and Lindsay stopped their conversation mid-sentence and stared with wide eyes.

"Gosh, Steph! Your hair looks amazing!" Lindsay gushed as she rushed over to get a closer look.

I could see the tears in Mom's eyes and knew this time they were there for a good reason. As she gave me a hug, she whispered, "You look beautiful, Steph." I could tell she was overcome with emotion. As hard as this ordeal had been for me, I knew it had also been tough on her. Now we both could breathe a sigh of relief—the worst was over, at least that's what we hoped.

Thanksgiving morning came and I got ready to wear my wig in public for the first time. Traditionally at Thanksgiving all the local relatives got together at my grandparents' home in a new subdivision in Gilroy. If we weren't interested in whatever football game was on TV, it wasn't hard to find something else to do. The pool table was right there; sometimes we brought a soccer ball to kick around; and there was Granddaddy's computer upstairs or the hot tub out back. With my cousins around, I wasn't bored. Grammy always put out an amazing spread of delicious food and yummy desserts. She loved cooking for everyone, especially Sundays after church. We all enjoyed her easy style of entertaining—nothing fancy, just good food. If my soccer team was in Gilroy for a tournament, between games I'd bring a couple of my teammates over to hang out instead of making the half hour drive home. She loved meeting my friends.

On Monday, September 11th, Grammy unexpectedly died of a heart attack. It shocked us all. We had just had dinner with her the day before and I remembered how pretty she looked in her powder blue sweater and teardrop earrings with blue stones. Other than being in the hospital the year before for a couple of days with a blood clot in her leg, she'd been healthy. I couldn't believe she was gone. Granddaddy wanted to stick with tradition and celebrate Thanksgiving in Gilroy that year, even though Grammy was gone. It was going to be hard on everyone without her there. On top of that, I was going to be wearing a wig.

As I walked up to Granddaddy's front door carrying the pilgrim and Indian sugar cookies I had decorated the day before, I was nervous about my wig. When we left San Jose that morning, I thought my hair looked pretty natural, but I wasn't sure. It felt kind of heavy, but it was great not to have a hat on. From the minute I walked in the door to Granddaddy's home, my nervousness started to disappear. Neither of my cousins Emily or Michael stared and neither did my aunt or uncle when we greeted each other with hugs. The girls busied themselves with the ongoing food preparation while the guys relaxed and watched the Dallas Cowboys play the Detroit Lions.

Later, as we gathered around the table with plates brimming full of incredible food, we took turns saying what we were most thankful for. Things got emotional as we talked about good times with Grammy. As my turn approached I wanted to shout out, "I'm thankful that I'm wearing a wig and not one of you noticed!" but I kept that thought to myself and gave my usual, "I'm thankful for my family," and smiled.

Thirteen

UCSF

Back in November, when we were desperately trying to halt the loss of Stephanie's hair, I asked the dermatologist if there were any new treatment options because the cortisone injections clearly weren't working. After trying all their recommendations, which included the injections, Rogaine, vitamin supplements and Nioxin shampoo—all which were ineffective—they referred us to Vera Price. Dr. Vera Price was a Professor of Clinical Dermatology in the Department of Dermatology, University of California, San Francisco (UCSF). Dr. Price was also the director of the UCSF Hair Research Center and had served as a Director of the American Academy of Dermatology (AAD). In addition, Dr. Price was a co-founder of the National Alopecia Areata Foundation (NAAF). Recognizing her outstanding qualifications, I knew that if anyone could help Stephanie, Dr. Price could.

Fortunately, Dr. Price's medical practice was only an hour away from our San Jose neighborhood and she accepted our insurance. Scheduling an appointment, however, proved to be extremely difficult.

After several weeks of failed attempts, we were finally able to get on her schedule due to a cancellation. Appreciating the fact that Dr. Price was a world-renowned expert on alopecia areata, I knew going into the appointment that if she could not help Stephanie, we would look no further. Stephanie was not anxious about the appointment; I, however, was nervous enough for both of us.

Neither of us was overly optimistic the day we drove up to San Francisco for the consultation, but we both knew if we did not explore this last avenue, we would always wonder, what if? Unusually fair weather greeted us as we entered San Francisco, which helped to lift our spirits. The perpetual dense morning fog was nowhere to be seen. Billowing cumulus clouds filled the sky and a gentle westerly breeze blew bunches of brittle autumn leaves down the sidewalks. Despite the fact it was a weekday, there were plenty of people out milling around, taking advantage of the unusually nice weather. Navigating through the Lower Pacific Heights neighborhood to the Mt. Zion Medical Center on Divisadero St. was challenging, but we finally located convenient parking next to the correct office complex.

Arriving slightly early for her 11 o'clock appointment, we fortunately found two seats together in the crowded waiting room. Knowing that a majority of the waiting room population was present for alopecia consultations made the urge to glance at everyone's hair almost irresistible. Out of politeness, I concentrated on the *Vogue* magazine in my hands and resisted the urge to stare. Half an hour after her scheduled appointment time, Stephanie's name was called and we followed the nurse down to one of the many small exam rooms. After recording the appropriate medical history in Stephanie's chart, the nurse left, assuring us that Dr. Price would be with us shortly. Compared to the exposed feeling of the patient waiting area, the solitude of the private exam room was a welcome refuge.

Not too many minutes passed before there was a knock on the door and Dr. Price entered and introduced herself. She was a thin woman of small stature, but projected authority with her upright posture and discerning eyes. Immediately I observed that she didn't seem to be wearing a wig, which I found oddly disappointing. I reminded myself that physicians did not have to experience a disease to treat it and tried to ignore my disappointment.

After asking the appropriate preliminary questions Dr. Price asked, "Stephanie, would you mind taking off your wig?"

"Not at all," Stephanie replied. She carefully loosened the wig tape and uncovered her head. At that point almost all the hair on the top of her head was gone, with a sparse smattering of long hairs left along the bottom and sides, similar to an advanced case of male patterned baldness. At home, I was accustomed to seeing Stephanie's uncovered head with the scraggly long pieces still attached, but the bright harsh lights of the office and the presence of a stranger made her condition look much more tragic. Once again I felt tears forming. Having seen this condition numerous times, Dr. Price examined Stephanie's head in a very matter-of-fact way and identified that Stephanie definitely had alopecia areata. Dr. Price assured us there were millions of other people with the condition across the United States.

"In your experience, are there any treatments that can reverse this condition?" I asked. I was fairly sure I already knew the answer, but I was still holding out hope.

"If I treated Stephanie with very strong medication for several months, I could get her hair to grow back. However, the body can not tolerate medication like that for long. The damage to the rest of the body would be much worse than her loss of hair. Then, when she stopped the medication, her hair would fall out again. Now, her hair may naturally go through cycles where it grows back in, but it will always end up falling out again. I see you have a nice wig, Stephanie." Dr. Price pointed to her long blond wig on the exam table.

"Thanks," Steph said. She was absorbing all the information we had just heard in silence.

"Fortunately there are nice wigs available now that look very natural. Have you heard of NAAF?" she asked.

"Yes, we have," I answered. "We receive their online newsletter."

"NAAF has support groups that meet all over the country, if you are interested. Also, they have an annual conference for teens every summer, which you might consider attending," she said. "Attendees always leave feeling great after hanging out with many other alopecia teenagers. You should consider it."

"One last question I have, Dr. Price," I said.

"Yes?"

"Is having alopecia areata an indication that you might have other auto-immune problems in the future?"

"No, having alopecia areata does not mean a person is more likely to have other auto-immune disorders. The chances of her having other auto-immune issues are the same as the general population. Stephanie, alopecia should not prevent you from having a long, full life. It was nice meeting you and I wish you best of luck in the future," and with a shake of her hand, the appointment was over and we were free to go.

Leaving the office complex that day, the gravity of what we had discovered began to sink in. Neither of us had been surprised by what we heard, but hearing from a top medical expert that Stephanie was going to be dealing with alopecia for the rest of her life made things certain and final. In the back of my mind there had always been the hope that we could get her into a new drug trial or on an experimental treatment, but now those hopes were gone. In addition, to find out that if Stephanie's hair did grow back, that it would fall out again, was extremely disappointing. On the flip side, it was wonderful to know that having alopecia did not make her more prone to other auto-immune diseases.

"Are you bummed?" I asked when we got to the car.

"Yeah, kind of. I mean I didn't really think she could do anything, but I was kind of hoping…"

"I know. Me too. At least we know we've been to the best."

"Yeah."

"Should we look for a Starbucks?" I asked as I approached the garage kiosk. We both needed something to cheer us up.

"I guess," she answered with indifference.

"Okay, let me know if you see one. I'll keep my eyes on the traffic and try not to run into anyone," I said, very serious about the real possibility of hitting something with the myriad of cross-streets, traffic, pedestrians, road signs, store fronts and general chaos that surrounded us in downtown San Francisco.

Leaving the city that day, our quest to halt the loss of Stephanie's hair officially ended. Some relief came with knowing that the fight was over—we had exhausted all our options. But it was sad knowing that Stephanie's hair was irrevocably gone. End of story; the search was over. Now we just had to deal. Wishing for a glimpse into the future, I longed to see that everything was going to be okay. Fortunately, I had no idea what was coming.

Fourteen

COURAGE

Stephanie adapted amazingly well to wearing a wig. Sometimes she wore her hair down and straight; other days she curled the front, put it in a ponytail or wore braids. Flexibility was a nice benefit of the human hair wig. No one suspected that it wasn't her own. In fact, during our family gathering for Thanksgiving, my sister Terri pulled me aside to ask privately how Stephanie's wig appointment had gone. When I informed her that Steph was, in fact, wearing a wig, Terri couldn't believe it. My sister had no clue that Steph had a wig on when she hugged her that morning. That was all the confirmation I needed to know that our money had been well spent.

For gym, Stephanie still brought a hat to make sure her wig stayed in place. High winds could be worrisome, but other than that, her hair was manageable. Basketball, however, had its challenges. Before heading back to school for practice in the evenings, Steph would remove her wig and put what was left of her hair up in a messy bun. Then to disguise some of the baldness on top, she wore a thick terry headband. The headband was becoming less and less effective because the bare area was becoming so large, but once Steph stepped out on the court all thoughts of hair disappeared. She wanted to get the ball and defeat her opponent.

With Stephanie's approval, one night after basketball practice the coach explained Stephanie's hair situation to the members of the team. Not knowing what kind of reaction to expect, Stephanie was amazed at the outpouring of support from the girls. Some asked questions, which she was more than happy to answer. Steph had been the most exposed in front of this group of girls and they had politely never questioned her. Being able to explain exactly what was going on to them had a cathartic effect. To them she was still the crazy wild one and always would be. Knowing that the team was going on two overnight trips, I was relieved to hear that the girls finally knew about Stephanie's alopecia. Keeping her secret while staying in a hotel room with two other girls would be impossible. With everything out in the open, I had hopes that the trips might actually be fun for her—one of the trips included a day at Disneyland.

Christmas break was over in a flash. Stephanie came home from the basketball trips with an all tourney award, and a lot of great memories. She spent New Year's Eve at her friend Fiona's house and took silly photos of the two of them modeling different kinds of wigs. Having been in several stage productions, Fiona had quite an extensive wig collection. One shot of Steph in a short blond wig with curls everywhere looked cute, but my favorite was the straight black cropped cut with long bangs in the front.

With basketball season in full swing, Stephanie was enjoying her position as starting point guard. The team had lost more games than they had won, but Steph was averaging about ten points a game as a freshman, so that, along with the great camaraderie among the girls, kept her happy.

One afternoon I was busy preparing dinner when Steph walked in and informed me that for the upcoming evening game against Notre Dame Belmont, she had decided to go out on a limb and try wearing her wig during the game. I felt the hair on the back of my neck stand up.

"Do you think that's a good idea?" I asked.

"Well, I think it would be better to try it at an away game just in case anything happens. I have to at least give it a try."

Appreciating that she had thought things through and impressed that she was even willing to try, I supported her decision. After all, it would be enjoyable to see her playing with hair instead of wondering how much attention the bare top of her head was attracting.

Game day arrived and Steph began the preparation with her wig. She lined the front underside with strips of double sided wig tape, hoping that the ultra sticky tape would be enough to hold her wig in place. However, for more stability, she put her hair in two braids, intertwining what was left of her own hair in with the hair from the wig. Having worn her hair like that to school with no problem, she seemed confident with her plan. After dropping her off at Leigh to catch a ride on the team bus, I headed home to prepare a quick dinner.

Nothing can adequately prepare you for life's tragic moments.

Immediately when Tracy noticed Stephanie on the ground—her wig hanging off the back of her head, her secret exposed to all—he stood up and from the back of the stands started yelling, "Time out! Time out!"

Down on the court, Coach Hernandez had also signaled for a time-out. With the whole crowd watching in stunned silence, Stephanie got up and ran to the sideline. Fast and furiously her fingers moved as she tried to unbraid her hair and get the wig off as the bare crown of her head reflected the harsh lights from above. I have no idea how she got it done so quickly, but within seconds, she had the wig off. Quickly she bunched up what was left of her hair into a tiny bun, put her headband back on and stood up ready to get back on the court. Coach Hernandez ask if she was sure she wanted to stay in and with no hesitation she nodded her head yes.

Stephanie returned to the court with a vengeance that inspired her team. Repeatedly she drove the ball into a crowded key and either scored or was fouled. She hit seven out of seven free throw attempts and was relentless on defense. Free from the worry of her wig, Steph flew in for rebounds and dove for loose balls. During the remaining three quarters of the game, she managed to score 15 points and rally her team to a respectable defeat.

After the battle was over with Notre Dame on top 70 to 59, the teams headed to the locker room while parents milled around waiting.

Tracy and I kept to ourselves, ready to sweep Stephanie away as soon as possible.

"She's an amazing kid," Jeff Werner commented as he patted Tracy on the back.

"Thanks."

Several of the parents told us that Stephanie's performance was the most inspirational they had ever witnessed. We were very proud of her. Faced with the decision to either run and hide or get back on the court, she made the difficult choice and stayed. She had not only handled the situation, she had soared. Now that the game was over, I started to worry. With a basketball in her hands, Steph was resilient, but how would she be with the adrenaline gone?

Steph was the first one out of the locker room. Still in uniform, her head was covered by the team sweatshirt that thankfully had a hood. With her head lowered, she managed to avoid the other parents and locate us. Quickly we dashed to the car, partly to avoid the rain that had begun, but also because we knew Stephanie wanted out of that gym as soon as possible. Not a word was spoken all the way to the car.

"How are you doing, Steph?" I asked after the doors to the BMW were tightly shut and I knew no one else but the family could hear. Turning backwards towards the rear seats, I could just make out the expression on her face in the dim light—it was grim. Her upper lip was trembling—she was barely holding herself together.

"I don't want to talk about it," she answered weakly, and the tears began.

Difficult, exasperating, tedious, humbling and tiring are all words that can describe the job of parenting, but it also can be the most rewarding, awe-inspiring, thrilling job a person could ever hope to have. Witnessing my child suffer, as I had that night in the gym, powerless to help, was the most heart-wrenching moment of my 45 years. I will never forget that feeling as long as I live. But watching her rise from the horrific situation, to not only face her demons, but to also smash them to the ground with such inspiring courage and tenacity, was thrilling. Yes, I knew she was hurting on that long ride home, but I also knew that she had been truly heroic that night and no matter what obstacles lay ahead for her, she would triumph.

Fifteen

A FRIEND

According to Disney, it's a small world, and I guess I have to agree. The only friend from high school that my mom still kept in touch with lived nearby in Saratoga and had alopecia. All through their high school years together, Mom never knew Katie had hair issues. They spent hours together training for track and cross-country and the subject of alopecia had never come up. Katie lost her hair for the first time in junior high school, but it had grown back in by the time she started high school. Away at college, Katie lost her hair again during a particularly stressful time, but again it grew back in. She met and married her husband after college and a few years later her hair fell out for the third and final time. She had been wearing wigs ever since. It wasn't until we moved back to California that Mom found out about Katie's alopecia.

A few days after my wig fiasco, Mom asked if I would be interested in having lunch with her friend Katie. Curious to meet someone else with alopecia and hopeful that she'd have some good advice, I looked forward to the lunch. I had many questions.

By mid-January, I had lost a lot of hair from my wig, and the hair that was left was becoming increasingly dry and brittle. The wig wasn't going to last much longer. Our request for reimbursement to United Health Care had been rejected. Had I lost my hair in an accident or because of chemotherapy, the wig would have been covered. Go figure. I knew Mom and Dad couldn't afford another $1600 so soon, so I was hoping Katie could recommend a cheaper alternative. If anyone knew something about wigs, it had to be her—she had been buying wigs for 20 years.

Luckily I had a random Friday off from school when both Katie's boys were in classes. Due to the fact that Katie had had ankle surgery and was still in a wheelchair, Mom decided to bring lunch to her house. Mom made one of my favorites—Chinese Chicken Salad—and a fresh apple cake. We arrived late-morning to her sprawling, one-story house and she greeted my Mom and me with a warm hug. Katie was slim and attractive with petite features, beautiful green eyes, freckles and an easy smile. Her short layered auburn hair framed her face perfectly. If I hadn't already known, I would never have guessed it wasn't her hair.

With introductions over and lunch served, Mom and I began gleaning all the information we could from Katie's years of experience. Obviously the two had been close in high school because Mom wasn't shy about asking Katie anything and Katie was more than willing to answer. After hearing that Katie bought only synthetic wigs, usually priced under $200, I breathed a sigh of relief. Katie had lots of useful information, such as which brands looked most natural and wore better and which online websites were the best. Eventually, as I suspected it would, the topic of conversation came around to my embarrassing moment on the basketball court. Of all people, I knew Katie could empathize. Applauding my courage, she assured me she had had her share of wig mishaps too.

"Here's a good one for you," Katie offered as she began to tell of her own near catastrophe.

"One summer, Bill and I went to Paramount's Great America amusement park for the day. It was his company picnic. We hadn't been to the park in years, and were excited to ride all the crazy roller coasters. The park was packed because the weather was nice. Most of Bill's co-workers were there. We wanted to get some rides in before the lines got long so we headed to The Demon first."

"That ride is really scary," Mom commented. "I always feel like I'm going to hit my head at the end when you speed down through the skull."

"I know! We were so lucky when we got there because the line wasn't too long so we got in line for the last car."

"You like the back?" Mom asked.

"Yes, we love to get whipped over the hills. Anyway, we were so excited and finally our train came and we stepped in. A couple of little boys got in the seats in front of us. We pulled the safety bar down and were off. I was hanging onto the bar as we reached the top of the first hill and went screaming down. We were going real fast up the second hill and right when we reached the top, we were jerked forward. Instantly I felt my wig lift off my head."

"No way!" I exclaimed, knowing from experience the terror she felt.

"Just wait," Katie interjected with a mischievous smile on her face. "Bill had his hands raised when we neared the top, and he *caught* my wig, *mid-air* before it went flying away. I couldn't believe it. I put the wig in my lap and hung on tight. Unfortunately, the two boys in front of us turned around and noticed I had no hair. They kept staring back at me between the jumps and dives. After the final jump, just as the cars were beginning to slow, I quickly put my wig on as we glided back into the station."

"As we stepped out of the car, the two boys rushed to their parents waiting on the side and starting yelling and pointing directly at me, 'She's bald! She's bald!'"

"My husband and I looked perplexed at each other and then looked at the boys with puzzled faces, like we had no clue what they were talking about, and walked away.

"Whoa! That could've been a complete disaster," my mom exclaimed.

"Yes, with his co-workers at the park, it wouldn't have been fun. None of them knew I wore a wig. I was really lucky, thanks to Bill. That's one problem I haven't been able to solve; how to wear a wig and ride a roller-coaster."

"I've got that figured out. Our basketball team went to Disneyland in December and I just made sure I wore a sweatshirt with a hood. On the fast rides, I pulled the hood over my hair and it stayed in place."

Being able to offer her advice felt good. I felt an instant connection—I wasn't alone anymore. Sharing our horror stories was surprisingly comforting.

Katie and Mom continued to talk about kids, husbands, schools, whatever was on their minds, and I cleared the dishes.

"I'm a little worried about our trip to Kauai this summer," Mom told Katie. "Stephanie loves to boogie board and I don't know what she's going to do about her wig and the waves. Some of them knock her right over. Have you body surfed with your wig?"

"Yes," Katie laughed, "and had to recover my wig as it bobbed along in the seaweed, so I don't really recommend it," she warned.

"Hmm, what if she puts goggles on over the wig? Do you think that would be strong enough to hold it in place? I really hate to see her give up boogie boarding."

"That might work. It's worth a try," Katie said.

"Well, I guess we'd better head home," Mom declared as she reluctantly got up from the kitchen table. "Thanks so much for meeting with us. We really appreciate it and are grateful for all the advice. You helped a lot. We'll get right on that website you recommended when we get home."

"It was great to meet you," I added and gave her a hug, feeling relieved that I had someone to talk to who knew exactly what I was going through.

Leaving Katie's neighborhood that day, I felt optimistic about the future. Katie not only looked normal, she looked great. As much as

Mom sympathized with what I was going through, she could never truly understand, but Katie did. I had someone on my team!

Sixteen

SHAVING

Avoiding what I knew to be inevitable, I hung onto the thinning strands of my hair. Each strand was a connection to life before alopecia, and I was not ready to break those ties yet. Logically, I knew my hair was gone, but there was still a part of me that hoped my hair would eventually grow back. I just couldn't bear to part with what little I had left.

In most situations, wearing a wig solved my problems. Having worn my wig for a couple months, I was getting inventive experimenting with new looks—braids, pulled to the side, half-up-half-down, pony tails, French braids, messy buns. In a lot of ways, my hair wasn't any different than anyone else's; I just took mine off when I got home.

Basketball was my only dilemma. Wearing a wig to play was obviously out of the question, so I continued to tie up my remaining hair, spreading it as far as I could to cover as much of my baldness as possible. Wearing a terrycloth sweatband helped in the front, but the top was pretty bare. Knowing there was one final step I needed to take, I wondered if I could actually go through with it.

"I'm thinking about shaving my head," I announced to Dad one lazy Saturday morning while we both sat at the kitchen table eating breakfast, me looking at the comics and Dad reading the front page.

"If it'll make you feel better, I'll shave my head too," Dad offered, momentarily forgetting the paper.

"Uh, that's okay, Dad. No thanks," I answered, thinking that was the last thing I needed to see—my dad with no hair. "But, thanks for the offer."

"I'm serious, Steph. I'll do it," he said again and I knew he meant it. "Just let me know when you're ready and we'll go out and get what you need."

"When I'm ready," I replied, busying myself with my cereal, just wanting to drop the subject. It was way too early in the day to think about anything other than when I could take a nap. Saturday was the only morning I didn't have to rush anywhere and I relished it. To avoid straightening my room—another typical Saturday event—I had planned on keeping my door shut all day and hoped that Mom would forget about my disastrous bedroom and not come down the hallway.

After finishing breakfast, I put my dishes in the sink and remembered there was a taped edition of *Survivor* that I hadn't seen, so I headed for the couch, grabbed the remote and a quilt, and spread out on our comfy sectional ready to relax and catch up on my favorite show. Valerie had gone with Dad to Home Depot and Mom was out buying groceries, so I had the house to myself—peace and quiet. After a hectic week of school and basketball, a quiet Saturday morning alone in the house was just what I needed.

As usual, I fell asleep on the couch watching *Survivor* and woke up when Dad and Valerie came storming in the garage door, talking loud enough to wake the dead. I was always grumpy when I woke up, so I growled at them for being so obnoxiously loud and Dad informed me that if I wanted to sleep, I had my own room upstairs. Actually, it was a good thing they were loud, because I realized I had basketball practice at noon and needed to get ready.

After putting on my practice uniform I stared at my reflection in the mirror. As I got my "hair" ready for practice, I thought maybe it was time to bite the bullet and get rid of that pitifully thin bit of hair hanging on my head. I was slowly warming up to the idea. With thoughts of shaving cream and razor blades in the back of my mind, I flipped my sweatshirt hood over my head and ran down the stairs on my way out to the car.

"Mom, I have to go," I yelled as I rushed through the kitchen. I wasn't worried that I couldn't hear her response. Mom, of all people, would get me to practice on time. Right on cue the door opened and in a flash we were on our way. During the entire ride I couldn't stop thinking about shaving my head. I wondered what it would look like and feel like to have it all gone. My daydreaming ended as we pulled into the parking lot. Jumping out with my bag, I thanked Mom for the ride and headed into practice. Lately, I had started to get a little self-conscious about taking my sweatshirt off for practice, but I knew that once the basketball was in my hands I'd forget about my hair, and that afternoon was no different. The two-hour practice was over in no time, and when I exited the gym, hood up, I saw Dad waiting for me in the parking lot with the van.

"Hey, Dad," I said as I climbed into the passenger seat, grabbed a stray water bottle from the back seat and took a long drink.

"Hey, Steph! How was practice?" Dad asked as he put the van in gear and pulled away from the curb while waving to some of the other parents.

"Okay." My standard response. We sped down Blossom Hill Road on our way home.

A couple blocks from our house, I made up my mind.

"Dad, do you think we could go get the shaving stuff?" I asked as we rounded the corner onto Camden Ave.

"Sure, Steph. You mean right now?" Dad asked.

"Is that okay? I might want to shave my head soon, so I want to be ready just in case."

"Of course! We've got time," Dad answered. "We can stop by Rite Aid."

After locating the correct aisle in the drug store, we saw endless brands of shaving cream lining the shelves. Claims like "dermatologist recommended", "lightly fragranced", "prevents nicks, cuts & razor bumps", "soothes skin" made the choice difficult, but I finally decided on one, pulled it off the shelf and went to check out the razors. Mom never bought the expensive Venus kind, so I knew this was my chance; besides, Dad always was the big spender. Mom tried to stretch every penny. The lavender Gillette Venus razor with three blades, two lubricating strips and a center pivot cartridge looked like just what I needed, so I grabbed it and headed for the registers. In a matter of minutes, we were back in the van on our way home.

"Remember, Steph, I'll shave my head if you want me to," Dad offered again as we approached the house.

"Uh, that's okay, but thanks for the shaving cream and razor," I answered with a tentative smile, thinking about the ominous items sitting in my lap hidden in the plastic shopping bag.

"No problem, just remember…"

"I know, Dad!"

Later that evening, Jamie, Fiona, Maiko and I were going to see *Dreamgirls* at the local movie theater and I couldn't wait. Because we went to three different high schools, it had become difficult for us to do anything together. I was extremely excited that our plans had worked out. Fiona's mom was giving us a ride to the movies, and Dad volunteered to pick us up. As I was putting the finishing touches on my outfit, my phone buzzed, and I knew Fiona was outside waiting.

"Bye, Mom. Bye, Dad," I yelled as I rushed down the stairs, ready to fly out the door.

"Wait, what time do I pick you up?" Dad asked as he dashed to meet me at the door.

"The movie should be over by 11:05, so get there by 11:00 and I'll call you when we're walking out."

"Okay. Have fun!" Dad said, giving me a hug as I ran out the door. "And be good!" Dad yelled after me.

"Of course," I replied with a smirk as I climbed in the back seat.

All too soon the movie was over, my friends were delivered to their homes and Dad and I were in the van, heading home. As expected, we had had a blast. Nothing beats hanging out with good friends, seeing a good movie, and acting crazy. But that part of the evening had come to an end, and my thoughts turned towards the razor and shaving cream that sat waiting for me on my dresser.

When we entered the kitchen, I noticed it was very quiet in the house.

"Where's Mom?" I asked Dad, surprised she wasn't up.

"She had a headache and went to bed," Dad informed me as he hung up his keys and headed to his usual spot on the couch with remote in hand. He turned on the TV and got comfortable on the couch.

"Well, I'm going to bed."

"Okay. Love you," Dad responded with his attention directed to the latest skit on *Saturday Night Live*.

As I climbed the stairs, I thought of how sick I was of seeing my bald head with a bunch of long strands hanging off the sides. Thankful to hear no noise coming from the second story, I knew both Mom and Valerie were sound asleep. Not wanting to wake them, I inched my way slowly into the dark room and felt around for the bag on my dresser. I picked up the bag and turned to my desk, searching for the pair of scissors I had seen that afternoon. My hand hit the ceramic cup full of pens and almost sent it tumbling. Luckily, I caught the cup with my free hand just before it fell. Shaken, I continued my search, and finally my fingers settled on the cold metal end of the scissors. Snatching them up,

I walked the few feet to the bathroom, supplies in hand, shut the door and turned on the light.

I knew looking at my reflection that it was time. Before I changed my mind, I gathered up what I could on the left side of my head, pulled the hair out away from my head, and with one slice of the scissors, the hair was gone. I stared at the hairs hanging from my hand. They were gone forever because of me. I paused for a second and then continued on before I lost my nerve. With swift cuts, I removed what was left of my remaining hair. With the long strands gone, I slathered my scalp with shaving cream. Next, I ripped open the razor package and got to work. Progress was slow because the razor clogged so often, but eventually all the shaving cream and hair went down the drain. Bending my head under the bathroom faucet, I rinsed off the residue with warm water and then wrapped my head in a towel.

Standing up straight, I removed the towel and studied the unfamiliar image staring back at me. Stunned by what I saw, my stomach started to heave over the realization of what I had done. For better or for worse, I was bald.

After the initial shock wore off, I looked at my head more critically. Yes, my scalp was extremely pale, but that was something I could change with a few days in the sun out by the pool. Noticing that my head actually had a nice shape to it, I felt a little better. Running my hands over my scalp, it was strange to feel the smooth skin. As I gazed down in the trash and saw the last of my hair lying in a pile, I felt no regret. I was no longer on alopecia's timeline. I had taken matters into my own hands—made my own schedule—and that felt great.

Anxious to pull one over on Dad, I tiptoed softly down the stairs. Without a sound, I crept all the way to the kitchen table undiscovered. *Saturday Night Live* was still on, and Dad was sitting there watching it right where I had left him. His back was to me.

With as much dejection in my voice as I could muster, I announced, "I couldn't do it, Dad."

Immediately Dad turned around and saw me standing there completely bald. Unsure of what reaction my bare head would get, I was relieved to see a giant grin spread across his face. As he rushed over to me, I could see tears in his eyes.

"Stephanie, you are beautiful!" he said as he grabbed me and hugged me and I could tell he meant it. We stayed there together a few seconds, holding each other, crying. That night I found the courage to do what needed to be done and say goodbye forever to my hair. I deserved a few happy tears.

Seventeen

CAL-HI SPORTS

"Mrs. Weed?" I heard as I picked up the phone seconds before the answering machine kicked in. Coming back from retrieving the mail, I had just made it to the phone on time.

"Hi, Gary," I replied a little out of breath, instantly recognizing the voice of Stephanie's basketball coach. Standing at over six feet, Coach Hernandes was a big man in width and in stature. Having been instrumental in helping Stephanie through the past difficult months, we were extremely grateful for his leadership and sensitivity. I continued flipping through the mail as I cradled the phone on my shoulder.

"How are you today, Mrs. Weed?" he asked, always one to be cordial.

"I'm good," I answered. "What's up?" I knew he had to have something specific on his mind.

"Well, I got a call from Kevin Thom today. He is one of the reporters at Cal-Hi Sports. Are you familiar with that program? I think it airs on Sunday nights."

"Yes, I've seen it before. It's the show that covers Bay Area high school athletic events, right?" I had watched the program several times and always looked for glimpses of athletes I knew.

"That's right. Okay, so you know what I'm talking about, good. Well, Kevin called this week and was asking about the members of the Leigh team and we went over some statistics. Then he asked if there were any human interest stories among the players on our team. I immediately thought of Stephanie. I briefly told him about the incident on the court during the Notre Dame Belmont game and he said he's interested in doing a feature piece on her."

"Seriously?" I found it hard to believe someone thought her story was newsworthy. Of course, as her mother, I believed Stephanie had been extraordinary that night. I wasn't sure the rest of the world would share that view. Far from convinced, I remained skeptical.

"Yes, he is definitely interested. How do you think Stephanie would feel about being interview for TV? Would she do it?"

Silent for a few moments, lost in thought, I finally answered. "I think she might be very excited about it, but I don't know." Ever since revealing Stephanie's condition to the basketball coaches without her consent, I was hesitant to predict her reaction to any situation involving alopecia.

"Well, here's what we'll do," Gary offered in his relaxed, easygoing manner. "Talk to her about it and if she is interested, give me a call and we'll set up a time to do an on-camera interview. They want to do the interview at the gym and they'd also be interviewing me and a teammate of her choice. So, if she is agreeable, have her think about another player from the team she'd pick."

"Okay, I'll talk to her this afternoon and give you a call. I'm betting the answer will be yes." I hedged, allowing myself to get a little excited, but knew it was out of my hands.

"I hope so, Mrs. Weed. Talk to you later."

"Okay. Take care." I placed the phone back on the receiver as my brain started spinning. Cal-Hi sports wanted to interview Stephanie for a feature spot on their show! Gary was convinced the station considered her story newsworthy, but I wasn't sure. Naturally they didn't have to use the piece if they changed their mind after the interview was complete. Doubt invaded my mind. Taking into account all that had transpired in the past view months, I wasn't sure Stephanie would choose to expose herself in such a public forum. Given the choice, I wasn't sure what I would do in her place. Disclosing her secret to the basketball team and the staff at Leigh was one thing, but announcing her alopecia to a TV audience was a whole other matter. Would she want to talk on camera about the most embarrassing moment of her life?

I tried to push the matter from my thoughts and go about my day. As hard as I tried, I couldn't stop obsessing about the interview. Knowing Stephanie to be confident and poised in the spotlight, I was reasonably certain she would handle the interview well, but what would the repercussions be once the piece aired? It was possible the feedback would all be positive, but there was a risk. Would the reporter exercise sensitivity in the questions he asked? There were so many unknowns. The fact remained that it was Stephanie's decision and I would support her no matter what she chose. I knew watching the clock was not going to make time pass any quicker, so I gathered the laundry from upstairs and got busy.

Finally, two o'clock rolled around and I rushed the 2 1/2 miles to school, ready to break the news. Impatiently I tapped my fingers on the steering wheel, hardly able to contain my excitement. I saw student after student exiting the school, but no Stephanie. Where was that girl? Just when my nerves felt like they would snap, I spied Maiko and Stephanie strolling out in front of the gym, books in hand, carrying on an animated conversation. Maiko continued walking with Stephanie all the way to the car.

Steph opened the car door and leaned it, "Mom, can we give Maiko a ride home? Their car is in the shop."

"Sure. No problem. Hi Maiko!" I'd have to hold onto my news a little longer. After waiting for hours, what difference did another fifteen minutes make?

"Hi, Mrs. Weed. Thank you so much!" Maiko pulled on the automatic door handle to the van and got in.

Maiko lived just around the corner from us and it was never a problem giving her a lift. Forced to keep quiet awhile longer about the phone call, I listened to the girls chit chat as we traveled down the road, anxious to get to Maiko's house as soon as humanly possible. Gwen Stefani and Akon came on the radio with their hit "Sweet Escape" and the girls enthusiastically sang along, knowing all of the words by heart and I was momentarily distracted. After sitting through many red lights, eventually we arrived at Maiko's house. She thanked me profusely for the ride.

"See you tomorrow, Maiko," Stephanie yelled and waved out the open window as I put the car in reverse and backed out of Maiko's driveway.

"See you, Steph!" Maiko shouted back as she unlocked her front door and stepped in.

Driving away, the time had come. Finally we were alone.

"Steph, you're never going to guess what happened today," I spat out as fast as I could, bursting with excitement.

"What? Calm down, Mom," she said, laughing, skeptical of my exuberance.

"Cal-Hi Sports called Gary today and they want to do an interview with you!" I practically shouted as we rounded the corner onto Larabee Court.

"What?" Stephanie asked, completely baffled. "Why would they want to interview me?"

As we entered the house through the garage I recounted the conversation Gary and I had earlier in the day.

"Of course you know you don't have to do the interview. It's totally up to you," I assured her. "As your mom, I think it's a great thing, but I also understand why you might not want to have your embarrassing moment broadcast on TV." I wanted her to know I would be behind whatever decision she made.

"Are you kidding? Yeah, I'll do the interview!" she said with enthusiasm as she leaned back against the kitchen cabinets. "That's so cool!" Her face lit up with unbridled excitement.

"Gary said they wanted to interview one other teammate about you, so you need to decide who that might be," I said.

"That's easy," she said. "I want Katie."

Katie Werner, the tall center, was the only other freshman on the Leigh basketball team. Katie's sister Richelle, also tall, was on the team too. Partly because of their basketball ties, but also due to their incredible support through the tough stages of alopecia, the three girls had a close relationship. Stephanie and Katie were particularly close because they had played a full season on the same National Junior League basketball team the year before.

"I knew that's who you'd pick," I replied, concurring with her decision. "I'm going to call Gary and let him know. They want to do the interview at Leigh sometime after school, but before practice. Are there any days that wouldn't work out that you know of?"

"No. I don't have to do anything right after school this week," she answered. "Just make sure I'll have time to come home and touch up my hair and make-up before the interview," she wisely instructed.

After several phone calls, it was determined that the interview would be the following day an hour after school let out, in the lobby of the Leigh gym. The next day, as planned, I picked Stephanie and Katie up immediately after school. Once we arrived home, Steph had the momentous task of deciding what to wear for the event, and was plagued with indecision. Fortunately, Katie was available for cutting edge fashion advice. I excused myself from the process. Then there was the whole issue of her hair—should she curl it, straighten it or wear it in braids? She opted to wear it down, slightly curled with a wide bronze headband. Ready for her fifteen minutes of fame, she looked great in a simple graphic t-shirt and brown cotton zip-up jacket.

"You both look fabulous," I said.

Stephanie, always a joker, responded by smiling provocatively and made a sizzling noise when she touched her "red-hot" skin. "I'm just going to have to beat the guys away after they see my interview," she teased.

"Have you thought about how you're going to answer their questions?" I asked as the three of us piled in the Odyssey van and started the drive back to Leigh.

"A little. I don't want to over think things, though. I'm just going to wing it," she answered, clearly not worried.

"Are you nervous, Katie?"

"Not really," Katie replied. Helping her dad DJ on the weekends, Katie was accustomed to the spotlight.

"Like I said, girls, you both look terrific!" I pulled into a parking spot and stopped the car. "Good luck. I know you'll be fantastic!" We walked quickly to the gym lobby.

Gary Fernandes greeted the three of us in lobby of the gym, wearing a freshly pressed, button-down plaid dress shirt. Although the weather was beautiful that afternoon, the lighting in the foyer was slightly dim due to the large overhang that protected the L-shaped walkway wrapping around the front and side of the gym. A considerable number of scrapes, nicks, staples and old pieces of tape stood out on the walls, evidence of budget cuts and neglect. Funny how the imperfections had gone virtually unnoticed as I passed through that same lobby numerous times before going to and from basketball games. The mural above the dark green entry doors, proclaiming "Longhorn Country" with a massive steer head breathing steam was impressive, though. All things considered, it looked like they had chosen a satisfactory location for the shoot.

Before long, Kevin Thom and Mark Kochina from Cal-Hi Sports arrived and things got rolling. After inspecting the gym lobby and deeming it adequate, they set up chairs and the appropriate lighting and were ready to film. To put the girls at ease, they interviewed Gary first and gave me permission to stay and observe.

"Tell us what happened at Notre Dame Belmont," Kevin began. The bright lights and camera focused on Gary's face.

'Well, I knew Stephanie was going to wear her wig in the game— we had discussed it beforehand. I had advised wearing it at a non-league away game just in case something happened. Everything went fine through the first quarter, but at the start of the second quarter Stephanie took a charge and went down on the floor. Her wig kind of came askew on her when she fell. I immediately called a time-out and went over to talk to her to get her to relax a little. She just looked at me and said, 'This thing (the wig) has got to go, Coach.' She just took it right off, put her headband back on and went out and played. She played a heck of a game after that."

Kevin continued to ask Gary questions about Stephanie and how she fit in the team dynamics, with Mark manning the camera and lights.

Katie was up next and told how she had supported Stephanie through the past few months on the court and at school. "Some people talk about it…I just stand up for her cause I know how hard it must be. She's a really strong person especially with that disease. She's so brave."

Finally it was Stephanie's turn in the spotlight. Positioning her to catch the light just right, Mark began filming.

"When did you first notice signs of alopecia?" Kevin asked from behind the camera.

"In sixth grade I noticed a really small bare spot on my eyebrow, and after a couple of years I started losing hair on my head that gradually got worse," she answered, seeming a little nervous, but mostly at ease.

Minutes ticked by and the interview continued, Kevin gathering the necessary background information for the piece. Eventually, he got around to the most significant question. "What was it like for you out on the court at Notre Dame the other night?"

Holding my breath, I waited to see how she would handle revisiting that horrendous night. Anytime I had broached the subject, she immediately dismissed the topic and would not engage—some of that reaction was typical teenage angst, but also I knew remembering the incident had to be painful.

To my relief, I saw her face light up as a smile crept across her face. "I can still remember the crowd, like, gasping," she responded, laughing, somehow able to find the humor in that tragic moment now that a few weeks had passed. "I love playing basketball and I just wanted to finish the game."

"How did your teammates react?"

"The whole team has been really supportive. I probably wouldn't be playing basketball without them."

"Do you worry about how your disease affects your appearance?"

"Going to practice is hard because our practices are right after the guys' practice and they're still in there, and you know, every high school girl likes to look good for the guys." She smiled bashfully, but raised an eyebrow at the same time. "This week, I finally decided to shave my head, so now I wear a bandana at practice and in the games."

"How has your mom helped you deal with this?" Kevin asked.

"My mom has been really great. Sometimes I get home from practice and I'll be in a really bad mood because I don't like to have my wig off. She just knows that's what I'm going through and leaves me alone. She's a really big support for me on and off the court."

With great anticipation we turned on the television that Sunday night to catch the Cal-High Sports program. Midway through the hour we were rewarded and saw a still shot of Stephanie displayed on the set below the anchor desk with the caption "Still in the Game". Robert Braunstein, the host of the show, explained the Orchard Supply

Hardware Spirit of Achievement weekly feature. "This award spotlights an athlete who has overcome adversity in his or her life to succeed in sports and in the classroom."

Kevin Thom then had the floor. "Alopecia areata affects many people, including NBA star Charlie Villanueva. But for a girl, it's tougher. Still, for this Leigh High School player, despite this ailment, she's still in the game."

"The way Leigh freshman Stephanie Weed plays basketball you wouldn't think she has any reason to be self-conscious on the court, but if you look a little closer you might notice that Stephanie is dealing with more than just making a shot or playing good defense. Stephanie has a widely unknown disease called alopecia, which causes hair loss at a young age and affects five million people in the US."

The feature continued highlighting the wig incident on the court. "Stephanie wore a wig in a game, but her aggressive play makes this a problem..." Both Gary and Stephanie's recount of the incident was aired. There were clips of Stephanie leading the team cheer, making a steal, sinking a jump shot, saving the ball, driving for a layup, diving to the floor, and adjusting her headband on her nearly bald head while running down the court.

Kevin concluded the feature with these words. "With three more years of varsity basketball in her future and a close bond with her talented classmate, Katie, Stephanie is on track to leave behind a legacy of perseverance and success at Leigh."

Unsure how much of the interview would end up on the cutting room floor, we were all extremely pleased with the content of Kevin's piece. Kevin had accurately depicted her struggle and precisely captured the essence of her spirit. Seeing Stephanie's hair loss highlighted on TV was considerably more dramatic than observing her at an actual game where there were so many other distractions. Watching the footage of her playing with half of her hair gone was a poignant visible reminder of just how much she had overcome. More than the pride I felt for Stephanie's bravery, was the hope I felt this feature offered to other teens struggling with cosmetic issues. Stephanie's reaction to a difficult situation illustrated that what mattered most was your heart, not any physical imperfections. Given the chance, your heart can outshine anything.

Eighteen

BRENDA, KEILY AND RACHEL

As the weeks went by, my wig lost more and more hair. The thinning was becoming noticeable and was going to get worse. Knowing a replacement would be needed soon, I was not looking forward to returning to the wig shop. Sure, I did end up liking my wig, but the styling appointment disaster was still fresh in my mind. Fortunately, one of Mom's good friends mentioned a place she had heard of in San Jose that sold wigs—The Next Step, a Women's Boutique. Once she found out that they had private fitting rooms, Mom made an appointment for Friday afternoon. Leigh had a minimum day that Friday, so we would have a good two hours before my younger sister got out of school.

As we entered the shop, I couldn't wait to see what kind of selection they had. The shop was chock full of merchandise. Dozens of mannequin heads lined the mirrored shelves displaying many types of wigs and hairpieces and hats. Underneath the mirrored rows there were several bins overflowing with scarves of different prints and colors. I liked the Victorian décor—everything looked so girly and pretty. Surrounded by gold framed mirrors, lace and jewel covered knickknacks, I felt like I was shopping in an exclusive boutique.

"Can I help you?" asked the young girl behind the counter.

"Yes, my daughter Stephanie Weed has an appointment to try on wigs," Mom answered, motioning in my direction.

"Hi, Stephanie, my name is Gina," the salesclerk volunteered as she extended her hand.

"Hi," was all I offered. Even though I was now accustomed to wearing a wig, I still wasn't all that comfortable talking about it, or shopping for one. Fortunately, the shop momentarily had no other customers.

"So, what are you looking for?" Gina asked.

"She's wearing a human hair wig right now, but we'd like to try an acrylic one—we've heard great things about them," Mom replied.

"Sure. The acrylic wigs are nice and much cheaper than human hair. Do you need a full wig or are you looking for a partial hairpiece?

"Definitely a full wig," Mom answered.

"Okay, great. Stephanie, what style were you thinking of?" she asked.

Reluctant to respond, but knowing I must, I answered, "I definitely want something long, kind of like that one over there," I said as I pointed to a blondish wig on the top row that looked a lot like the wig I had on. "I'd like to look at some different colors, too, if you have them." I was relieved I could get the words out.

"Okay, why don't you step into this room and I'll bring a few in for you to look at," she said as she directed us to a small, private room with two chairs, a side table and a large mirror.

"Thank you," Mom called as Gina headed for the storeroom.

"I don't want to take my wig off in front of her!" I blurted out as soon as Gina was out of earshot.

"I'm sure that's fine, Steph. Don't worry about it. They see people everyday with no hair and I'm sure they'll understand your need for privacy," Mom assured me.

"She better..."

"Don't worry, Steph, I'll make sure she leaves the room before you take your wig off."

Gina bounced back in, her hands full of hair. "I brought several types and colors for you to try on. This one is long. What do you think of the color?" She combed through the layered dark brunette wig with her fingers.

"I think I like it," I answered, eager to see how the chocolate brown color would look with my eyes and skin.

"Do you want some help getting it on, or would you like some privacy?"

"I can do it. Privacy would be nice," I answered, relieved that she asked.

"Sure. No problem. Just call me if you need help," Gina responded as she slid the pocket door closed.

"Turn around, Mom," I insisted before I took my wig off. After shaving my head, I wasn't used to exposing the baldness, even to my mom. At home I opted for wearing a beanie when I had my wig off, which worked well since it was wintertime and our house was always cold.

As soon as she turned, I pulled my blond wig off and grabbed the long brown one. Once I had it in place, I turned toward the full-length mirror in front of me.

"Okay, Mom. You can look."

We both scrutinized my reflection.

"I like it, Steph. What do you think?" Mom asked as she played a little with the placement of the hair.

"I think I like the color. I can't believe how much lighter it is than my other wig—that feels good. What do you think of the cut?" Layered and shorter than my other wig, this cut looked completely different.

"I like the layers and the bangs are a good length for your head. The color is fabulous—I told you dark colors look great on you!" Mom said after examining the hair with a critical eye.

A knock on the door halted our conversation.

"Come in," Mom answered and Gina slid the door open.

"That style looks great on you. How do you like it?" Gina asked with an approving smile.

"I really like it. It's so lightweight," I answered, still primping and adjusting the hair.

"Human hair does weigh a lot more. Have you tried any of the others yet?" Gina asked pointing to the pieces she had left on the small side table.

"No, this is the first one. I don't think she wants to take it off," Mom answered, teasing.

"That's fine. Take your time. I'll be in the front of the shop so just call if you need help or have any questions." Gina backed out of the room and slid the door shut once again.

Mom picked up a short blond bob. "Why don't you try this one on next? It would be great for working out in since it's shorter. You might even be able to put it in a short ponytail."

"Okay. Turn around," I instructed as I pulled off the brunette wig and placed the short blond one on my head. "You can look now."

Again, we both observed the new look. Curling under at my chin, I had never seen myself with such a short cut, and it wasn't half bad. Unmistakably, it did make me look older, which could be both good and bad.

"That looks great, too, Steph," Mom said, sounding surprised.

For over an hour, I tried on wig after wig, different styles and different colors. Somehow, I kept coming back to the original brunette one. The cut seemed perfect and the color was truly growing on me.

"Do you want to get that one?" Mom asked.

"You mean get it today?" I was shocked. "I thought you said we were just looking today."

"I did, but that style looks so perfect around your face and the color is great. If you really like it I'll get it," Mom said and I could tell she was excited.

"I'm going to try it on one more time, just to be safe," I said, wanting to be sure before I made my final decision.

Looking at my brunette reflection once again, I thought, why not? Lots of my friends had gone from blond to brunette in the last couple of years; I might as well join them.

"Sure, let's get it," I decided.

To my surprise, Mom also bought the short blond bob that I could use for the gym or when I went running. Compared to the cost of my last wig, the synthetic wigs were a real bargain at roughly $200 a piece. Even though I knew it was a necessity, I had felt guilty when Mom shelled out $1600 for my first one, especially when it lasted only a few months. Now that we had found an inexpensive alternative, we were both breathing a little easier. It was nice to have options.

Several days later I got up the nerve to wear my ginger brown hair to school. I was amazed by how many people still did not know my story and asked if I had dyed my hair or got extensions. I would simply reply "yes" instead of going into a lengthy discussion about what was really going on. All the girls on the basketball team loved my brunette look, and named that wig "Rachel", which led to them naming my long blond one "Brenda" and the short blond one "Kiely". I loved the camaraderie—the girls made me feel like I belonged and supported me whenever they could.

Nineteen

THE MERCURY NEWS

S teph, a reporter from the *Mercury News* wants to interview you about your alopecia," Mom announced as I got in the car after school, exhausted and starving as usual.

"Seriously?" I asked. Cal-Hi Sports was one thing, but the Mercury was a completely different matter. "Why?"

"You remember my friend Katie from high school?" Mom asked once she was clear of all the speeding cars leaving the school lot.

"Yes," I answered, wondering what Katie had to do with The Mercury.

"Her cousin is a sports writer at the newspaper and he saw your feature on Cal-Hi Sports the other night. He thought your story would be great for the sports section. He's a sports writer."

"Really? I didn't think it was all that exciting, but whatever. I don't really care anymore who knows about my alopecia." I was thinking it might be pretty cool to have an article in the sports section about me.

"Great. I'll call him back and let him know. He's going to interview you over the phone and then talk to Dad and me. He seemed like a nice guy when I spoke with him earlier."

Wow! After going through so many disappointing days in the past few months, things were starting to look up. Maybe there was a silver lining to this cloud. If I had known back in September that by December my hair would be completely gone—just a series of clumps bundled up in the trash buried in the local landfill—I don't think I could've handled it. Now that I had let go and moved on, some great opportunities were popping up and I was ready to embrace them.

Like my mom had said, David Kiefer was a nice guy. His familiarity with the disease helped him know just what questions to ask when he interviewed me. As predicted, he was very impressed by my actions on the court after losing my wig, but I still felt I did what anyone else would have done in the same situation. It wasn't a big deal. In any case, it was nice to be able to laugh about it. He talked to Mom and Dad—I don't know what they said to him, but I prayed it was all good and nothing embarrassing. Parents love to say the most obnoxious things. It makes you wonder if *they* were ever teenagers. Keeping my fingers crossed, I hoped for the best. David informed me at the end of our conversation that he was sending a photographer to the basketball game on Monday night to get some shots for the article. Great. As much as I liked having my picture taken, I was nervous enough playing point guard. With a photographer there it would be worse.

Game night came and, as promised, the photographer showed up. Unobtrusive, he stayed out of the way, although conversations were buzzing among the players about who made it into what shots. Excited myself, but a little apprehensive, I hoped they didn't catch me wiping my nose or dislodging a wedgie. Before long the buzzer sounded ending the final quarter and it was time to stash all the gym equipment and head home.

As I fell asleep that night, I knew the article would be in the paper the next morning. Yes, I was excited, but I also was afraid of what exactly David would print and how this "outing" of my disease would be received by the students at Leigh. It could go either way for me—it could be a day of celebration or embarrassment. I prayed for a favorable outcome as I drifted off into a restless sleep, dreaming of photographers snapping pictures while I dribbled down the court.

"Stephanie, wake up! Your picture is on the front page!" I heard Mom shout as she shook me awake. "Get up! You're not going to believe it!"

"Wha…" I started to say as I groggily clawed my way back to consciousness. "Okay, I'm getting up…"

Mornings never were my strong suit; in fact it was my least favorite time of the day. Slowly, I sat up on the side of the bed, my mind still foggy, and my body barely responding. Finally, I was awake.

Had Mom just said "front page"? I bolted from the bed and grabbed my robe. Taking the stairs three at a time, I flew into the kitchen.

As I approached the table I saw the paper. Underneath an 8x10 color photo of my face, complete with green bandana, was the headline "The Courage to Be Herself".

At the top of the picture was this banner:

"A rare skin disease has robbed Stephanie Weed of her hair, but it couldn't take away her dignity."

Just under my chin in the picture was the quote:

"This was the turning point of me finally accepting it. There was nothing worse that could happen."
--Weed, after her scalp condition became apparent when her wig came loose during a basketball game.

Underneath the large picture and headline was another picture of me dribbling the ball, underscored by these words:

"Leigh High freshman Stephanie Weed tried hiding her alopecia areata by wearing a wig, but now shaves her head and wears a bandanna."

The article continued inside the front section with another large photo of me hugging Richelle Werner, celebrating senior night.

The caption read:

"Teen—Disease means no hair, but she still has plenty of heart."

I was floored. Expecting to dig through the sports section to find a small article with maybe one tiny picture, I was staring at the front page with my face on it, twice! Proclaiming to its 1,600,000 readers, the *Mercury News* announced to everyone in the Bay Area that I had no hair, but had the courage to be myself.

The article detailed the path my alopecia had taken and included a play-by-play description of the wig incident on the basketball court. Any mystery surrounding me was over. Twice shouted in headlines, alongside pictures of me, was the fact that I had no hair. It was abundantly clear from the pictures and headlines that the identity of the bald girl was me. Even though I was a little nervous to face the uncertain reaction of my peers, I knew I could handle it. At least I didn't have to hide my condition any more. By the end of the morning over a million people would know my secret.

"Are you okay with all this, Steph?" Mom asked.

Neither of us had any idea the article would end up on the front page, and certainly never dreamed it would include a large close-up of my face. Remembering that I freaked when she told Gary about my alopecia without my permission, I could understand why Mom was worried. So much had transpired since then, I felt like a different person. After what I had been through, I was stronger and not afraid. Knowing other hurdles lay ahead of me, I wasn't frightened.

"Are you kidding? This is awesome!" I shouted to Mom as I reached into the pantry for my favorite box of cereal. Practically shaking from excitement I overflowed my cereal bowl with milk and had to clean up the mess. Able to get just a few bites down, I finally gave up and tossed what was left down the kitchen sink.

Racing up the stairs, I knew I had a ridiculously perfect shirt to wear that day. Rushing past my door I impatiently pushed hanger after hanger aside looking for the shirt. Not finding it on the first try, I frantically searched again. Where was it? Again I started at one end of my closet, searching hanger by hanger, but couldn't find it. It wasn't anywhere. I knew I had seen it just the other day. Taking a deep breath, I calmed myself and slowly searched once again through the endless row of hangers, one by one. Half way down the row, my patience finally paid off when I found the shirt I was looking for pushed back behind the others. Printed in bold letters across the chest were the words:

Brunette Today

Blond Tomorrow

Perfect!

As I dressed that morning, I was worried about facing people when they found out I was bald, but I also thought of what else the article claimed about me—that I was courageous and had plenty of heart and dignity.

At the end of the article, David concluded with these words:

> *"Stephanie knows there are many others with alopecia areata who are still wondering if they should run and hide. She can't tell them what to do, but she can show them that life's most embarrassing moments can sometimes turn into the most glorious."*

Brunette today, blond tomorrow was just a better way of saying, "I have alopecia and I'm okay." I didn't want pity. If my supposed bravery could help some other unlucky person deal with alopecia, then maybe all I had been through had a purpose after all.

Twenty

HAWAII

Stephanie received an amazing amount of positive feedback from the February 14th, 2007 front page article. David Kiefer forwarded emails that he received. Many included the words, "compelling, inspirational, extremely courageous," and "moved to tears". Perhaps the most meaningful were the emails from fellow alopecia sufferers that applauded her for sharing her condition with the public.

Back in November of 2006, when Stephanie's condition was so devastating to us all, I felt my prayers were useless. As the feedback from her article came pouring in I began to see glimpses of a master plan. My fearless toddler, who was impossible to keep out of harm's way, had grown into a young adult ready to face this difficult challenge. With her innate boldness, she had soared right over every hurdle and was paving the way for others to follow. Maybe God was listening after all.

The remainder of Stephanie's freshman year at Leigh High School was largely uneventful. A few more wigs entered the picture—she was amassing quite a collection. Due to constant contact with her clothing, the longer acrylic wigs got nappy fairly quickly. Two months was about the longest they lasted. Being resourceful, once the ends looked bad, Steph cut them off into a new shorter style, thus extending the wear-time by months. In the span of a week, I saw her in a number of different looks—short blond, long brown, short brown, long blond, long red. One afternoon when school was out for the summer, we were standing in the kitchen, drinking some soda when she blurted out, "I'm so lucky!"

I knew she was referring to having alopecia, and I was astonished that she felt that way. "Wow, really?"

"Yes. Think about it. I can shower and get ready in two minutes flat, with my hair absolutely perfect, and I can change my hair color three times a day if I want. How cool is that?"

Her attitude amazed me. Never in a million years would I have thought I'd hear those words coming out of her mouth. The fact that she felt lucky to have no hair showed the power of optimism. Yes, there still were times when being bald was inconvenient, but she dealt with those times good-naturedly (for the most part), and focused on the positive aspects of baldness. Being able to get ready and be out the door in a couple short minutes was definitely a plus for my social sixteen year old.

Looming on the horizon that summer was our trip to Kauai. Having vacationed on the Hawaiian island several times before, no time would be wasted finding the best snorkeling and boogie boarding beaches. We knew just where to go and were looking forward to a week of recreation and relaxation. We weren't leaving until August 4th, so the first two months of the summer were spent mostly in the back yard at the pool enjoying the palm trees and the California sun. Fortunately, this gave Steph almost two full months to tan her head before we left. Neither of us were sure how she would handle being at the beaches in Kauai, but she wanted to have the option of going bald. She would only consider doing that if her head matched the golden brown of the rest of her skin. By the beginning of August, her head was nice and brown and on August fourth we boarded our flight to Lihue, Kauai.

Walking off the plane in Lihue, we were greeted by the warm humid air. Lihue Airport is the primary airport on Kauai and consists of two runways and eight gates—it's impossible to get lost. Excited to be at our destination, we quickly made our way to baggage claim. The smell of plumeria from the lei vendors' stands filled the tepid breeze in the open air terminal. All ten of our bags arrived. With five of us traveling together, it was always a challenge to fit our luggage in the rental car. Tracy managed all our bags in record time and soon we were off to the grocery store.

Prices in the local market were predictably high. Supplies weren't cheap on an island in the middle of the Pacific Ocean. Five dollars for a loaf of bread seemed outrageous, but eating out was even more costly, so we filled up our cart, hoping that $400 worth of groceries would get us at least part way through the week. By the time our shopping was complete, it was dark. After making our way through the parking lot to the car, once again we loaded up—bags of groceries stuffed in every available nook and cranny—and headed the thirteen miles to our two bedroom condo on Poipu Beach.

Climbing out of the car into the familiar parking lot on Pe'e Road, we could hear the sound of waves crashing against the jagged rocky shore. Although we could see nothing beyond the paved lot surrounding the hotel complex, the smell of the ocean was right there. Having missed the sunset, we couldn't wait to wake up the next morning and take in the beautiful ocean view. Check-in was accomplished without incident, and before too long we were settled into our corner ground floor unit enjoying the soothing sound of the waves from our very own living room.

Ten am in California was only 7am in Hawaii, so we were up early the next day. Tracy and I enjoyed our morning cup of coffee on the lanai outside our unit while watching the waves roll in. There was nothing between our porch and the ocean except a small walkway and a few yards of lava rocks. Sipping fresh gourmet coffee in a lounge chair by the ocean was heavenly.

Not too long after we finished our coffee, the girls began to stir. Digging into the cereal, they filled their urgent need for food in a flash and were ready to start our adventures.

"Dad and I are going for a run and then to the pool hut to rent boogie boards and beach chairs. You girls put your dishes in the dishwasher and get your suits and sunscreen on. We'll hit Shipwreck

Beach first when we get back," I instructed as Tracy and I headed out the door.

Only a few other souls were out exercising that early on the roads winding through the many resort complexes at Poipu. Running by the ocean was exhilarating. Watching the endless patterns of waves hit the shore—the raw beauty and power of it—made us momentarily forget the effort we were exerting. Unfortunately, the last mile of our normal running course was uphill and away from the shore, which seemed to magnify the steepness and humidity, but we always finished, glad that we had expended the extra effort.

"Hey girls," I called as we walked back into our unit. "Great job picking up." I glanced around the kitchen, surprised that everything was put away. I knew better than to look in the bathroom they shared—that would certainly kill my mood.

"Hi, Mom and Dad!" Valerie shouted as she got off the couch and ran to greet us with a vivacious smile. Noticing the sweat pouring from every inch of our bodies, she wisely stopped short of giving us a hug.

"Can we go to the beach now?" Valerie asked, excited to get outside.

"Why don't you get Stephanie and Lindsay and walk down to Shipwreck Beach and see if its red flagged or not while Dad and I are showering? If it is, we'll walk over to Poipu Beach and swim there," I said, as the air-conditioned room began to stem the seemingly endless flow of sweat coming from my body.

"Okay!" Valerie shouted in eager anticipation of splashing in the warm ocean waters. She dashed into the second bedroom to retrieve her sisters.

As was always the case, that beach was red flagged, so we gathered the rented equipment and drove the half-mile to Poipu State Beach Park on the other side of our resort. It was only nine am, but the sun was high and warm. Claiming our spot in the sand under a large palm tree, we set up our chairs, dumped our snorkeling gear and headed for the water. Stephanie was wearing her short blond wig up in a ponytail. Due to a long breakwater out from the shore, the waves were very gentle at that beach, so I was confident her wig wouldn't pose a problem. Just the perfect temperature to be refreshing, the water was as blue as the sky. Immersed up to our shoulders in the crystal clear water, we leisurely floated up and down with the swells of the waves. Stephanie gave Valerie some boogie-boarding pointers in the small waves that broke on the shore, but they weren't really strong enough to do much with.

Taking a break, I toweled off and relaxed in one of our chairs, basking in the warmth of the warm tropical sun. Traffic was picking up at the beach by then, but there was plenty of room for all the tourists. Momentarily I saw Tracy and Steph approaching from the water.

"You doing okay?" Tracy asked as he got closer, water dripping down his face and chest.

"Just peachy!" I smiled back from beneath my hat and sunglasses.

❧❧❧mother❧❧❧

"We're going snorkeling. Lindsay is out there with Valerie in the water," Tracy said as they grabbed their masks and fins.

"Okay.'

So this was the first test. I saw Steph pull her mask out of the backpack. I was a bit nervous as to how she was going to get the sticky rubber strap of the goggles over her head without the wig coming off. I watched, glad my sunglasses concealed my staring. Like a pro, she placed the goggles just under her nose and pulled the wide strap right over her wig to the back of her head and let go. It usually took me at least a couple tries to get the goggles on right and I didn't have a wig to worry about, so I was relieved she succeeded on her first attempt, but not surprised.

"See you in a while," Tracy called as he blew me a kiss and they headed for the water, flippers in hand.

"Have fun!" I shouted over the roar of the waves. Always amused by the sight of someone putting on the awkward flippers, I settled in to watch the coming entertainment. Thigh deep in the crystal clear water, Tracy managed to get the first flipper on without any mishaps. As he tried to get the second foot secured he started to lose his balance, saved himself twice, as his arms wind milled, but then couldn't hang on and splashed backwards into the water. Without fail, it was the second flipper that got you every time. Stephanie had a different approach. Attaching the flippers on dry sand, she carefully waddled backwards into the water, which worked like a charm. When she was about ten feet into the water a large swell came in and she also lost her balance and tumbled backside first into the water. At that point they were floating neck deep in the shallow water, both busting up with laughter.

After positioning their snorkels I saw them swim away. I watched as they slowly drifted over to a reef that was home to a vast array of colorful tropical fish. Unsure how the salt water would affect Stephanie's wig, I did my best to relax on the shore. The swaying palm trees and cool trade winds did an adequate job of distracting me, but I still worried. Thousands of miles away in the middle of the ocean, I knew there was no possibility of getting a replacement wig in time if the salt water damaged her hair, so she would have to make the best of whatever happened.

I had just about dozed off, my legs stretched out in the warm sand in front of me, my baseball cap tipped over my face, when I was jolted awake by a spray of cold water droplets assaulting my skin. I looked up to see both Tracy and Stephanie shaking their wet heads above me.

"You're in trouble now!" I shouted as I sprang from my chair and attempted to chase them down. Not wanting to draw too much attention to my 46 year old body, I gave up after just a few yards in the sand and headed back to the chair. Busy with thoughts of retaliation, it suddenly registered that Stephanie's hair looked fine. Yes, it was still wet even after shaking much of the salt water onto me, but the color hadn't changed as far as I could tell, and nothing had torn or melted. Good.

After we all had taken turns with the snorkeling gear, we packed up and drove to the North Shore to try and locate a place called

"Queen's Bath" in Princeville. Unable to find the famous lava pool on our last trip to the island, we were determined to find the obscure attraction this trip. Before setting out on the hour and a half drive to Princeville, we made sandwiches to eat in the car. Stephanie rinsed the salt water out of her wig and stashed it in the beach bag. After she put her short brown hair on we were on our way.

Heading up Highway 520 we passed through the familiar Tree Tunnel. Over 500 eucalyptus trees planted by a wealthy cattle rancher over a century ago formed a beautiful canopy that shaded a mile long stretch of the highway. Almost immediately after exiting the tunnel, we merged onto Highway 50 with its characteristically heavy, slow moving traffic. It served no purpose to be in a hurry on Kauai—the only route around the island was a two-lane highway with few opportunities to pass. After reaching Lihue, we traveled on scenic Highway 56, which followed the eastern shore up north through the most populated city on the island, Kapa'a. Hugging the shore, the road wound past one amazing view after another.

Finally, we arrived in Princeville and located what we believed to be the parking lot for Queen's Bath. After sliding down the slightly treacherous dirt and mud trail 25 yards to the rocky coastline, we could see a group of tourists about 300 yards off to the left. Certain we had finally located the illusive pool, we carefully made our way over the mass of large lava rocks to the site of Queen's Bath. Having read that the area could be extremely treacherous depending on the surf, we forged ahead cautiously. Fortunately, conditions were ideal when we arrived. Carved into a lava shelf, the crystal clear natural pool was the size of an Olympic sized pool. Formed by a ring of raised porous lava rock, the oval pool was an unexpected sight along the wide black rocky shore. From the high shore side wall the view was stunning. Even with the surf fairly calm, waves crashed over the slight ocean side wall, sending spray high into the air.

After climbing down the 15 ft. wall, we jumped into the refreshing ocean water. A small inlet at the mouth of the pool fed fresh seawater in fast enough to keep the water clear, but not quick enough to disturb the calm surface of the bath.

On the inland side of the pool, there was a large outcropping of black rock that rose a good ten feet above the water level. Positioned perfectly, the rock was a jumping platform for the more adventurous visitors. Intrigued, we watched as several teens in succession jumped. Not jumping out far enough could result in a nasty collision with the submerged lava rock below.

"I'm going for it!" Lindsay murmured as she rose from her spot on the rocks.

"Wow! Okay. I'll take your picture. Be careful!" I shouted as she started making her way past the inlet up to the platform on the adjacent side of the pool.

"Trace, quick!" I yelled and motioned him over with my arm. He was swimming in the pool and I wanted him to make sure the jump was safe. Fortunately he heard and swam over with Valerie. "Lindsay is going to jump. I'll stay here with Val. Can you go see if it's safe?" I asked, hoping there was time.

"It's fine. I was swimming over there earlier. The water's pretty deep," he informed me as he hoisted himself out of the pool onto the lava rock edge.

"You're sure?" I questioned, doubtful.

"Yes. She'll be fine. I'm positive," he declared as he grabbed his glasses out of our bag.

I grabbed our camera just in time to catch Lindsay mid-air. In seconds she hit the water and submerged. To the sound of us cheering she rose out of the water, with a big smile on her face.

"Mom, I want to jump, but I'm afraid I'll lose my hair," Steph whispered. Her wig was definitely going be an issue.

"Hmm," I said, "you could hold onto your wig with one hand." Steph was always the dare-devil of the group and I knew it was killing her to not be on that rock.

"That would look stupid!" she answered and I had to agree. "What if I put these swim goggles on over my wig—do you think that would work?"

"That's a great idea. I think you should go for it. I'll be ready with the camera."

"No pictures!" Stephanie commanded as she glared at me.

"Okay, okay." I gave in and put the camera away.

As she made her way around the pool to the giant boulders, I noticed her tightening the strap on the goggles.

"Please, not today," I prayed as she got into position. Even though Queen's Bath wasn't too crowded—maybe 20 people at the most—it still would have been pretty awkward if her wig came off and she had to swim to the side before she could get it back on. She jumped. Holding my breath, I saw her hit the water and go under. For several seconds she was completely submerged, swallowed up by the circle of foaming water. Finally, her head immerged with wig and goggles perfectly in place. Breathing a sigh or relief, I gave her the thumbs up sign from my spot on the side.

After a little over an hour, we decided it was time to go and made the trek back across the uneven lava rocks and up the muddy trail to the top of the bluff where our car was waiting. Pleased that we had successfully located Queen's Bath, we began the long drive back to Poipu along the coast.

Just south of Princeville we came upon Banana Joe's Fruit Stand. Banana Joes is a small locally owned business that sells island grown exotic fruits, homemade breads and the best "frosties" on the planet. Made completely of frozen fruit with no added ice or milk, the frosties are made by feeding frozen fruit into one side of a small white grinding machine. Out the other side comes a substance that is the consistency of soft-serve ice cream and has the taste of sherbet, but contains no added sugar or fat. It's amazing and delicious. Once we had our pineapple frosties in hand, we sat in the grass shack conveniently located out front and enjoyed the healthy snack.

After the break, we got back in the car and headed south. Traffic was light on that section of the highway and the miles flew by. Soon we were approaching one of our favorite boogie-boarding beaches—Kealia Beach. As we crested the hill above the beach, we could see the powerful waves crashing onto shore below. Stretching for miles, the deep blue water met the sky in a perfectly flat line on the horizon that seemed to go on forever.

"Dad, can we go to this beach, please?" Valerie asked, always ready to chase the waves.

"It's fine with me. Does everyone else want to go?" he asked the rest of us.

We all agreed and as we neared the turn-off, he slowed down. Parking for the beach was adequate, but unpaved. Driving over the uneven iron rich red dirt could be tricky, but Tracy managed without any problems. As we got out of the car and began to gather the chairs and boards, Steph looked a little worried.

"I don't know what to do," she told Tracy and me. Listening to the violent crash of the waves against the shore I understood her dilemma.

"You can always wear nothing on your head," I suggested out of earshot of anyone else.

"Maybe I'll just sit on the beach," she said as she looked out at the waves. Lindsay and Valerie had already run ahead and claimed their patch of sand on the beach.

"You would look great either way. Honestly, Steph," Tracy said.

She stood there, thinking about her options. In the end, the pull of the waves was too much to resist. "I'll just go for it," she decided as she leaned into the car and pulled off her wig. Tracy was correct—she did look beautiful without her hair, striking even. Because of her fastidious tanning at home, her whole head had a bronze glow. Without hair, her eyes looked larger than life. Following her out onto the beach, I couldn't help but feel proud.

In a flash she was out in the waves with Tracy and Lindsay, trying to catch that perfect ride. The more powerful waves tossed them about and ground them into the ocean floor, but they rode a majority of them all the way onto the beach, grinning from ear to ear. Valerie stayed closer to shore, and had fun riding the gentler waves. Not a thrill seeker myself, I took a couple rides with Val and was then happy to sit out and take pictures.

The afternoon wore on and soon we were all exhausted and ready for a shower. Knocking the sand off as best we could, we loaded our salt and sand coated bodies back in the car. As I was trying to do something with my crusty, ocean tossed hair, I saw Steph grab her wig and put it on. In an instant she was fresh and ready to go.

"Hey, that's not fair. Your hair is perfect," I teased as I desperately tried to get a comb through my tangled mess. She just smiled.

Over the next several days, we hiked the Kalalau Trail along the Na Pali coast, snorkeled at Tunnels and Poipu, and relaxed in the sun. Enjoying being away from the hectic pace of the Bay Area, we loved the laid back island lifestyle. Several other family members were also vacationing on the island that same week. My sister Terri, her husband and their three kids were staying at our resort, along with my Dad, older brother Bob and his wife Olivia. On Thursday of that week Terri and I planned to take the kids on a catamaran snorkel trip up the Na Pali coast, while Tracy, Bob and Olivia rented Harleys and toured Waimea Canyon.

As we approached Port Allen early Thursday morning, we were all excited. Having hiked along the cliffs a few days before, we couldn't wait to see the beautiful coastline from the water. The steep rippled velvet green cliffs drop thousands of feet straight down into the ocean making the coastline inaccessible except by hiking or by boat. The prehistoric looking jagged cliffs have appeared in many movies such as *Jurassic Park, Raiders of the Lost Ark, Six Days Seven Nights* and the remake of *King Kong*.

Valerie was especially looking forward to the spinner dolphins that loved to swim alongside the boats. For me, it was the goggles with corrective lenses provided by the tour company that I couldn't wait to try. Being able to observe the colorful tropical eco system in focus was going to be an added bonus.

Promptly at 8am we boarded the luxury 55-foot, sleek white catamaran. Along with roughly thirty other passengers, we stepped onto the boat and found a spot in the cabin below to store our gear. Next, we headed up top to put on sunscreen. After the crew made introductions and gave their obligatory safety speech, we departed the port slowly. Once we left the no wake zone and reached the open ocean, we picked up speed and were treated to a nice continental breakfast complete with coffee, juice, bagels, cinnamon rolls and a variety of fresh fruit. August weather on Kauai is generally pleasant and sunny and that day was no exception.

As the catamaran skimmed along the surface of the water, I breathed in the fresh air and enjoyed watching the miles of vast ocean fly by. Distant white clouds hung in the clear sky that stretched out endlessly against the darker ocean. You could see for miles. Occasionally our progress was interrupted by pods of spinner dolphins. When the dolphins appeared, a crowd would immediately form on that side of the boat, with the passengers holding onto the rail with one hand, camera in the other, hoping to snap a few stunning photos of the mammals' aerial maneuvers. With great acrobatic skill, the dolphins would leap out of the water and fly alongside the boat, making over a dozen full twists before diving back into the water. Stars of the show, the mother-calf pairs that spun in unison were amazing to watch.

On the bow of the boat there were two trampolines available for sunbathing or enjoying the ride if you didn't mind getting wet. Stephanie, Lindsay and Valerie along with my niece Emily and nephew Michael chose that spot to travel and were lying with their stomachs on the trampolines, clutching onto the ropes as the boat plowed through the waves. Hanging on tight, the kids were enjoying a thrilling ride and getting soaked at the same time. The bigger the wave, the more they screamed. Wave after wave sprayed them. Occasionally the other passengers seated up front on the padded benches got splashed, which was where I chose to sit. I was staying relatively dry, but getting sprayed nonetheless. Under the bright tropical sun the ocean water was refreshing—such an enjoyable ride. Content to sit back and relax, I tipped my head back against the boat and let my mind go as the boat gently bounced along.

Suddenly, without warning, the boat crested a rogue swell. My mind snapped to attention as I felt the boat rise higher and higher in the air. I held onto my seat and watched in horror as the front of the boat with all five kids tipped violently down and pitched into the deep trough below. Instantly the bow was submerged into the deep water. Where the boat had been was now a sea of white foam. The trampolines and occupants were completely covered by the white water engulfing the front of the boat. The kids had disappeared and none of them had life jackets on. Sitting helplessly a few feet away, visions of the girls being pulled down to the ocean bottom and vanishing raced through my mind. Valerie barely weighed sixty pounds—I prayed that her hands were strong enough to keep her anchored to the boat, but I knew even the strongest arms were no match against the powerful ocean.

Immediately the captain cut the engine. Time seemed frozen in space. No one moved. After several agonizing seconds that seemed to last a lifetime, the boat slowly began to tip back, and right itself. You could feel the boat struggle under the immense weight of all that water. Slowly, as several tons of water receded off the front of the boat, the bow miraculously surfaced. To my welcome relief all five of the kids reappeared, each one of them gripping the ropes tightly, the muscles in their backs taut from exertion.

"Sorry about that, folks. Didn't see that one coming," the captain announced over the PA system as the boat continued to wildly pitch up and down from the force of the wave.

As soon as she could stand, Valerie cautiously exited the trampoline and made her way slowly over to me one step at a time as the boat continued to rock. Stephanie followed right behind.

"Are you okay?" I asked as Valerie finally made it safely to my side. Val grabbed me and scooted as close as she could, her body drenched and shivering with fright.

"I don't want to go back there!" Val answered as I covered her with a towel and she buried her head in my chest.

Steph wrapped herself in a towel and sat on the other side of me.

"To think I was so worried about the *wind* catching my wig there," she whispered. "I can't believe it stayed on when that giant wall of water hit us. I'm not taking any more chances," she said.

If the wave had washed her wig off, chances are we might never have seen it again. Glad to have avoided that disaster, Steph and Val settled down next to me and left the trampoline to Lindsay, Michael and Emily, who seem unfazed by the incident.

When everyone was repositioned, the Captain hit the throttle and the boat continued on. I sat with my arms around Val, glad to have her next to me. As we rounded the northwest corner of the island, we got our first glimpse of the incredible Na Pali coast. Rugged and beautiful, the jagged coastline contains several enticing sea caves, small beaches and high waterfalls. We were able to see a few of them close up. After traveling down the coast a ways and checking out a couple of the caves, the captain anchored the catamaran just off the shore and we were free to get off the boat and snorkel.

Amazing coral beds formed an ideal backdrop for the brilliant colors of the many types of fish we saw. From the bright yellow and black of the teardrop butterfly fish to the amazing aqua, orange, yellow and fuchsia plaid rainbow parrot fish, the variety was amazing. My personal favorite was the Hawaiian reef triggerfish—also known as humuhumu-nukunuku-apua'a. Reminiscent of Batman's sidekick, this triggerfish looks like a would-be super hero trolling the coral reef with its black mask and yellow cape.

After about half an hour, we got back on board and rinsed off in the fresh water shower on the back of the boat. It felt good to get the salt off. We then enjoyed a nice lunch, complete with fresh pineapple and macadamia nut cookies. Against the ocean's current, the ride back to Port Allen was always rough, but fun, especially on the front end of the catamaran.

With legs a little wobbly, at 1 pm we exited the boat, having had a great day out on the ocean. On the way back to Poipu, we stopped in Koloa and treated ourselves to another Hawaiian specialty—shave ice. Basically like a snow cone, shave ice is served in a large cone shaped container, drenched with whatever flavor(s) of syrup you desired.

"Michael, were you scared when the boat went under?" I asked as we sat in the shade outside the Koloa Shave Ice shop, enjoying the refreshing treat.

"That was awesome!" he answered. "Too bad I didn't have to wrestle a shark off the boat. That would've been cool!"

A little too cool for me.

Morning dawned on our final day in Kauai and we all were anxious to get a few more hours in at the beach before we returned to our mundane lives back in San Jose. Tracy and the girls wanted to boogie board, so we decided Brennecke Beach would be best. Just around the corner from our complex, Brennecke's is world renown for its excellent body surfing waves. Having surfed at this beach before, Stephanie knew how wild the waves could get. After her previous appearance at Kealia Beach without her wig, Steph decided that being at the beach bald was just not her style, but she didn't want to miss out on our last adventure.

"What are you going to do, Steph?" I asked, knowing she wouldn't go bald again, but hoping she wasn't planning on sitting on the sidelines with me.

"Don't worry. I've got it covered," she replied as she gathered up the dirty beach towels and headed out the door to exchange them for clean ones at the pool hut.

Opening the van doors, we were hit with the pungent stench of rotting ocean debris—an unavoidable occurrence when snorkel gear is stored in a closed, hot car. The funky smell was enough to make you gag. Once we opened all the doors and got some air circulating through the car, the smell was tolerable and before too long we were on our way. After parking in the Poipu Beach lot, we headed left to Brennecke's. Not a disappointment, the strong waves curled and crashed onto the small beach with a vengeance. After loading up with sunscreen, we were ready to hit the waves. Stephanie put her plan into action. She grabbed her navy Speedo latex swim cap out of the beach bag and pulled it carefully over her wig. With a few wisps of blond hair peeking out from under the cap, she looked like a serious swimmer ready for the ocean.

Along with her dad, Steph swam out past the smaller waves—for beginners and novices like me—to the large powerful ones responsible for Brennecke's fame. Right away, Steph caught a big one and rode it all the way onto the beach. I snapped a picture of her beaming face as she yelled, "Sweet!"

Satisfied that her cap had stayed in place, I knew the true test would come on her first wipeout. I didn't have to wait long for that to occur. Just minutes later Steph got pummeled by a giant wave. She disappeared under the churning water as her board kicked up above the waves, fortunately anchored to her wrist by a small leash. As the wave subsided, I saw her get up and, thankfully her cap and wig were both in place. She had barely caught her breath before she headed back out for more.

Twenty-one

MITTY

Just before we left for Hawaii in August, my dad got an unexpected promotion at work. Dad's boss resigned, so Dad was bumped up into his boss's position and got a substantial raise.

"How would you like to go to Mitty next year?" Mom asked as she was busy making dinner, stir-frying chicken, broccoli, carrots and onions in the big heavy wok Dad had given her for Christmas that year.

"Seriously?" I asked staring at her in disbelief while she stood, stirring the vegetables that sizzled and popped in the hot oil. I wasn't sure I had heard her correctly over the roar of the exhaust fan above the stove.

"Yes. That's what Dad and I decided to do with his raise, but only if you want to," Mom answered.

Never in a million years did I think I'd have the chance to attend Mitty. Impeccably landscaped and maintained, Archbishop Mitty was a private Catholic high school on the west side of San Jose known for its amazing athletic program. Since seventh grade I had played on the

Mitty club basketball team, the Cagers. The ultra-competitive environment definitely helped raise my game. Practicing under the numerous championship banners in the Herman J. Fien gym, I always dreamed of playing on the high school team there, but knew it was out of reach for financial reasons. Private school at $13,000 a year wasn't in our budget. So starting freshman year, when most of my Cager teammates enrolled at Mitty, I had gone to Leigh.

"Of course I want to go. Won't Lindsay be mad, though?" I asked as I placed four placemats on the table and went to get the plates. My older sister had done extremely well at Branham High School, but was never given the chance to attend a private school.

"Don't worry about that," Mom answered as she poured Thai curry sauce over the golden chicken and tender vegetables and continued stirring. "I've already talked to her about it. She got into the college she wanted and that's all she cares about. If she hadn't gotten into Cal Poly, there may have been an issue, but she did and there isn't. Are you sure you want to switch schools?"

Mom knew I had enjoyed my year at Leigh and had some great friends there, especially with the girls on the basketball team, but to be able to go to Mitty and play on their elite basketball team was a great opportunity and I wasn't going to pass it up.

"I'm sure!" I answered as I grabbed dinner plates out of the upper cabinet.

"You know, this is a long shot," Mom warned as she put the glass lid over the wok and turned off the burner. The sweet, spicy smell of the curry was making my mouth water. "Registration has been over for months now, but I talked to the assistant principal and he said we should fill out the transfer application anyway and get a copy of your transcripts from Leigh. His name is Greg Walker. We have an appointment to meet with him on Wednesday. Normally, they don't accept transfers without recommendations from English and Math teachers, but they might make an exception in your case."

"You could try emailing them. I think I have their email addresses somewhere," I suggested as I grabbed silverware out of the drawer.

"Hopefully your 4.0 grade average will speak for itself. I just don't want you to get your hopes up," Mom warned as she placed the heavy pot filled with the colorful entrée in the middle of the table. "Enrollment is already full, so like I said before, this is a long shot, but we might as well give it a try." Mom returned to the kitchen and used our old ragged potholders to grab the corning ware pot full of white rice off the stove.

Along with forks and knives, I distributed the plates around the table. The smell of the food was so enticing; I couldn't wait to dig in.

"Go call Dad, Linz and Val and tell them dinner is ready, would you, Steph? I'll get the drinks."

Our meeting with Mr. Walker went well. As predicted, they were very happy with my grades. Mom had emailed both my Math and English teachers asking for recommendations, but had not heard back from them. August was a prime month for teachers to be on vacation, so she wasn't surprised. As for basketball, Mr. Walker said that if I did get into Mitty and made it on the basketball team, I would have to get special clearance to play from the CIF/Central Coast Section Commissioner. Because I had had pre-enrollment contact with a club coach, Sue Phillips, who was the Women's Varsity Basketball Coach at Mitty, they would have to clear me of any recruiting violation. Coach Phillips had not recruited me in any way, so I felt pretty confident we would be able to get the clearance, but wasn't sure how all that worked. As we left that day, Mom gave Mr. Walker Dad's cell number in case a decision was made the following week while we were in Kauai. We shook hands and he said he would be in touch as soon as possible.

"Well, Steph, it looks highly unlikely that they'll accept you at this late date, especially without hearing from either of your teachers, but if you are meant to be at Mitty, I truly believe you will get in somehow," Mom remarked as she started the car and buckled her seatbelt.

"I hope so…" I replied, staring out the window at the Mitty campus, wondering if that would be my home for the coming year.

"I say we stop by Starbucks on the way home for good luck," Mom said. Was it possible that she liked Starbucks more than I did?

"I'm always up for a frappacino," I answered with a smile. It was great to have the interview over with and the issue out of our hands.

Wednesday of that next week, on our way to Hanalei, Dad got a call from Mitty High School letting me know I had been accepted. All five of us looked at each other after Dad put the phone down and cheered and high-fived. "I'm going to Mit-ty! She's going to Mit-ty!"

we all chanted. Sitting in the second seat of the van, I couldn't believe it. Honestly, I thought there was absolutely no chance without teacher recommendations, especially taking into account that my application had been received just three weeks before the start of school. But none of that mattered now; I was going to be a Mitty Monarch for my sophomore year.

Arriving home from Hawaii on August 12th, it was just nine days until school started on August 21st. I got in touch with my Cager basketball friends and let them know I would be joining them at Mitty. Hearing their excitement gave me confidence and I was thrilled that I would already know a few students on campus my first day.

"Steph! It's time to get up!" I heard Mom shout as she poked her head into my room. Wow, it seemed way too early to be awake— 6:00 am. Sleeping till noon that last week after we returned home from Kauai was so enjoyable. My lazy mornings were over. Normally I dreaded the start of school, but that day I was full of excitement and nervous energy. Bouncing down the stairs, I grabbed a box of cereal and made myself breakfast.

"What are you going to wear today, Steph?" Mom asked while she spread mustard on my turkey sandwich—part of my lunch that I would be so happy to devour later that day.

"I think I'm going to wear my polo and some jeans. I can't wear any of my tanks. They're against dress code. So are most of my jeans."

"What's wrong with your jeans?"

"We can't wear any clothes with unfinished edges or rips, and my shoulders have to be covered."

"Really?"

"Yeah, and skirts and shorts can't be any higher than 6" above your knees, so most of my shorts are out too."

"Wow, I didn't plan on buying you a new wardrobe for Mitty, but it looks like I might have to."

"Yeah, I know," I said, knowing we didn't have much extra for new clothes.

"Don't worry. Little by little, we'll get you up to speed with the Mitty dress code. Now, go get ready. We have to leave at 6:45!" Mom urged.

"Okay," I answered and quickly rinsed out my bowl and placed it on the counter. Slightly nervous, I pulled on my polo and tugged on my jeans. Next was my hair. Deciding on the short blond ponytail, I placed the wig on my head and used plenty of wig tape—I didn't need any disasters on the first day. After applying my make-up and perfume, I looked in the mirror. Reasonably pleased with what I saw, I brushed my teeth, slipped on my shoes and was ready to go.

"I'm ready, Mom!" I shouted as I raced down the stairs, pausing momentarily in front of the mirrored wall in our living room.

"Okay. Don't forget your lunch! I'll meet you in the car," she answered as she grabbed her purse and disappeared into the laundry room.

Here goes… I thought to myself and followed.

Traffic was light that morning—most public schools were still on summer break—so we arrived at Mitty in record time. As we drove into the front lot, I could see several students milling around.

"Bye, Mom," I muttered as I threw my backpack over my shoulder and hopped out of the car. I was in a hurry to meet my girlfriends at our previously designated area.

"Hope you have a great day, Steph!" Mom shouted.

A quick wave and I was off. Feeling like I was in a bizarre dream, I walked across the Mitty campus, wondering how I had ended up there on the first day of school when just three weeks prior I was registered to continue at Leigh. As I walked past the cafeteria and glanced at the attractive picnic tables scattered around the tidy patio area, complete with waterfall and plush greenery, I couldn't help but compare it to the campus I previously called home. Cash strapped budgets for the past ten years had contributed to the declining appearance of the Leigh campus. With education a top priority, maintaining the school grounds had taken a back seat with the tight budget.

"Hey, Keilani! What's up?" I asked, relieved to see Keilani exactly where she said she would be.

"Not much. We're just hanging till the bell rings," she answered with a friendly smile and introduced me to the rest of the crowd.

That first day progressed without incident. Before long, the final bell rang and the mass exodus of students began. Running into Kelly and Kaitlyn in the hall, we compared notes about our teachers, classes and the fact that we already had homework on the first day. Within minutes our little crowd grew to seven. All the girls were easy to hang out with and seemed happy to add me to their list of friends. Claire had the most beautiful wild long curly red hair—we cliqued right away. Having assumed that Mitty students all came from wealthy families, I was expecting to find more of a snobbish, elite attitude among the student body, but the classmates and friends I had met that day were down-to-earth teenagers, just like I was used to at Leigh.

"Stephanie, there's something going on with your hair right there," Alea commented and pointed to the side of my head. Knowing that she was probably pointing to a small spot where some of the webbing of my wig was exposed, I felt twinges of panic begin to rise. Mustering my self-control, I calmed my edgy nerves and did my best to change the subject.

"Oh, a bobby pin probably fell out. Are you going to the game this weekend?" I asked, giving Kelly a knowing look. Both Kelly and Kaitlyn knew about by hair. They were both on the Cager team and saw me in my bandana all the time. I wasn't sure how and when to inform my new friends about my wigs. The subject was bound to come up sooner or later and I didn't relish having to explain the whole situation over and over again.

"Probably," Alea said as the group turned to leave and we parted ways.

"See you tomorrow, Steph!" Kelly called and when everyone else's back was turned, mouthed to me, "Don't worry. I've got your back."

"Thanks," I mouthed back to her, grateful she could do the explaining and I wouldn't have to.

Later that afternoon when I was back in my bedroom, lying on my bed, relieved to have the awkward first day over with, grateful that everything had gone so well, I got a call on my cell from Kelly.

"Hey, Steph."

"Hey, Kelly. What's up?"

"I just wanted to let you know that I explained to our group about your hair. They couldn't believe you were wearing a wig. They said your hair looked so real."

"Thank you *so* much, Kelly. I was dreading having to go through the whole story again," I said, glad she had taken the initiative to help me out. "I'm getting a new long blond wig soon, and I knew people were going to ask questions about that."

"No problem. See you tomorrow!"

"Yeah, see you tomorrow and thanks again. You're a lifesaver," I added.

"Any time, Steph."

Closing my phone, I let out a huge sigh of relief. Instead of spending the night worrying about, and planning how and when I was going to explain alopecia to my new friends, I could kick back and relax—Kelly had taken care of everything for me. Life is so much easier with people you can count on.

Twenty-two

POWDER PUFF

Everything about Stephanie's transition to Mitty had gone so smoothly that I kept waiting for the other shoe to drop. It never did. Nearly every day she came home with pictures of more friends she had met. Hooray for digital photography. Supposedly cliques didn't exist—everyone hung out with everyone. Decisively strict, the student behavioral policies and dress codes were judiciously enforced. Inappropriate behavior of any kind was not tolerated. The threat of Saturday detention was enough to keep most students' behavior and attire in line.

Slightly apprehensive in the beginning about how this new group of students would respond to Stephanie's alopecia, it appeared I had nothing to worry about. They had accepted her with open arms, just like the students at Leigh. Bombarded daily by the media with depressing news, it was easy to picture a bleak future, but watching the students respond to Stephanie's uniqueness with kindness, understanding and acceptance went a long way in restoring my faith in humanity.

"I'm on the powder puff team!" Stephanie blurted out, as she climbed into the driver's side of the van after school.

Since the first day of school, Steph had been driving home from Mitty with me in the passenger seat. Although letting her drive was very stressful at first, I was anxious for her to start driving on her own. January of the coming year she would turn 16 and get her license, so I wanted her to have as many hours of experience behind the wheel as possible before she took the driver's test. When she could drive herself to school, our gas bill would be cut in half, not to mention the number of miles piling up on the car. Steph getting her license was a win-win situation for all of us, as long as she didn't get in an accident. The best chance of staying out of harm's way was for her to gain experience.

The first two weeks it was extremely stressful with Stephanie driving, but with each day that went by she got better and was beginning to manage the traffic quite well.

"Great! What is that?" I asked, not sure what she meant by the "powder puff" team.

"It's flag football for girls. We're going to play in front of the whole school next Wednesday for Spirit Week. The guys are cheerleading. It's going to be awesome," she answered as she put the key in the ignition and started the van.

Spirit Week was one entire week of non-stop activity for the student body to show their school spirit and build anticipation for the Saturday night homecoming football game. Each day the students dressed according to a different theme (70's, 80's, etc.), and at lunch there were various activities (karaoke, teacher dunk tanks, etc.) to watch or participate in.

"So, you're finally getting to play football. Remember in fifth grade when you got so mad at Dad and me because we wouldn't let you join Pop Warner?" I asked. Convinced we were the absolute worst parents in the world when we wouldn't let her play football, she had barely spoken to us for a week. We didn't want her to end up badly hurt. Eventually she forgave us.

"We have practice this Saturday morning. Can you or Dad take me?" she asked as she pulled out of the parking lot like a pro.

"I'll have to check when we get home, but we'll make sure you get there somehow," I assured her. "Just remind me to put it on the calendar."

"Great! Thanks. Now, can I please get in the carpool lane?"

"No, Steph. I've told you before; you're NOT going in the carpool lane. It's too dangerous getting over there!"

"That's stupid. I know I can get over and it sucks to sit here in traffic when the carpool lane is clear, but whatever…"

This was a daily argument. Adamant that she didn't need to negotiate her way over to the carpool lane, I stood firm. At three o'clock the traffic on Highway 85 from Saratoga to Camden just wasn't that bad and getting three lanes over could be very tricky, especially for an inexperienced driver, and then she would have to get back across to exit. Besides, when she did start driving by herself she wouldn't be able to use the carpool lane anyway, so what was the point? As wrong as she thought I was, I didn't waver on this, but she never quit asking.

Saturday rolled around and we managed to get Steph to her practice before Valerie's soccer game. Fortunately, she was able to get a ride home with one of the other players.

"So, how did practice go?" I asked after we returned home and I saw her at the kitchen table eating a quesadilla.

"Okay. They put me on defense," she said, a little forlornly. I could tell she was disappointed.

"Well, somebody has to play defense. I bet you'll be great!" I commented, hoping to lift her mood.

"True."

I opened the bread drawer hoping to find something other than flour tortillas.

"The girls all said they would wear red bandannas with me," Steph said as I grabbed the loaf of wheat bread that I found and began to set slices on a small wooden cutting board.

"Really?" I asked, momentarily neglecting the sandwiches I was in the middle of preparing. When Steph had originally talked about Powder Puff, I wondered what she was going to do about her hair. Hearing that her teammates would support her by wearing bandanas themselves was totally unexpected. Most fifteen year olds want to look their best, especially if they're in front of the whole school. Without even knowing these girls, I liked them. "That's terrific!"

Spirit Week arrived and, like always, Steph enjoyed dressing up for the theme days. Wednesday morning while I was making lunches at the kitchen island, Steph walked in and leaned up against the counter facing me with her arms folded across her chest. Something was obviously bothering her.

"Mom, I don't know if I'm doing the right thing," she said while I was busy bagging up cheezits and banana chips. "Having my wig off and wearing a bandana for basketball practice is one thing, but in front of the whole school…I don't know if I want to do that."

Surprised that she was second guessing herself—that wasn't like her—I tried my best to be reassuring.

"Aren't the other girls going to be wearing bandanas in the game too?" I asked.

"Yeah, but it's not the same. They'll all have hair sticking out from under theirs. I won't. Everyone will be able to tell I'm bald."

Not used to seeing her so tentative and unsure of herself, I reached over and gave her a hug, wishing I could do more.

"Just do what you think is best, Steph. You don't have to play if you don't want to."

"I know, but I would feel like I'm letting the team down," she said.

I could tell she was torn. Being in front of the whole school at an assembly without her wig was a huge deal. If she chose to play, the minute she walked on the field with only a bandana covering her bald head, the entire student body would know that she had no hair. She had a difficult choice to make and I silently prayed that she would make the right one.

"Whatever you decide, I'll be praying for you," I said, knowing that was all I could do.

"Thanks, Mom." Steph stared at the tiles on the floor, lost in thought.

Hearing a car horn out in our driveway, Steph grabbed her lunch and walked up the steps to the front door.

Meeting her at the door, I gave her another hug. "Bye, Steph. Love you!"

"Thanks, Mom. Love you too!" she answered as she got into the neighbor's car.

I watched as the taillights and trailing exhaust disappeared into the early gray morning.

After Valerie left the house to walk to school with her friends, I couldn't stop thinking about Stephanie and the Powder Puff game. Alone that morning, I was consumed by thoughts of her on the football field. Would she be brave enough to play? I knew she wanted to. At an age when looks are so important and self-esteem so fragile I knew it would take a huge amount of courage to walk out on that field in her bandana in front of 1600 peers. Teenagers, in general, want to look just like everybody else—"carbon copies" of each other. Sure there are the punk and Goth kids, the saggers, the skaters, etc. Yes, they stand out, but in their quest to be different they've merely joined a smaller group of look-a-likes. None are standing alone. I knew if Stephanie chose to play that day, she would be the only one on the field with a shaved head, and I hoped desperately that she would have the courage to face the fallout, whatever it might be.

After listening all day to the clock chime the hours as the time slowly ticked by, I heard three strikes from the clock and knew that Stephanie would be home momentarily. Dying to know what had happened, the suspense had been eating at me all day. At last I heard the garage door go up, followed by the opening of the laundry room door. Steph came barreling in and dumped her things on the kitchen counter.

"That was the best decision I ever made!" Stephanie exclaimed, her face beaming. Without a doubt I knew she was referring to the game.

"What happened?" I asked. I still had no idea what had happened on the field and the suspense was killing me.

"Well, first of all, you know I said the other girls were going to wear bandanas?" Steph reminded me. I could tell by her tone that whatever was coming wasn't going to be good.

"Yes," I answered, a little worried.

"Okay, when I got to the locker room, they were all wearing the bandanas, but they had them tied on their arms, not on their heads."

"Oh," I sighed, knowing that must have been a huge disappointment.

"Yeah, well, I decided just to go for it anyway. I don't mean to brag, but it seemed like I was the only one that could chase people down on defense."

"Nice to see your speed came in handy," I interjected, wishing I could have seen the game. "You played the freshman team, right?"

"Yeah. When time was just about up, one of the freshmen caught a pass and made a break for the goal line. I gave it my all and chased after her even though she had a pretty good head start. Just as she was about to cross the goal line, I made a flat out dive for her flag. Seriously, I was horizontal in the air. I stretched my fingers out as far as they could reach and I felt her flag whip by my hand. I closed my fingers and could feel her flag give way as I hit the ground and rolled into the mud. When I stood up, my right side was completely covered with mud. I raised the flag above my head and waved. Everyone went wild. I caught her just before she crossed the goal line. The team surrounded me, jumping up and down. It would have been humiliating to get beaten by the freshmen. Then as we walked to the sidelines, another group of students mobbed me, calling me their hero. I couldn't believe it."

"Wow, Steph, that's incredible!" I congratulated her, astonished by the extent of her success that day.

"Coach Phillips even came over and said, 'Good tackle, Weed.'"

Sue Phillips was the extremely demanding and successful Women's Varsity Basketball Coach at Mitty, who gave out compliments sparingly. With basketball tryouts starting soon, that compliment was worth more than gold to Stephanie.

"Do we have anything good for snacks?" Steph asked, done with her gloating, ready to move onto more pressing matters like the empty pit in her stomach.

"There's some leftover stir-fry from last night," I answered. Food never went to waste in our house with Stephanie around.

Later that night as I reflected on the events of day, it was obvious that Stephanie had made a difficult choice and it had paid off. After that one event, every single student at Mitty knew she had no hair. But more importantly, they knew she was perfectly comfortable with her situation and didn't care.

Twenty-three

TRYOUTS

Knowing how much was at stake made basketball tryouts more nerve-wracking than usual. Believing I had a shot at making the varsity team, I gave 100% everyday on the court, but would that be enough? The level of competition in the West Catholic Athletic League was much tougher than the Blossom Valley Athletic League that Leigh High School participated in. Although my year on the Leigh team wasn't easy—I had played nearly every minute of every game—I didn't know if those minutes on the court had prepared me enough for a spot on Mitty's varsity team. *Sports Illustrated* ranked Mitty the #5 athletic program in the nation and the #1 athletic program in California for the 2006-2007 season, so I knew competition was going to be fierce. Yes, I had played with many of the girls trying out at Mitty in my years on the Cagers, but they all had one more season playing for Coach Phillips. In her fourteen years of coaching at Mitty, Coach Phillips had won 13 league titles, 12 section titles, 6 Norcal titles and 2 state championships. She knew what she was looking for.

Practices ranged from 2 to 2 1/2 hours with no more than a couple 30-second water breaks. Every minute my skills were put to the test. Dribble, hit threes, block out, make layups, run the offense, make free throws. It was exhausting. Not only was I running at full speed, my mind was constantly working, making spilt second decisions, hoping my instincts and training would pay off. Honestly, I knew I needed work on my shooting, but I knew there was no one better on defense than me.

My days were extremely long—I left the house at 6:45 in the morning and most nights didn't get home until 7pm on a good day, 9pm was more likely. Normally on days we had late practice, I finished my homework before practice so when I finally got home I could eat and roll into bed. Those twelve to fourteen hour days were tiring, but I managed to survive by eating right and often and getting as much sleep as my schedule allowed. Although the classes at Mitty were demanding, I kept my grades up by using every second of my time—I didn't have any to waste.

Eventually Saturday came when the final cuts for the team were going to be made. Having lasted through two rounds already, I was hopeful, but by no means certain of the outcome. Early practice (8am start) would be cut short to allow for individual player meetings with the three coaches. When it was my turn and I was called into the office, my hands were shaking. All morning I tried to convince myself that I didn't care and it didn't matter if I made varsity or not. At that point I was at least guaranteed a spot on the junior varsity team, and had persuaded myself that JV was good enough because usually people didn't make varsity till junior year. As I walked into the office, all attempts to convince myself I didn't care were forgotten—I desperately wanted to make varsity and prayed that I had done enough.

"Come in, Weed, and have a seat. Don't be so serious," Coach Phillips said with a smile, trying to lighten the mood. She motioned toward the empty chair. There was another Stephanie on the team—a senior that year—so I had been nicknamed Weed, which was fine with me. Sitting down in the chair, I hoped none of the coaches noticed my hands shaking. After two months of open gym and three days of try-outs, I was about to learn my fate.

"We like your effort out on the court, and would like to offer you a spot on the varsity team. You won't get much playing time this season, and if that's going to be a problem you're welcome to take a spot on JV—you would be playing a lot more there—but we would like to have you practicing with the Varsity team," Coach Phillips explained. "So it's up to you."

Sitting in the office, facing the three coaches, it took a moment for the invitation to sink in. Coach Phillips had just offered me a spot on the Varsity team—yes, with the disclaimer that I wouldn't get much playing time—but a spot nonetheless. Every drop of sweat, every bruise, every floor burn and every sore exhausted muscle had paid off.

Realizing the coaches were waiting for my reaction, I snapped back into focus. "I'll take the spot on varsity. Thanks."

"Congratulations," Coach Phillips said as she got up and extended her hand, thus signaling the end of our meeting.

"Thanks," I said again, shaking her hand along with the other two coaches and then leaving the office. Nina, another guard and a good friend of mine, was waiting outside.

"So, what did they say?" she asked, itching for the news. Nina already had a spot on the team and was hoping I would join her.

"I made it!" I whispered, aware of the fact there were other players in the vicinity, still waiting to learn their fates. "They said I might not play that much, but I don't care. I just can't get enough of Coach's killer workouts," I joked.

"Yeah, I know what you mean," Nina said with a wry smile. We swore Coach had invented the saying, "No pain, no gain". On one hand we all hated the brutal and extremely difficult and demanding workouts Coach put us through each day, but we also knew that following her direction, we were on the way to being the best athletes we could possibly be.

"Well, got to go. My mom's waiting out in the car," I commented as we walked across the gym and opened the door. We enjoyed breathing the fresh outside air after being in a stagnant gym all morning.

"Yeah, me too. See you, Steph." Nina waved as we parted ways in the parking lot. With my jersey and shorts soaked, I couldn't wait to get home and shower, but first I had some good news to deliver. Spotting the van, I saw Mom reading in the passenger's seat. She knew today was the day. With my head down and no smile, I opened the car door.

"Well?" she asked.

I broke into a wide grin, "I made it!" I cried as I dumped my bag in the second seat.

"That's great, Steph!" she practically shouted.

"Don't get too excited," I warned her as I sat down in front and began to unlace my black Nikes. "They said I probably won't play that much."

"That's okay. At least you'll be practicing with them. You have two more years left to play after this season."

"I know. I'm excited," I assured her. "They gave me a choice and I knew if I played on JV this year, I'd have to work my way into a spot on Varsity all over again next year, so I decided on Varsity. I'm glad."

"Sounds like you made a good choice."

"Can we stop by Starbucks to celebrate?" I asked, knowing she'd pretty much have to say yes.

Being a member of the varsity team was demanding and stressful, but it also had its perks. Nike sponsored the team and gave us complimentary basketball shoes, warm ups and duffle bags—my parents appreciated that. During the first week in December, the team was flown down to San Diego for a basketball tournament (got to miss three days of school!)—travel and hotel rooms were provided by the school.

Just as the girls on the Leigh basketball team had, the Mitty team accepted me bandanna and all. They treated me as an equal. No one made me feel out of place when I took off my wig in the locker room.

In fact, Nina bought me seven different bandannas for Christmas to wear at practice.

During the portion of our workout that was done outside on the track I was able to wear my wig. Every once in awhile it had a mind of its own and would start to shift out of place. When that happened, one of my teammates would discretely let me know so I could position the wig back in place before any of the football players on the field noticed. It was a great feeling to know that people had my back.

Contrary to what the staff would like to think, getting a good education was not the top priority for students at Mitty—at least not for the crowd I hung with. Impressing guys was the top priority. On days we had early practices, the guy's team would show up in the gym towards the end of our second hour. That was my least favorite time to be wearing a bandanna. We all knew the guys were watching, and I knew I stood out. Who wouldn't notice someone in a bright bandanna when everyone else had hair? I did my best to not let it bother me. *I'll just try to impress them with my skills*, I thought. On the bright side, at the end of practice, with the men's team still around, I got to walk out of the locker room with hair that wasn't sweaty and matted down.

One particular evening when we left practice, the men's team was getting ready for a scrimmage. Some of the opposing players happened to be outside our locker room as we were leaving, looking pretty fine with their big arms, small waists and tight butts. Feeling extremely lucky to have my wig back on I did my best to catch the eyes of any of the fresh prospects as we walked by. So there I was being all cool, or so I thought, when I heard my name and turned around.

"Steph!" Classye whispered with her teeth clenched, trying not to attract too much attention. As I looked her way she shot her eyes down at my gym bag and back up to me. Not sure what was up, I glanced down and to my horror my bright yellow, pink polka dotted Victoria Secret bra was hanging out of my bag ready to drop on the ground at any minute. Nice. Shocked into immediate action I quickly bent down as we walked, snatched up my bra and stuffed it inside my duffle bag under enough junk so it wouldn't fall out again. Of course I heard the guys snickering—nothing like the sight of a bra to get guys going. My days in the spotlight came in handy and I didn't even blush; I just kept right on walking.

As the season progressed, true to their word, the coaches kept me on the bench most of the time. When I did get into the game, coming off the bench cold, it was hard to keep my confidence up and often my nerves got the best of me. Trying not to let the lack of playing time get me down, I kept plugging away, hoping that some day Coach Phillips would believe in my abilities and give me a chance.

Occasionally at games I was questioned by the refs about my bandana, which was ridiculous. Did they really think I chose to wear a bandana? Anyone could see that there was no hint of hair on my head. To me, the reason for my bandana was blatantly obvious, but for some I guess it wasn't. For that reason, I kept two letters in my basketball bag. One was signed by my dermatologist and stated:

To Whom it May Concern:
I am writing in regards to our patient,

Stephanie Weed, who has been seen in
our office for treatment of her medical
condition. It is deemed medically necessary
that Stephanie wear a bandana when she
plays basketball.

Along with that letter, was a letter written by my mom explaining that I had alopecia (the dermatologist could not release that information due to patient confidentially laws).

On January 12th up in San Francisco in Sacred Heart Cathedral's gym, I was questioned. Having traveled the hour and a half on the bus to face the number one women's basketball team in the nation we were pumped and ready for action. Everyone needed to be at the top of their game for us to avoid getting slaughtered. Observing the JV game, we waited anxiously for our turn out on the court to begin. With a couple minutes to go in the fourth period of the JV game, I ducked in the bathroom to take off my wig and put on my black bandana. Our JV team finished on top and it was time for us to take the court. Lining up on both sides of the gym, we began our pre-game warm-up sequence. The atmosphere was electric—could we do the impossible and come away with a win? Not likely, but if you're going to dream, you might as well dream big. After completing our passing drill, we lined up for layups. That's when one of the refs pulled me aside.

"You can't wear that bandana in the game," he informed me, with an attitude.

I thought about pulling it off right there in front of him and shocking him with my bald head, but decided not to.

"I've got a medical condition. I have a letter in my bag from my doctor stating that it's necessary for me to wear a bandana. Do you want to see it?" I asked as I pointed over to our bench.

"Oh, uh, no. That's okay. Go ahead," he answered, still a little puzzled, but he let me go. Did he think I actually liked wearing a bandana? Someday I *was* going to whip off my bandana and show them the obvious—that would shut them up pretty quick. I knew I would never actually do that, but the thought of it was tempting.

As the game progressed, we were getting hammered by the Sacred Heart Team. With about a minute and a half left in the game, with the contest for all intents and purposes already over, I got subbed in, tried to hit a three and missed. At least I could say I had played against the number one team in the nation.

With 17 seconds left in the game, Sacred Heart Cathedral President John Scudder stopped the game and announced that there had been an incident on Ellis Street. The game was over. He directed all fans and players to exit through the rear door of the gym, which the police were guarding.

Confused, we all looked at each other wondering what could have happened that would make them stop the game. It had to be bad. The coaches huddled us up on the sideline and informed the team that someone had been shot outside and we needed to leave immediately.

In a daze, I grabbed my water off the bench, put it in my bag and began looking for my sweats. It was surreal. Someone had been shot right outside the gym—I was scared. We all scrambled to get our stuff together, shoving things indiscriminately into our bags. People were talking in hushed tones—the gym was abnormally quiet. In the far corner of the gym I could see an armed police officer standing by the side door where he was directing people to exit. The main doors were blocked off by two other officers who made sure no one entered or exited that way. Access to the bathrooms was through those doors and was now sealed off. I had nowhere to change into my wig. How could I get my bandana off and wig on with so many people filing by? Wearing a black bandana out onto a dark street in downtown San Francisco where someone has just been shot was not a good idea. I felt trapped.

"Mom, I can't go out there with this on." I pointed to my bandana.

"Mm…good point," she agreed. We both looked around for options.

"What am I going to do? I can't get to the bathrooms." My anxiety was growing by the second. Fortunately, no one had panicked, but you could definitely feel a sense of urgency. Wanting to get to the safety of their cars and out of the city as soon as possible, people were moving to the side door as quickly as they could.

"Just use your sweatshirt and put the hood up," Mom suggested. Since I didn't have a better plan, I agreed. Grabbing the sweatshirt out of my bag, I quickly pulled it over my head, and put the hood up, hoping it would adequately conceal my bandana from anyone waiting out on the street.

Following the flow of the crowd, we exited the gym onto Ellis Street, which was eerily quiet and dimly lit. The crowd moved silently, everyone listening intently for suspicious sounds and watching for unusual movements. Just outside the door, a police officer directed us up Ellis Street—going down Ellis was not an option—it was a crime scene and was roped off. Following the yellow police tape up the sidewalk about thirty feet to the intersection of Ellis and Gough, we were relieved to find another police officer standing guard. The police presence was reassuring, but I in no way felt safe. Turning down Gough, we were on our own. While walking several blocks through the darkened streets of San Francisco to retrieve our car, we were all on edge.

Reaching the car, I couldn't get the door open and inside fast enough. Once the four of us were inside our locked vehicle and safely on the way home, I began to relax a bit. I still couldn't believe someone had been shot right outside the gym. That kind of thing just doesn't happen.

The next day we found out that it was a father of one of the Sacred Heart Cathedral players that had been shot and killed outside the gym on Ellis Street. The previous summer, that SHC player had been on the Cager basketball team, so many on our team knew her personally. Shocked by such a senseless tragedy, none of us could imagine being in her shoes. As much as we complain about how strict, old-fashioned, unreasonable or out of touch our dads are, we still count on them being there when times get tough. This player wouldn't have her dad's strong arms for reassurance anymore, ever. Sometimes it takes someone else's horrific loss to make you appreciate what you have, and that night I went to bed very grateful that my dad was snoring away down the hall.

We ended our season that year as California Division II State Champions. Being in Arco Arena with the filled stands, bright lights and TV cameras was nothing short of amazing. Even though I never made it onto the court during the championship game, I felt like I had played a significant role in the team's success. Having teammates like me to practice against, made them the successful team they were that night. Besides, I knew my time was coming.

Twenty-four

ALLY

M rs. Weed?" I heard when I answered the phone. Dripping with
sweat from my hour long run in the hot California sun, I hoped
whoever was on the phone didn't need to see me anytime soon—I
looked horrible and smelled even worse.

"Yes," I replied.

"This is the secretary at Leigh High School. We have a girl who
is going to start here as a freshman this fall and she is really nervous.
She heard about Stephanie and her mom wondered if she could meet
with Stephanie or at least talk to her sometime before school starts?"

Puzzled at first as to why someone at Leigh would contact us
about a prospective student, I didn't know how to respond. I was sure
the secretary was aware Stephanie no longer attended Leigh, so I
couldn't imagine the reason for the call. However, the wheels began to
turn, and suddenly it clicked.

"Does this girl have alopecia?" I asked.

"Yes, she does. Sorry, I should have said that up front," the secretary apologized.

"I was a little confused as to why you were calling, but then I figured it must be about that," I answered. "I'm pretty sure Stephanie would be happy to meet with her. At the moment, she's away at a basketball tournament, but I can find out and will let you know."

"That would be great."

"If, for some reason, Stephanie doesn't want to follow through, and I can't think of any reason she wouldn't want to, I'd be happy to meet with the girl's mom," I replied, knowing my experiences might help ease the mom's anxieties about her daughter starting high school. "Do you know if the girl has already lost her hair?"

"I'm not sure, but I don't think so. Why don't I give you their names and phone number and you can contact them when it's convenient?" she offered.

"Okay, sure. That would be great. I think it would make Stephanie feel good to help someone else out."

"I think so too. Stephanie did so well here with everything."

"Thanks. The staff was very supportive through it all—that made a big difference," I answered.

"You're very welcome. Here's their number. Do you have a pencil?"

Later, when I let Stephanie know about the phone call from Leigh, she was more than happy to meet with the girl. Her name was Ally. Scheduling anything in the summer was going to be tricky. With the family's name and number in hand, I studied our calendar for an available date and time. Steph was at a basketball tournament in Oregon, but would be returning the following week. Valerie started field hockey camp that next week and would be out of the house from 9am till noon. With July 14th looking like the only day available before we left for New York on Friday August 1st, I made the call.

Unfortunately the answering machine picked up. As briefly as possible I introduced myself and said my daughter Stephanie and I would be happy to meet with the two of them on July 14th if they were available. Hoping that date would work, I left my name and number and hung up the phone. Knowing the potential meeting would not only be good for Ally and her mom, but for Stephanie also, I knew somehow we'd make it work.

Several days later I got a call from Ally's mother. They had about an hour window between activities on the 14th and were looking forward to meeting us. After giving her directions to our house, I hung up and thought about how far Stephanie had come. Alopecia wasn't even an issue anymore. The only time the subject came up was when she needed a new wig. Outside of that, we never talked about it. Furthermore, this was a great opportunity for her to help someone go through the same challenges she had recently faced. Knowing how confident and sure of herself Stephanie was by then, I was certain she could help Ally. Thinking back to that first wig appointment, I realized how nice it would've been for Stephanie to have known another teenager like herself, before we walked in that door.

Early on the morning of the 14th, I dropped Valerie off for field hockey camp and returned home to find Stephanie still sound asleep in her room, which was an abysmal mess. How someone could sleep surrounded by such chaos astounded me. Carefully I found my way through the piles of dirty clothes and assorted debris littering the floor.

"Steph, wake up!" I shouted while shaking her shoulder.

She mumbled something inaudible and pulled her comforter tighter around her shoulders.

"Steph, get up! Ally is coming this morning and you have to get this mess cleaned up!" I shouted again. The name "Ally" must have reached something in her subconscious because I saw her eyes flicker open.

"Get up now! I'm not kidding. You have to get moving!" I insisted, reaching the end of my patience.

"Okay, okay. I'm up!" she barked as she sat up on the edge of her bed, eyes closed, waiting for her body to join the land of the living. Even though her eyes were closed, I took the fact that she was actually sitting as a good sign and went back downstairs to finish my morning duties. After taking care of the breakfast dishes along with any stragglers left from the night before, I put some tea bags in a pot of water on the stove to make iced tea. The weather was gorgeous so I planned to take our visitors out back by the pool and knew we would enjoy something cool to drink.

"Morning, Steph," I commented as I heard her stumble into the kitchen and open the pantry. "How did you sleep?"

All I got in response was a partial grunt and decided not to press the matter—her eyes were barely open. Managing to get milk and cereal in her bowl without leaving too much of a mess on the counter, she sat down at the kitchen table and grabbed the newspaper. Continuing about my business, I gave her some space until I was sure she was fully awake.

"Steph, Ally and her mom will be here in a little over an hour and I want you to have your room and the bathroom upstairs straightened up before they get here."

"Sure, okay," Stephanie agreed. Wow! Usually I got at least some kind of argument when I asked her to straighten her room. She must be looking forward to the encounter, otherwise she'd be complaining.

"What do you think about sitting out back under the umbrella by the pool since it's such a nice day?"

"Sounds good," Steph answered, looking out the windows. Even though we lived in a compact subdivision, we had a generous backyard. With most of the landscaping established thirty years before, the bordering trees and bushes were mature and offered shaded privacy on the patio, which we enjoyed often. Most summer evenings we ate outside by the pool. Nothing beat our pleasant summer California nights—no humidity, no bugs, gorgeous sunsets, and no rain from June to October.

"Make sure your room is presentable…" I reminded.

"I know. I know, Mom."

"If you think you want to talk to Ally alone, ask her if she wants to see your room and I'll stay out back with her mom. You don't have to, but if you want to, don't worry, we won't follow you up there."

"Okay," she answered and brought her nearly empty cereal bowl over to the counter. "I'll go up and clean my room and get ready. What time did you say they're coming?"

"Ten thirty."

"Wow! I better get moving," she acknowledged and dashed up the stairs.

"I'll get it," Steph called down when she heard the doorbell chime. Everything was ready out back. I had iced tea and water pitchers set up with assorted sweeteners and some sliced lemons. Nothing substantial, but it made the table look inviting. Wearing her new leopard print shirt and white shorts, Steph looked cute with her dark tan and long legs. My hope was that this mother and daughter would see how normal Stephanie appeared and be reassured for Ally's future.

As Stephanie opened the right side of our front wood paneled double door, I walked into the foyer and joined her.

"Hi, I'm Steph," she said as she greeted our visitors with enthusiasm.

Glad to see Stephanie's excitement, I extended my hand to the mother.

"You must be Nina."

"Yes, and you must be Stacy," she answered, smiling.

Ally looked like the typical all-American teenager. Her long, straight, dirty-blond hair was pulled back into a ponytail and her smile revealed a mouth full of braces. Pale blue uncertain eyes looked back at us, unsure of where to look and what to do.

"Why don't we sit out back since it's such a nice day," I offered, hoping to break the ice quickly due to the time constraints we were under. After they stepped into the foyer, we all headed through the dining room to the backyard. Most people wouldn't suspect anything amiss when glancing at Ally's hair, but I noticed several telltale patches of scalp just barely showing in a couple of spots on the side of her head underneath her ponytail. At that time, it was comforting to see she still had a good head full of hair, but I knew from experience that she might soon be in for some heartache.

When we were all seated and comfortable on the patio in the shade of the umbrella, I asked, "So you're starting high school this fall?"

"Yes," Ally answered with a shy smile, but quickly was quiet.

"She'll be going to Leigh next month. She's my oldest, so I'm a little nervous about the high school thing," Nina answered.

"Oh, you're going to love being in high school," Stephanie said. I was grateful she quickly joined the conversation.

Even though we were all aware of the purpose of the visit, we were still reluctant to broach the subject of alopecia. How to begin? Since we didn't have an extended amount of time, I decided to jump right in.

"I want you to know, the staff at Leigh High School was very supportive in dealing with Stephanie's hair issues."

"You don't know how glad I am to hear that," Nina replied, visibly relaxing a bit.

"Yeah, pretty much all my teachers were really cool about the whole thing," Stephanie added.

"You must have questions about her alopecia, so go ahead and ask," I suggested.

"What are the wigs like?" Nina asked.

"The first one we got was human hair and really expensive. It was nice because I could style it, but it was also pretty heavy and sometimes it was a bummer to *have* to style it. Now I wear synthetic all the time like this one," Steph answered pointing to the dark brown wig she had pulled into a ponytail.

"That's a wig?" Nina exclaimed, looking more critically at Stephanie's hair and staring in amazement. "I thought your hair had grown back!"

"Yeah, when you opened the door, I thought that was your hair," Ally added with a smile, some of her shyness starting to melt away.

"Nope, this is definitely a wig," Steph answered. It was great to hear that they both had mistaken her wig for real hair.

Conversation was easy from then on. Stephanie did most of the talking, describing her challenges at school while losing her hair and how she had dealt with it. Relieved to be on the other side, Steph assured Ally that the toughest part was the months of losing the hair, and explained that once it was all gone, everything got easier. As the hour wore on, I could see the anxiety fade from Nina's face.

"Do you want to go up to my room and see my other wigs?" Steph asked Ally.

"Sure," Ally answered, and they were both out of their seats in a flash.

Glad for the chance to talk candidly to Ally's mom with the girls gone, I asked, "So how is Ally doing with everything?"

"She's doing okay. You know how hard it is sometimes. She's really nervous about starting high school."

"She still has quite a lot of hair," I pointed out, optimistically. "Maybe she won't lose anymore. That's one thing we learned from the doctors—no one can predict exactly what's going to happen."

"True. But there's alopecia in our family. I remember my aunt always having to wear a wig, so I'm thinking that's probably where Ally is headed."

"Well, like Stephanie said, you're going through the worst part right now. After all the hair is gone, it does get easier. We don't even talk about it anymore, except when she needs to get a new wig. Then we just order one online.

Almost to tears several times, Nina explained how much it meant to her to know that Stephanie had coped so easily and successfully with losing her hair. It gave her a tremendous amount of hope that Ally would survive too.

"Steph, they need to get going," I yelled up the stairs when Nina and I returned to the foyer.

"Okay. We're coming," Steph answered amid fits of laughter.

"Sounds like they're having a good time," I commented to Nina, glad the girls had hit it off.

"Yes. I'm glad," and again emotions almost got the best of her.

"Text me *anytime* you have questions. Seriously!" I heard Stephanie tell Ally as they came walking down the stairs.

"Okay, Ally. We've got to run," Nina said, hoping to speed things up. And then to me, "I wish we had more time…"

"I know. Me too. Actually I'm amazed it worked out at all. Stephanie is gone so much for basketball during the summer and soon we're leaving for vacation." I realized I wouldn't have wanted to miss meeting them for anything.

"Yes. At least we had an hour. Well, enjoy your vacation!"

"Thanks. Call anytime."

"Bye, Steph," Ally waved as she walked out to the car.

"Text me!" Steph yelled back.

"So, how did it go up there?" I asked, knowing by the smile on her face that things had gone well.

"Great. She's really nice."

"What did you talk about?"

"Just stuff. You know…I showed her my wigs and she tried some on."

"Really? That's great! Now she won't be so nervous if she has to get one."

"Hopefully," Steph answered.

"I'm so proud of you," I said as I hugged her, wishing she had an inkling of just how much she had done for that mother by befriending Ally. "It meant so much to Nina for you to talk to Ally." I knew full well that she wouldn't completely understand until she was a parent herself.

"It was no big deal. Ally is kind of shy, but she's really nice. Besides, it made me feel good to help someone out—like I hadn't gone through all that for nothing."

It's funny how far-reaching the ripple effect can be. If Stephanie hadn't chanced wearing her wig in the game that day, there never would have been the news article and Ally wouldn't have known about Steph. Sadly, Ally would then have had to navigate the world of alopecia at Leigh High School alone, without the benefit of advice from someone who had walked the same path. Steph was a living, reassuring example of Ally's future and would help her through the difficult times that lay ahead.

Twenty-five

WATER POLO

During my sophomore year, just as Coach Phillips predicted, I spent a good deal of the Mitty basketball season on the bench. What a contrast to my freshman year at Leigh when I had scored a total of 182 points over the course of the season; sophomore year at Mitty I scored a meager 28. It was a rough adjustment. I was optimistic and hopeful things would change during the Cager spring/summer season. Four players had graduated, three of whom went on to play at D1 schools. This was my chance.

"Weed, you are an inspiration. Players like you are why I still coach basketball," Coach yelled across the gym during a particularly tough practice. No one put in more effort at practice than I did.

Unfortunately, that didn't seem to matter. I still spent a majority of our games on the sidelines—and I couldn't understand why. I was inspiring, but not inspiring enough to be out on the court. It was discouraging. Making one mistake in a game was the coup-de-gras. I would be subbed out faster than the refs could run down the court. It gets pretty frustrating when you see other players commit turnover after turnover, miss baskets, get sloppy on defense and still stay in the game. If I just had enough time on the court for my nerves to settle and to get into a rhythm, I knew I could execute. My confidence took a huge hit.

Several players got so discouraged that they gave up basketball altogether and left the team. Even though it seemed like an exercise in futility, I was determined to stick it out. Each practice I gave it everything I had and more. Every loose ball I dove for. Blocking out was automatic and instinctual. I could deliver to the posts consistently and successfully. Staying with my man, I fought through screens like crazy. My percentage on three point shots was improving. With all my hard work I was hoping to catch a break, but it was like rowing a boat upstream.

For years, basketball had been the sport I lived for. I just couldn't get enough. Nothing beat the rush I got after driving in for a layup and sinking a shot, especially if I was fouled and it turned into a three-point play. Making the resulting free throw was icing on the cake. I spent many evenings on our lighted court at home, practicing free throws, set shots, jump shots, and three pointers. When it rained I practiced dribbling in the garage—cross-overs, behind the back, speed dribbling, hesitation step—Mom timed me and pushed me, doing what she could to help.

Sometimes I pushed too hard. During one insane track practice during our summer club season (Coach was upset with our performance the day before at the EOT Oregon City Basketball tournament and was administering her form of punishment) I pushed myself to the breaking point. After doing dozens of jump squats over cones in the hot sun on turf for over an hour, my muscles cramped so tight I could barely walk. Weakness was not tolerated so I did my best to stumble through the rest of practice as the sweat rolled off my head and completely soaked my jersey. By the end I was barely moving, but I didn't complain. I didn't want to risk losing any of the few minutes I got on the court by giving in to the pain. Not knowing that something was seriously wrong, I tried to fight through the extreme muscle cramps during our evening game, but I just couldn't get my muscles to function.

Upon returning home after the tournament, I was in bad shape. I couldn't walk up and down stairs without bracing my arms on both sides against the railings. Even walking was painful. Being an athlete I lived with sore muscles, but I knew this was different. The stiffness was getting worse instead of better—my body wasn't recovering. Forced to the doctor by Mom, he immediately suspected rhabdomyolysis and ordered the necessary blood and urine tests.

The next morning we got a call from Dr. Triantos asking us to come in immediately. He explained that three conditions point to a diagnosis for rhabdo: severe incapacitating muscle pain, elevated levels of creatine kinase (CK) in the blood, and myoglobin in the urine. I had all three. The muscle cramping I was experiencing was caused by muscle membranes breaking down, allowing myoglobin and potassium to leak out of the cells and overwhelm the kidneys—a result of extreme exertion. He explained that dehydration plays a big part in the occurrence of rhabdo (during the harsh track workout in the blistering sun in Oregon we had no water for over an hour). My condition was serious and I needed to have another blood test immediately to see if my kidneys were recovering. If not, I'd be admitted to the hospital and given intravenous fluid. Severe cases of rhabdo could lead to kidney failure and we wanted to avoid that at all costs. I wasn't allowed to practice for at least a week.

After having my blood drawn a second time, I went back home and pounded down water by the bucketful, hoping and praying there was no permanent damage. Sitting home, waiting for the results, I wondered if it was all worth it. Why was I working so hard and risking my health for a coach that didn't believe in me? I knew I was capable, but what could I do to convince her? Obviously I couldn't give any more than I already did—but that wasn't good enough. Would it ever be?

Fortunately the next day the news was good—my kidneys were recovering. Knowing I wasn't the first athlete to feel unjustly treated by a coach (and wouldn't be the last), I finished out the summer season with as much enthusiasm as I could, but in truth I couldn't wait for the season to end.

Two weeks later, with summer basketball over and my body fully recovered from rhabdo, I was back at the airport traveling with my family to New York for our summer vacation. We bought handbags on Canal Street, saw *Wicked* on Broadway and spent a week visiting family and friends. August 9th we landed back in San Jose, August 11th I had my wisdom teeth out, and August 17th I completed another Rim-to-Rim hike in the Grand Canyon. Two days later I was back at Mitty for the first day of the 2008/2009 school year.

During that first week back at school, which was such a drag, I discovered that my good friend on the basketball team, Liz Gordon, was trying out for water polo. She encouraged me to join her. Having had absolutely no experience in the water other than fooling around in our backyard pool and occasionally swimming the short laps our pool allowed, my first reaction was, "No way!" I knew nothing about swimming and even less about water polo. We were juniors. Thrown into the mix of experienced swimmers, how could I compete? But the more I thought about it, the more I began to realize a break from basketball might do me some good. After such a frustrating season a change might breathe new life into me. There were lots of positives with water polo: you got tan while playing, which was a bonus; wrestling was legal and necessary; and everyone on the team during practice and games wore a cap, so I would look just like everyone else. Being around the men's water polo team was also a major draw. So despite knowing that I was going to be completely destroyed in the pool, I decided my pride could handle it and I showed up the second week of practice.

As predicted, I was well behind everyone during the drills, especially the distance ones. Surrounded by experienced swimmers, their strokes were swift and graceful, while mine were awkward and choppy. Skilled at getting a breath in while swimming freestyle the seasoned swimmers finished each lap in one fluid motion, whereas I managed to swallow a whole mouthful of water every time I tried to breathe. Flip turns were a piece of cake for the other players. I, on the other hand, swam to the end, stopped, and pushed off with my legs, which caused me to fall even farther behind. Even though I should have been humiliated, I was having the time of my life. Taking a break from basketball was good for my soul.

My first lesson on staying afloat involved mastering the "egg-beater". Egg-beatering is treading water with a circular movement of the legs that resembles the motion of an egg-beater. This method of treading water allows you to keep a constant position relative to the water level, whereas a scissor kick causes you to bob up and down. Initially the kick felt unnatural, but after a few days I had it down. There's nothing more motivating than the threat of drowning to speed up the learning curve.

I loved many aspects of water polo. One of my first days at practice we did a partner drill where each player had her hands on the other person's shoulders and the point was to try to dunk each other. Actually, it was anything but simple. Grueling and vicious was more like it. It took extreme physical effort to try and stay above water while an opponent was trying to drown you. If by chance you gained the upper hand, you couldn't sit back and relax. Let up for a second and you were the one back under. Yes, it was brutal, but I loved it.

Due to the fact that I was just beginning water polo at the age of seventeen (most players had at least three years of experience by then and even more years as swimmers), I was on a crash course to learn all I could about the game. Literally, it was sink or swim. In water polo you are in constant motion just so you can breathe (in other sports breathing is a freebee), which is tough enough, but while you are desperately trying to survive in 9 feet of churning water, the six opposing players are pushing on you, kicking, pinching, pulling—basically doing whatever they can besides flat out punching you to impede your progress. On top of that, you need to be able to catch the ball and somehow rise out of the water high enough to deliver an accurate shot into the goal, hopefully past the goalie. No other sport allows such physical contact and demands such precise skill without the benefit of having the ground to stand on.

As the days passed, my swimming dramatically improved. Starting at the bottom really sucked, but it also offered a tremendous opportunity for growth, and my skills were developing rapidly. My years on the basketball court definitely came into play—ball handling was something I knew a great deal about and took to easily, especially given the smaller size of the ball. Having good vision over the field of play was nothing new. In addition, fighting for position was a big part of basketball, especially under the rim, so that came naturally also. However, in water polo the physical contact is magnified times ten, especially underwater.

During any water polo game there are actually two games going on—the one the officials and spectators see, which can appear calm and civil at times, and the ugly war going on underwater. Holding, sinking or pulling back an opponent that does not have the ball is considered a foul, and if the refs see it they'll call it. That's a big if. Anything but calm, the surface of the water becomes nearly opaque with the constant motion of 28 arms and 28 legs churning and swirling in all directions.

The choppy surface of the water provides the perfect screen underneath which any number of fouls can be committed, all unseen by the referees. Players will grab at anything, and I mean literally anything, to gain an advantage. Pinching, scratching, kicking and grabbing are all part of the game, and if you don't like it you might as well get out of the water.

Completely overwhelmed by all the rules I had to learn, my nerves were on edge at the start of our first JV game. Was I going to completely humiliate myself, or would I be able to keep up and perform adequately? For sure, I was entirely out of my element, but reasoning that there were no great rewards without risks, I jumped in the pool and gathered what little amount of confidence I had built over the previous days and gave it a shot. Whistles were blown every few seconds signaling fouls, and I quickly caught on. For a minor foul, the ref blew the whistle once, and play stopped. The player who was fouled then got a free throw. If the defender was fouled, it was a turnover. Minor fouls included acts like touching the ball with two hands; hitting the arm or body of player with the ball; being within 2 meters of the opponent's goal without the ball (off sides); pushing off the side or bottom of the pool; and holding the ball underwater even if another player is forcing you to. For major fouls the whistle is blown twice. Play stops, the ball is awarded to the other team, and the player who committed the foul is ejected for 30 seconds. Three ejections for any player and you're out of the game.

Feeling that I managed to keep pace fairly well in my first game, I was looking forward to the rest of the season. Much of what went on during games was instinctual and involved a lot of aggression—

something I had never had a problem with. After surviving that first game, there was no stopping me. I could tread water with the best of them and my shots on goal were improving—I was scoring. At first, playing most of the game really taxed my endurance, but as the strength in my legs increased, so did my stamina. I could last even through overtime periods.

There are many different techniques to use when making a shot on goal. Among them are the power shot, skip shot, lob shot, tee shot, and screw shot, but my absolute favorite is the backhand. To perform a successful backhand shot you have to lean forward, with your back to the goal, grab the ball and swing your arm behind you quickly, without looking. This shot, if accurate, is practically indefensible—the goalie simply isn't ready to block. Accuracy is the key. You're shooting without looking so timing the release is difficult, but when done correctly, it's deadly. Not long into our season, at the very beginning of one of our games, our team recovered the ball from the sprint start and I received a pass in the center of the pool, well beyond the 7-meter mark. Taking advantage of the fact that no one was marking me, with my back to the goal I swung my right arm quickly, flicking my wrist to release the ball. Everyone went silent and I turned around to see the ball bobbing up and down inside the goal behind the goalie. Just like that, six seconds into the match, we were up 1-0—I had successfully executed my first backhand from the center of the pool.

Midway through the season, the varsity coach called me over to practice with the varsity team. I was more than a little bit intimidated, but convinced myself that the coach thought I was capable, so I should have faith. Scrimmaging with them was exciting and as I started to score my confidence grew.

When I voiced my insecurities to coach Scott, he responded as he glanced at my cap (an unspoken reference to my alopecia), "Weed, you were born to swim."

"Mom, I think I'm going to be playing on Varsity tonight, so you might want to skip the JV game," I said when I used my cell to call her during lunch, thinking that she wouldn't want to sit through two games. We were playing Presentation High School that night—JV game at 4:30, Varsity at 6:00pm.

"Really?" she asked, her excitement evident.

"I'm not sure, but Coach Scott said maybe."

"That's great!"

After a couple seconds, Mom added, "I'll get there at 4:30 anyway, just in case you play JV—I wouldn't want to miss one of your games."

"Okay. That's up to you. Pray for me—I hope I don't drown trying to keep up with the varsity players."

"You got it. See you later."

"Love you."

"Love you too, Steph."

Presentation is a Catholic school for girls in a residential area of Willow Glen in San Jose. Our water polo teams are always well matched, so games against them are usually nail-biters. As we arrived at the Pres campus later that afternoon, I suited up for the JV game. At the end of our half hour warm-up there were no refs anywhere in sight, so we continued to warm-up for another half-hour until finally we had refs to start the game. Having been in the water already for an hour, I was concerned about my energy level. I observed the JV game from the warm-up section of the pool. At the end of the contest, Mitty was victorious 6-5, and I hadn't been called in once. As soon as the JV game ended, the Varsity players joined me in the pool to warm up. By then it was already 7pm—I had been in the 80 degree pool for two and a half hours, with my body constantly trying to maintain temperature—so not only was I nervous about my first game at the varsity level, but I was seriously concerned about my stamina.

As the game began, I could see the speed and intensity was definitely a notch above the JV games I was accustomed to. In general, passes were more accurate with less time in between, which made for more sprinting up and down the pool. Panic threatened as I watched and waited on the side. Anticipation was feeding my fear, which grew at an alarming rate. Would I get completely dunked in my first battle for the ball? Would I even play? Swallowed by terror, the initial elation I had felt when chosen for Varsity was long gone. As time passed, I started hoping the coach would forget about me.

Late in the first period, I heard my name called and I dove under the lane line into the field of play and swam into position. My time had come—would I make the most of it or be subbed out quickly to avoid disaster for the team?

As the battle raged on, my confidence grew. I was not only keeping up with the varsity players, but had made a few good defensive saves and had a couple shots on goal. After being subbed in that first time, I played a majority of the remaining time left. Several lead changes occurred in the last period—it was neck and neck the whole way. At the end of regulation, the score was tied, which sent us into overtime. Having been in the water for three and a half hours at that point, I wasn't sure how I could last through another three minutes. Eggbeatering does conserve energy, but that energy comes from a limited source. Every athlete runs out of gas at some point and I knew my time was almost up. Could I keep my head above water with three minutes left on the clock?

Somehow I found enough reserves in my tank to battle through the last minutes of that game and we finished with a win after a teammate scored the winning goal. Victory! My first Varsity water polo game ended in success for my team and me. Even though I hadn't scored, I had played a majority of the game, including the overtime periods, and contributed a lot defensively. The win was truly a team effort and I felt great.

Twenty-six

BASKETBALL ENCORE

All too soon it was November and water polo was over. Our season was mildly successful—we won some and lost some. By no means was I the top scorer on the team, but throughout the remaining varsity season I had scored my share of goals. Although the team didn't make it very far into post season play, I was hooked on the sport. Whether it was the challenge that drew me in or the brutality, I wasn't sure. What I did know was my water polo career had just begun and I would do whatever it took to make it a long ride.

Wednesday I played my final water polo game of the season and Thursday afternoon I was out on the track with the basketball team getting ready to run my first timed mile. For conditioning, three days out of every week basketball workouts began with a half hour on the track, which included running a mile on the clock—an event that was equally dreaded by every member of the team. Each player was given a particular time to beat—the times varied according to player ability.

Once you met your time, you were done running miles for the season. Even though the incentive was great, some players suffered through miles for weeks without success.

As I tied my shoes that first day, I dreaded getting on the track. During polo season I had spent all my time working out in the pool—we had done very little dry land. Occasionally on Sundays I had gone on long runs just to get a workout in, but in general I had done no running in the past couple of months. My first mile was not going to be pretty. I was given the fastest time to make—six minutes. I had run a sub-6 the previous year so I knew I could do it; just how many tries it would take, I wasn't sure.

Stepping out onto the all-weather track with the late autumn sun in my eyes and a nice breeze blowing in from the coast, I knew I had to run 90 second quarters to come in at six minutes. Along with several other players that hadn't made their mile times yet, I lined up ready to begin the grueling run. We stood there for a few excruciating seconds waiting for the torture to begin.

Finally, Coach Guerra shouted, "Go!" and we were off.

At the beginning of the first lap I felt pretty good. My breathing was out of control at first, but after the first half lap my breathing settled down. Surprisingly my legs were moving pretty well, but I knew the battle had just begun. Fighting through air to gain ground was so much easier than battling through water—at least in the beginning. As I came to the end of the initial lap I was anxious to hear my split.

"Eighty-six, eighty- seven, eighty-eight..."

Unbelievable! I was right on track. Knowing that if I just kept up my pace I could make my time on the first try, I pushed on. Players that had already met their mile times were used as pacers and ran single laps next to teammates that were trying to complete their miles. Unfortunately I had the fastest mile time to make and there wasn't really anyone that could run fast enough to pace me for a full lap so I was on my own. By the end of the second lap I was exhausted.

"Two minutes fifty-eight seconds, fifty-nine...three minutes."

Two laps down and I was still on the mark. Would it be possible to hit 6 minutes on my first try? When I arrived at the track that day I thought my performance was going to be mediocre at best, but with two laps to go and the goal within reach, I gave it everything I had. The third lap was always tough. You're over half-way, but you're a long way from the end and fatigue is starting to set in, big time. I could feel the burn from the lactic acid building up in my legs. Ignoring the pain was just about impossible, but I pushed on. Success in lap three is more mental than it is physical. With the finish so far off, you have to constantly tell yourself to keep going, keep pushing. You must ignore that nagging voice inside your head that is telling you to quit.

By the end of lap three, my pace had slipped a bit. As a result, my last lap had to be well under ninety seconds or I wasn't going to make it. As I rounded that first curve of my last lap I reached for every ounce of strength I had left and pumped my legs as hard as I could. If it was at all humanly possible I was going to make my time. The spring was long gone from my stride and I was barely hanging on. At that point I was breathing so hard I felt like I was going to barf. Somehow I made it through the back half of the last lap and was rounding the final curve. A couple hundred yards to go and I would be done.

As I approached the last straightaway, I could see my coaches and those lucky teammates that had already made their mile times lined up shouting at me. From the urgent looks on their faces I knew I had a chance to make it. My lungs were heaving and my legs were burning, but I kicked in that last stretch using every last ounce of energy I had. Pumping my arms furiously I gutted out those last fifty yards like a crazed animal.

"Five fifty-three, fifty-four, fifty-five, fifty-six!"

Everyone on the sideline cheered as I came across the line and immediately doubled over with my head between my knees, exhaling in short wheezing bursts.

"Great job, Weed. 5.56!" Coach Phillips congratulated me.

As I straightened up, my teammates reached to high-five me, but my arms stayed down at my sides, spent. Movement of any kind at that moment was too much. Mustering a weak smile, I acknowledged their kudos, and then made my way to the grass. I fell in a heap on the field and for a few moments I laid there on my back looking up at the sky, grateful to be done. Even though I was winded and my entire body was a tingling mass of spent muscle, I smiled. There would be no more timed miles for me that season. How I pulled it off I'll never know. Minutes later I headed into the gym for two hours of basketball practice. Feeling like I had nothing left, I knew I had to suck it up and deal.

Although it felt awkward at first to be back in the gym dribbling and shooting such a comparatively heavy ball, it wasn't long before my years of experience kicked in and I was comfortable out on the court. Yes, I missed the sunshine and fresh air outside, but running up and down the playing field versus swimming was way easier, so basketball did have its perks. Saying goodbye to chlorine was also nice—no more burning eyes and dry skin.

My attitude towards basketball changed radically. When I stepped out onto the basketball court I didn't feel the overwhelming pressure to succeed. I had already succeeded at water polo—basketball was no longer the only sport that defined me. That major change in attitude helped on the court. My previous basketball season was a season full of overwhelming pressure and fear. A player that's afraid is not an effective one.

In general the season progressed much like the previous season. Although I started a few games, I did end up spending a fair amount of time on the bench during the regular season, but this time I wasn't as upset. However, some games were still hard. Seeing the team struggle and knowing I could help was tough, but I kept going, pushing hard at practice, cheering them on. I wasn't throwing in the towel.

We finished a disappointing third in the league. Since I didn't play much during league finals, I didn't feel responsible for the dismal performance. However, as we started post season play in the Central Coast Section (CCS) Division II Championships things started looking up for me. I don't know if it was the shock of the team's failure at league or the phase of the moon, but Coach Phillips finally started giving me some solid minutes out on the court and I was making the most of them. All those endless hours in the gym—floor burns, bruises, broken nose, sprained ankle, gallons of sweat—started paying off, and I was psyched.

In the quarter finals we easily blew by Menlo Atherton in a 54 to 34 victory. Three days later we stomped on North Salinas in the semi finals, 67 to 46. The following Friday we were matched up against the undefeated Gunn Titans in the championship CCS game. There was a lot of hype about the Gunn team going undefeated that season. Our record wasn't nearly as impressive, but statistics can be deceiving. The caliber of teams that Gunn had played was far below that of our typical opponent, so we were still ranked above them and seeded first in the tournament. Even so, they hadn't lost all season and we knew we were in for a battle.

Driving into the parking lot of Santa Clara University that Friday night, seeing the Leavey Center all lit up, I was excited to play at such an impressive venue. Standing four stories high, the entire outside wall of the circular building is glass, so with the lights on inside it shines like a beacon across the campus. Four massive cement pillars on each side of the building brace the square roof. Every architectural detail from the soaring glass walls to the enormous roof supports shouted that this was a place where champions played. As I followed the curved cement ramp to the left of the building up to the players' entrance I felt truly honored with the opportunity to play for a championship and hoped my performance would prove worthy.

Stepping onto the brightly lit court of the Leavey Center, I could feel the adrenaline surging through my veins. Both the Mitty and Gunn bands were there along with the Gunn cheerleaders and the Mitty cheering section (nicknamed The Pit). Filled with more fans than I had seen at all our league games combined, the 4,500 seat stadium was pulsing with activity. Staring up at the exposed ceiling, my eyes were drawn to a giant banner picturing former alumnus and basketball great, Steve Nash. Getting to play on the same court that he had spent four years of his career on was inspiring.

After all the hours my parents had spent watching games sitting in uncomfortable bleachers, I knew they were enjoying the padded seats with backs. Among the audience were Cal-Hi Sports, Max Preps, various college coaches, a videographer and numerous photographers—we were definitely in the spotlight. Glancing at the suspended scoreboard in the center of the arena, I knew it soon would have our numbers flashing. I vowed to myself that my #13 would be displayed, not for fouls committed, but for points earned by the end of the night.

During warm-ups I felt pretty good. Noticing that the court was extremely long, I knew that it suited me well. I had endurance to spare. The question was, would I need it?

"Number 13 Stephanie Weed" boomed over the loud speaker as the announcer began introducing each team. As I made my solo run over to shake the hands of the opposing coaches, I thought of all the long hard hours I had put in to get to that point. Somehow I had kept the faith and believed that my efforts would pay off. I was beginning to think that tonight might just be the night.

At the opening tip off, our 6'3" senior Keilani Ricketts tipped the ball to Iman Scott and we were off and running. After a few unsuccessful attempts to score by both teams, we put the first points up on the board with an inside pass to Keilani who layed it in the hoop. Soon after, Iman hit an outside jumper to make it 4-0. On the second substitution I was put in with five of the eight minutes remaining in the first quarter. The confidence that I gained from my days fighting battles in water polo showed on the court. My defense was good. When my hands touched the ball I handled it with confidence, no longer playing with fear.

We played a fast paced game—strategy switched constantly.

"Thirty, thirty!"

"Forty, forty!"

"Stay down, stay down!"

"Get up, get up!"

"Help side!"

"Weak side!"

"One of you! One of you!"

"Two of you!"

"Yes, yes!"

"Let's go! Let's go!"

It was a challenge to keep up with Coach's directions, but we listened carefully and did our best to execute.

By the end of the first period, Mitty was in the lead 10 to 3 and I had scored two of our ten points off free throws. Just as I predicted, my number was up in lights—a proud moment for me. Gunn was doing their share of running us up and down the court, but we were up to the challenge.

Once again I was subbed in the second period with a little more than five minutes remaining in the half with the score 16 to 7. Determined to make my time on the floor count, I blocked an inbound pass. Again I blocked another pass, but it deflected out of bounds. Seconds later I passed to Nina and she hit a three point shot. Next I fired a pass down to Liz under the basket and she scored. Moments later I swished a one handed jump shot from the right, just inside the three point arc.

We went into the locker room at half time up 25 to 10. Satisfied with my contribution of four points, I was happy, but eager for more. Coach Phillips was pleased with our collective performance but she cautioned us not to get overconfident. Even though we had a comfortable lead, we still had sixteen minutes left to play and the battle was by no means over. By the end of the third quarter we were up by thirteen points. Early in the fourth quarter our lead was cut to eleven. Having seen that kind of lead evaporate quickly during the season with a sudden shift in momentum, we all knew the importance of staying focused. Winning the game meant playing hard all forty-eight minutes. With just over five minutes left in the game, I was subbed in and got a rebound under Gunn's basket. Instinctively I got the ball to our point guard, Nina, and raced up the court. The ball was delivered to one of our posts and she threw up a brick. In the process of getting her own rebound she was fouled, so we in-bounded the ball from under our own basket. Nina shot a bounce pass to me and ran to the 3 point line on the opposite side of the key. I powered it back to her over the key and she dribbled in, taking the defenders with her. Noticing that I was temporarily unguarded she threw the ball back out to me on the 3 point line. Just before Gunn's defense recovered, without any hesitation, I threw up a one handed jump shot from well beyond the arc and hit nothing but net.

"Weed scores from downtown," I heard the announcer call as I raced back up the court to defend. Hitting a three in the Leavey Center in front of hundreds of cheering fans I thought would be the highlight of my night, but there was more to come.

With our lead at fourteen and 4 minutes 51 seconds left to play, we knew that defense was key. Ashley passed the ball to Nina and it was knocked away by Gunn. Before the ball crossed the sideline, the Gunn player saved the ball and chucked it into the middle of the court towards her guard. As I saw the ball sail over the middle I accelerated forward. Just before the ball reached the Gunn player I tipped the ball high over her head in the direction of Gunn's hoop. Knowing that if I didn't recover the ball, Gunn would be in a perfect position to score, I knew what I had to do. When I started the chase, I had an impossible amount of ground to cover. In five giant strides, I sprinted up the remaining half of the court. Just before the ball crossed the end line I made one final desperate leap and caught the ball with my right hand. Before my feet hit the ground I looked up the court and threw the ball twenty feet in to our post player who passed it to our point guard who then got it to Nina. When Nina hit a three point shot the crowd erupted. Our bench went crazy—screaming, hands waving, bodies jumping up and down— and the Pep band belted out our familiar victory beat. Every member of The Pit was on their feet, fists raised in celebration. Immediately Coach

Phillips called a time out, the ref blew his whistle and we ran victoriously to the sideline. Just like that our lead was extended from 14 to 17 and the contest was for all intents and purposes, over.

The adrenaline surging on our bench at that moment couldn't be contained. Clapping, jumping and screaming, we were flying high. I took one of the coveted seats on the bench while Coach Phillips prepared us to return to the court. During a time-out, only players that would be returning to the court got to sit and take direction from the coach; all others had to stand behind. Having spent more than my share of time standing during time-outs, I relished being on the bench at that moment. Coach Phillips came directly over to me.

"Great hustle, Weed!" she shouted as she shot me a high-five.

Normally I kept my emotions in check during a game, but I couldn't hold back the excitement or the smile that spread across my face.

In the three remaining minutes left in the game I didn't manage to score again, but did get another rebound and a steal. Due to our substantial seventeen point cushion, several of the Mitty players that hadn't played at all that night were subbed in. Although my road to success had been rocky and hard to swallow at times, I had finally arrived and it felt great. Knowing those hours sitting on the bench were behind me made victory all the more sweet.

With a final score of Mitty 56, Gunn 40 we added another CCS championship to Coach Phillip's impressive fourteen previous CCS titles. Personally, I was responsible for seven of our 56 points that game and with a roster of fourteen players I was happy with my percentage.

Looking around, I knew we were just a group of ordinary girls, but that night, working as a team, we had done something special. With Keilani clutching the first place trophy we lined up on the court for a team picture as flash after flash went off. There I stood in front of the world, being photographed for posterity without my hair and it didn't bother me in the least. I had earned my spot in that picture and I didn't care who saw me in my black bandanna. Maybe they would be captivated by my dazzling smile or maybe not, but at least we were holding a first place trophy.

We had won CCS, but our season was not over. Four days later, on March 10, 2009, we faced the Valley Vikings in the Northern California quarterfinals. We scored an impressive 82 to their 41 and were on our way to the Nor Cal semis on Thursday to face Carondolet—an all girls Catholic high school. In preseason that year we had lost to Carondolet in overtime, so we knew a win was within our grasp, but it wasn't going to be easy.

After being on the bus for an hour and a half, we finally reached Concord—Carondolet's home town. As we filtered into the gym of De La Salle High School (the neighboring boys school), the stands were packed with fans—mostly Carondolet Cougar fans. Only about forty Mitty parents had made the long drive that Thursday night. What the Mitty fan crew lacked in size they were going to have to make up for in enthusiasm.

That night we knew it was win or go home. If we lost, our season was over, which meant no Arco Arena. After playing at the home of the Sacramento Kings the previous year, we were hungry to return. None of us wanted our season to end.

Precisely at 7pm Keilani lined up for the tip in the center circle. The referee pointed each team in the direction they were to score, threw the ball up and the contest began. We were off and running. With skills closely matched, each team drove and scored nearly every possession. The noise in the small gym was deafening. Coach Phillips communicated plays to us with hand signals—we couldn't hear anything she shouted over the roar of the crowd. With the frantic pace of the game and the constant full court press, it was good we had a deep bench.

As each quarter progressed we were neck and neck. With a score that tight, any mistake could be costly. Working just as hard on defense as we did on offense, we couldn't manage to get a substantial lead and the battle raged on. I was careful not to foul—we couldn't afford to be in the bonus and give up free shots.

When the buzzer sounded at the end of the fourth quarter the score was tied. Having played for close to two hours already, we were soaked and exhausted, but we weren't giving up. Half empty water bottles littered the floor under our bench. Rivers of sweat ran down my face onto my white jersey as I listened to coach pump us up for overtime.

"You've got this! This is what you've worked so hard all year for, now go out and take it!"

For the first bonus period we gave it our all and unfortunately could only hold Carondolet to a tie again. Heading into our second overtime period there was so much at stake. If we couldn't pull out that win, our season was over. None of us wanted to finish with an overtime loss, knowing victory had been so close.

Once again, after three additional minutes out on the court, we ended in a tie. At the start of the third overtime our legs felt like lead from the strain of the past two plus hours spent running up and down the court. Coach Phillips pushed us to the limit everyday at practice to prepare us for times like these. Physically we knew we could handle it. Mentally, we could not lose our focus—any lapse in concentration could be the end.

After a minute had run on the clock in the third OT, I was subbed in. Defense was key and I was on my girl like glue. When we had possession on our end of the court I took a chance and shot a three, knowing it could be a game winner. The ball had good arch as I released and watched as the ball spun towards the basket, right on target. As the ball reached its apex, players from both teams instinctively reached to block out. Holding my breath I watched the ball hit the rim.

The ball spun around the rim for two complete revolutions, dipped into the center a good six inches below the rim and then popped back out again. It was heart breaking. How could the ball go so far into the net only to emerge back out the top and shoot off to the side?

When the buzzer sounded at the end of the third and final overtime after two and a half hours on the court, Carondolet managed to best us 76 to 73. It was over. Having battled so hard for so long we made our way to the locker room, dejected. Our season was over and the overwhelming feeling of failure was almost too much to bear. Not looking forward to hearing Coach Phillip's end-of-the-game speech, we crowded around in the locker room, reluctantly waiting for the words of obvious disappointment to begin. No one was saying much. Lost in thought over mistakes made and missed opportunities, we could barely stand to look at each other. To our surprise and utter shock, instead of pointing out bad decisions we made in the game and factors that contributed to the loss, Coach Phillips told us she had never been more proud of a team. She said it was the most exciting high school basketball game she had ever coached in all her seventeen seasons of coaching women's basketball. Yes, she was disappointed to have lost, as we all were, but she felt we gave it our all and said she couldn't have asked for more out of a team.

Hearing those words of praise from a coach that had such high standards and demanded excellence not only in games but also everyday in practice was a great way to end the season.

Waking up the next morning, my only consolation for having lost the night before was not having practice after school for the first time in seven months. That was going to be awesome. As much as I liked to push myself and loved to sweat I knew I could use a break and was looking forward to it. As I knew there would be, an article in the *Mercury News* that morning proclaimed our loss to the Bay Area. However, Coach Phillips was quoted as saying just what she had told us in the locker room, "I couldn't be more proud of this team."

Although the basketball season was over, I was still in for another surprise. A couple of weeks later, the team, coaches and parents were gathered together at the school for the end of the season banquet. Both the freshman and JV teams had won their respective leagues and with the varsity CCS title it was a night for good food and celebration. Looking particularly festive, the school cafeteria tables were decorated with gold tablecloths topped with bright pink, yellow and orange Gerber daisies. Black and gold helium balloons scattered throughout finished off the affect. The enticing aroma of lasagna, chow mein and several other tasty entrees was making my stomach growl like crazy. After a quick blessing, we were allowed to fill our plates and eat—players first! Although we had all moved on to other activities since our last game—I was back in the pool with club water polo, some were running track and some were playing club ball—it was nice to see everyone together again.

After filling up on the ridiculously good food, Coach Phillips got up and said a few words about the Mitty Women's Basketball program as a whole and then excused the various teams to different rooms to hand out individual awards. Varsity stayed in the cafeteria and Coach Phillips and Assistant Coach Guerra took turns recognizing each player individually. Coach Guerra gave me my certificate and said I earned the award for most bruises and floor burns—a fact that I wouldn't argue with. No one spent more time diving for balls than I did. After all fourteen players were recognized, Coach Phillips proceeded to hand out the achievement awards. Scholar athlete went to Courtney Wilson.

"This next award goes to a player that comes to practice everyday and gives 100 percent effort all the time. I couldn't ask for more out of a player. She is consistently motivated and gives it her all. Any lost ball is never too far out of reach, which is evidenced by all the bumps and bruises on her arms and legs that she wears with pride. Nothing stops her whether it is a broken nose or sprained ankle…"

I couldn't believe what I was hearing. After the words "broken nose" and "sprained ankle" there was no mistaking the fact that Coach Phillips was talking about me. Early on in the season I had broken my nose and halfway through I severely sprained my ankle. Receiving such praise from Coach Phillips was unbelievable. Lost in a daze of disbelief, I missed some of what she was saying, but quickly snapped myself out of it.

"This player made the most impressive save I've ever seen in a game when she chased down a loose ball at the CCS finals and threw it back down the court, which resulted in us hitting a three to clinch the win. I called a time out just so she could get the applause she deserved. Her enthusiasm is infectious out on the court. This award for Most Inspirational Player goes to Stephanie Weed."

As the crowd applauded, I walked up to receive my award. Still in shock, I couldn't believe the award was for me. Having spent almost the entire previous season riding the bench, and a good portion of this season in the same spot, I never thought in a million years that I would receive any award at the banquet. As I turned around to face the parents, award in hand and Coach Phillip's arm around my shoulder, I looked over at Mom and Dad. The smiles on their faces were priceless.

After all the awards were given out and people were milling around, I made my way over to Mom and Dad.

"Congratulations, Steph!" Mom blurted out as she hugged me.

"Good job, Steph," Dad said as we pounded fists.

"Yeah, it's just because of my hair," I mumbled.

"No it's not!" Mom answered emphatically. "Didn't you listen to what Coach Phillips said? She went on and on about your attitude and abilities, not your bandanna."

"It's nice to see your willingness to sacrifice your body appreciated, Steph," Dad commented, smiling as he affectionately put his arm around my shoulder. Flashing back to numerous emergency room visits, I knowingly smiled back. Looking down at my award I couldn't hold back the feelings of doubt lurking in the back of my mind. Was I given the award for my athletic performance or because I had alopecia? At the end of my season playing for Leigh High School I was given the MIP award also. In that case, everyone in the room knew I was given the award because of my hair—they had all witnessed me losing it week after week, and most had been there the fateful night my wig fell off. After what I had been through that season, I gladly accepted the most inspirational player award even if it was solely for playing with alopecia. It had been a difficult and emotional time, but that was two years ago and ancient history. So I play with a bandanna—no big deal. Maybe some people call me brave, but there's nothing brave about stepping onto the court with a bandanna on. Stepping in front of a charging opponent that is dribbling down the court full-speed, knowing you're going to get knocked to the ground at the very least, now that's brave. Wearing a bandanna in front of a crowd of people was just a fact of life, and what I had to do if I wanted to play basketball. I did want to play and I didn't want anyone's sympathy.

As I drifted off to sleep that night my thoughts kept going back to the award I had received. Unable to stop my subconscious from replaying the unexpected praise I received from Coach Phillips, my mind was stuck in an unending loop. Putting a bandanna on my head took no skill, whereas impressing Coach Phillips on the basketball court took every ounce of skill I could call on. She demanded excellence at all times—anything less was unacceptable. Little by little I was beginning to believe that maybe my athletic ability had earned me the award. Certainly Mom and Dad were convinced, but I knew there would always be a question in my mind. Was it admiration or sympathy? I hated sympathy.

Twenty-seven

SURFING

For the first time since sixth grade, Stephanie took the summer off from playing basketball. Instead, she filled her days with the new sport in her life, water polo. Transformed from a gym rat to a pool rat, she had the golden brown tan to prove it. Returning home each night, predictably exhausted from another grueling workout in the water, she was happy and had enough energy for a game of pool in the living room with her friends or a bonfire out back. After a couple of weeks of late nights with her friends at the house, she decided it was time to look for a job. With the economy in a full-blown recession and unemployment nearing 10% I knew it wasn't going to be easy, but she was going to have to try.

For the next couple weeks, Steph put in an impressive amount of effort looking for a job. Scouring every shopping center within a reasonable distance, she filled out application after application. Two shops would've hired her on the spot if she had been eighteen, but that was six months away. It soon became clear that she was going to be spending the summer broke and unemployed.

Maybe it was having so much free time on her hands or just plain boredom, halfway through the summer Steph decided that she wanted to have her head tattooed. Being strongly opposed to any and all tattoos, I didn't like the idea and was certainly not going to give the okay for my seventeen year old daughter to get one and I told her so.

"It doesn't matter, Mom. In a few months I'll be eighteen and I won't need your permission," Steph challenged. By the look in her eyes, I knew she wasn't going to give up easily. I was equally determined to keep her from doing something she'd regret later on. Mother knows best.

"How are you going to pay for it?" I asked, knowing that there was no way she could even dream of coming up with enough money. She had trouble scrounging up money for the movies on Friday night, let alone a couple hundred dollars for a tattoo. Aggravated, I put down my *Better Homes and Gardens,* got up from the table and started unloading the dishwasher.

"I'll get it somehow," she answered, not the least bit deterred by what I considered an impossible obstacle. If she thought she'd do odd jobs around the house for me, she was mistaken.

Realizing that Steph was committed to seeing her idea through and very resourceful, I switched to a new tactic.

"You know, if you do get a tattoo when you're eighteen, any college money you're expecting from us is going to disappear, so you might as well forget about it until you're out of college. Once you're 21 and we're not footing the bill for your education you can tattoo your whole body for all I care, but as long as we're paying, I better not see ANY permanent ink on your skin."

"That's dumb!" she shouted, her eyes angry and defiant.

I didn't answer. We were at an impasse. Predictably, she turned her back and stomped upstairs, slamming her door shut. Continuing with my task, stacking up the dinner plates, I thought how depressing the job of parenting could be at times. More often than not it was a thankless job being the voice of reason—no one likes being the bad guy, even though our children think we relish the task.

It was always something with that girl. Why couldn't Stephanie ever be satisfied with the way things were? Usually the first to try anything, she loved to live life on the edge—not because anyone pushed her there, but because she walked there willingly. As a young child with her daredevil stunts and unpredictable imagination, it seemed like we feared for her life daily. Somehow we managed to get her to young adulthood with only a couple of broken bones and a minimal number of stitches. Now, it wasn't her life I feared for. Making a silly irreversible choice and having to live with the consequences is what I worried about. For the time being, I was confident the money issue kept the ball in my court whether she was eighteen or not. Ironically, I prayed that none of the jobs she applied for came through, which was looking very likely.

As the summer progressed, we became accustomed to the habitual late night events at the house. At least with the crew under our roof, we knew what they were up to. Even though they had a hard time keeping the noise down, it was a good group of kids. Trevor, Ryan and

Sydney—all friends from Mitty—would eat anything Stephanie served them that wasn't growing fuzz in the frig. No leftovers ever went to waste. Quesadillas were a favorite. They loved the pan fried flour tortillas filled with melted cheddar and jack cheeses that Steph prepared on our gas-powered Wolf range. The trick was to get the tortillas brown and crisp without burning them, which usually involved setting off the smoke alarm. Being startled out of bed by the obnoxious alarm after eleven was something I definitely could do without, but if it kept the troops fed and satisfied I was willing to deal. Between the loud voices, smoke alarm and the sound of poorly shot billiard balls hitting the wood floor in the living room, our summer nights were anything but quiet. However, it was good to know the kids were having fun that wouldn't land them in jail so I was willing to put up with a little noise, and actually grew to like having them around.

Nothing came through on the job front for Stephanie, so she filled her days going to the gym, working out in the pool, playing water polo, driving to the beach and hanging out.

Eventually the end of July came and we began packing for our bi-annual family vacation in Kauai. This trip to Kauai was going to be particularly memorable because fifteen other family members were joining us, including Tracy's sister from New Hampshire with her husband and three kids. With nineteen of us going, there would always be plenty of activities and someone to do them with.

As I began sorting out the suitcases, Steph came walking down the hall to retrieve the one I had reserved for her and dropped a bomb.

"Dad said he'd pay for my tattoo in Hawaii."

Stopped dead in my tracks, I didn't initially know what to say. Had Tracy really talked to her about a tattoo and volunteered to pay for it, or was she playing us against each other, trying to get her way? Of course she was. I wouldn't expect anything less from her, but it was hard for me to believe that Tracy would commit to something like that without talking with me first. Back in our first year of marriage he had come home with a brand new BMW motorcycle without saying a word about it to me. It was quite an issue but we worked through it. Since then we hadn't made any major decisions without coming to an agreement together. Obviously it wasn't the cost that bothered me; it was the principle of the matter. He knew how I felt about tattoos—he felt the same way—I guess except when it came to Stephanie's head. As exasperated and frustrated as he got with her at times, she still had him wrapped around her finger.

"Oh, really?" I shot back as a warning. "We'll see about that." I let her know that the case was far from closed.

"I'm thinking about getting a hibiscus flower…"

"I don't want to talk about it," I interrupted and continued pulling gear out of the hall closet.

"Mom, I thought…"

"I'm not going to discuss it with you—I'm NOT okaying a tattoo, period. Now go pack." Later, I was going to have a few words with Tracy, but in the meantime I had some packing to do myself. Delighted that our flight for Kauai left the following day, I wasn't going to let anything dampen my mood, not even the fact that Tracy and Stephanie seemed to be colluding against me. Gone were the days when

I had to pack three suitcases plus my own. Even Valerie was old enough to pack her own things, so once I got the correct suitcases assigned, I leisurely gathered my things. Tank tops, shorts, swim suit, flip flops—island packing was so easy.

"So, Steph said you told her you'd pay for her tattoo while we were in Hawaii. Is that true?" I asked Tracy quietly while we were sitting on the couch watching TV by ourselves later that night.

"Yeah, I might have," Tracy admitted. "I think it's a great idea. I wouldn't okay it anywhere else, but since she's lost her hair I think it's the right thing to do."

We were sharing a bowl of popcorn and I threw a few more kernels in my mouth before I answered.

"Well, I don't agree at all and I never will. If you're going to let her do it, you'll do it without my approval," I said.

"Fine, but I think you're wrong on this one."

I didn't want to argue. The show we were watching ended and being tired from making all the last minute arrangements for our trip, I was ready to call it a day.

"We'll see... I'm going up to read. Love you," I said as I gave him a kiss.

"Love you too."

When we were just starting out, the issue would've turned into World War III, but if nothing else, over the past 25 years we had learned that a good night's sleep helped clarify things and prevented us from saying things in the heat of battle that we might regret. So I headed up to bed thinking we'd cross the tattoo bridge when we got to Hawaii. Why fight about it now? Convinced that we'd be busy enjoying all the island activities, I was hoping that the subject of tattoos wouldn't even come up.

A little after noon the next day our plane landed in Lihue. Within minutes we had retrieved all our bags and the rental car and were off to Costco to stock up for the week. Always a challenge to fit a week's worth of groceries and luggage—complete with boogie boards and snorkel gear—in the rental car, we did the best we could. Every cubic inch of the rental car was occupied. Hoping for an early check-in, we headed out to our timeshare in Poipu.

The warm tropical breeze blowing in from the west glided through the dry palm branches high overhead creating its own rhythmic beat. Watching the gently swaying palm fronds and hearing the ocean meet the shore in wave after crashing wave, was so relaxing. Being on the islands was good for the soul. Recently having routinely put in fourteen hour days, I knew Tracy needed this vacation more than any of us.

With most of us staying in the same resort complex, I knew we were going to have to be keenly aware of the condo door when Stephanie had her wig off. Although at home she chose to hang out with a select few friends without a wig, no one else outside our immediately family had seen her without her hair and we needed to respect that.

Tracy had planned a dive trip for the morning after we arrived with the other scuba certified members of the family, so we used the opportunity to find Stephanie a surf lesson. On the beach in front of the Marriott Waiohai we were able to schedule a semi-private lesson. The big question for Stephanie was, should she try wearing her wig or not?

"Do you want me to ask the guy what he recommends as far as the wig?" I whispered to Stephanie as I stood on the beach next to the hut watching her put on the water shoes the instructor provided.

"No, thanks. I'll handle it," she answered, slightly annoyed. Even though it hurt a little knowing she didn't want my help, I was glad she felt confident enough to take care of business.

An overweight, forty-something man was the only other tourist joining Stephanie in the lesson. I overheard him say that he owned a surfboard on the mainland, but had never gotten up on it. I wasn't too surprised.

With my camera handy, I watched while they were given brief dry-land instructions. After about fifteen minutes, they both were ready to head out to the waves.

"Ah, I wear a wig. Do you think I should put a swim cap on before we go out in the water?" Stephanie asked the young, tan, very capable looking instructor. Obviously she wasn't bothered by the admission.

"That's totally up to you, but it's going to get pretty rough out there," the instructor answered. His initial reaction to hearing she wore a wig was masked behind his dark Oakley shades.

"I guess I'll be putting on my cap," she answered, smiling.

"Good idea. Let's head out," the instructor directed and they made their way down the beach and into the water.

Valerie and I picked a spot on the shore where I could snap pictures and she could play in the waves. Not long after, we were joined by my sister Terri and my four-year-old niece Katie. Katie and Valerie had fun writing their names in the sand, collecting shells and chasing the waves. Terri and I set up our chairs for some nice relaxing time in the sun together.

Knowing that Steph had a good strong upper body, I was reasonably confident that she would do well out in the surf. With a white cap on, it was easy to pick her out among the other surfers. On her first try she got right up and rode the board like a pro. After that she paddled back and caught wave after wave. When I saw her occasional wipeout, I knew she had made the right decision about the cap. No matter how lame she thought it looked, wearing the cap was better than having to find her wig when it fell off in the waves. The poor guy with her never managed to stand up no matter how hard he tried. When the two hour lesson was over, Steph stayed out in the water for another hour, paddling, surfing, paddling, surfing. When she finally came in, she was exhausted but enraptured with the new sport.

"I know what I want for Christmas, now," Steph announced as she walked up the beach breathing hard, holding on to the board with salt water dripping from her body, her eyes alive with excitement.

"Let me guess...a surfboard?" I asked as she set the board down in the sand.

"Yes!" she exclaimed and plopped her weary body down on the board, looking up into the sky, shading her eyes from the sun with her arm.

"I guess that means you'll want a wetsuit too," I added, knowing the Northern California ocean temp was a good 20 degrees colder. "It was easy to pick you out with the cap on. I think I got some good shots."

"Yeah, I'm glad it stayed on," she answered and smiled.

Kipu Falls was the group destination the following day. Tracy's sister and her family from New Hampshire had arrived on Kauai after spending a week on the Big Island. Having seen an impressive amount of Hawaiian coastline already, they were up for hiking inland to the falls. Their oldest boy of seventeen, Scott, was anxious to try out the rope swing. Having not visited the obscure tourist site on any of our previous visits, we didn't know what to expect, but had heard and read great reviews.

After taking Highway 50 for a short distance up the east side of the island, we turned right onto Kipu Road and found a dirt parking lot of sorts. To reach the falls we hiked about five minutes on an overgrown trail cut through tall sugar cane. There was no shortage of flying insects and some of them bit, unfortunately. Following the Hule'ia stream, the trail led down to the brink of Kipu Falls. Once we crossed the uneven tumble of lava rock at the end of the trail we could hear the soothing sound of cascading water and see the enormous, picturesque pool that lay at the base of the falls. The only view of the falls themselves was from the water below. Twenty-foot rock walls surrounded the pool at the bottom, which was deep and large—approximately 80 ft. long and 40 ft. across. To the right of the falls stood a large towering tree with 25 ft. of exposed roots leading down to the water. High up in its branches hung the famous rope swing we had heard so much about. To get to the swing you had to ford the Hule'ia stream at the top of the falls, which entailed stepping over numerous slippery moss-covered rocks. Fortunately most of us came prepared with water shoes. With the sun high and temperatures rising, a fall in the stream was almost welcome.

All the kids in our group lost no time making their way over to the rope swing. Scott was the first one to jump and executed a perfect back flip on his inaugural run. Stephanie waited patiently while Matthew, Andy and Michael had a chance, then I saw her put on her swim cap and grab the rope. From prior experience on a rope swing near our house, she knew the force of hitting the water was enough to dislodge her wig. Although the idea of wearing a swim cap at the popular tourist site was not her idea of fun, neither was the possibility of losing her wig in front of everyone, so the cap was on for better or worse. I hoped and prayed that it held. As she took off, the forty foot pendulum created by her body swung down, accelerating with gravity, sailing over the inviting water below. After flying past the equilibrium point, she swung up away from the water and just when the rope reached its highest amplitude, she let go and plunged into the deep water. For a few anxious seconds she was swallowed by the tropical pool. Would I see her cap and wig surface before her, detached by the force of hitting the water? Standing 25 feet above the pool I was in no position to help her. It was only a matter of seconds, but those seconds felt like hours as I stared at the swirling water, watching and hoping.

Thankfully, Steph immerged with a big grin on her face, cap and wig intact.

"How's the water?" I yelled down, enormously relieved.

"It's amazing. Feels great," she answered while leisurely sidestroking in the water.

"Is there any other way down?" I asked. Standing on the lava rock surrounding the falls I was starting to feel the heat and wanted to find some way into the refreshing pool. Not only did the prospect of holding onto the rope while flying in the air scare me, but climbing out via a 25 foot extension ladder up the side of the rocks looked terrifying. Knowing my incurable fear of heights and history on ladders, I was stymied. Steph looked all around the pool. There was a relatively flat overgrown bank on the other side covered with trees and sugarcane, but there didn't appear to be any way to reach the bank besides the rope swing or ladder.

"You could jump off the waterfall," she yelled from the bottom and laughed.

"Funny!" I answered.

A handful of the adults in our group stayed at the top of the waterfall taking pictures of all those brave enough to attempt the rope swing. To my surprise, after watching numerous jumps, I saw Valerie go flying across the water while hanging onto the rope. Just like a pro, she let go and dropped into the water below. That did it. If my 11 year old daughter could do it, then so could I. Making my way over to the tree, I told myself that it was only a rope tied to a tree. All I had to do was hang on. Tracy, who had already successfully completed a jump, was helping by retrieving the rope for the jumpers.

"I'm going to do it," I informed him when I finally made it over to the rope.

"Really?" he replied, quite surprised. He knew me well. "Okay. Just hand me your glasses first and I'll get the rope."

I took the final step down to the lowest jumping platform conveniently formed by some overlapping horizontal roots. Holding precariously onto the smooth bark of the tree, I looked over the edge to the water below. It looked impossibly far away. Instantly waves of dizziness came over me, and I tightened my grip on the tree. I knew the dizziness was irrational—the roots of the tree stood in the same place they had for what appeared to be decades and were definitely not moving. I, however, had no control over the sensations flooding through my body. Tracy handed me the rope and offered some words of encouragement.

"You can do it, Stace. It's easy. All you have to do is hang on."

Fighting back my fear and trying to ignore the whirling spinning movement that became stronger every second I stood on that ledge, I grabbed the rope tentatively with one hand. With the thick coarse hemp settled firmly in my palm I took one last look down and knew I couldn't do it.

"I can't," I told Tracy and handed the rope back to him. Having no upper body strength to speak of I was afraid that I wouldn't be able to hold onto the rope long enough, not to mention the overwhelming fear of jumping out into space. Grabbing my glasses, I headed back to the other part of the group; they were waiting and watching at the top of the falls. Disappointed, I found a relatively flat spot in the tumbled lava rock to sit and watch the swimmers below.

In the meantime another group of tourists had arrived, all males who looked to be in their mid-twenties. To my surprise, instead of wading over to the rope swing, the guys made their way to the very edge of the rock wall adjacent to the waterfall. Getting a little nervous watching them I wondered how long it would take for help to arrive if they ended up doing something stupid, and got hurt. Like seasoned veterans, they took one look over the falls and to our amazement, jumped off. Immediately disappearing beneath the rocks, they howled with excitement the whole way down. Within seconds we heard a series of three splashes, followed by deep congratulatory calls and we knew they had landed safely. It wasn't long before some of the guys in our group climbed out of the water and wandered back over to the top of the falls. Not to be outdone, back flips and choreographed group jumps ensued. The whole time I sat watching, getting hotter and more uncomfortable. Finally, I couldn't take it anymore and walked over to the edge. One thing was certain, it was a long way down, but unlike the rope swing, jumping off entailed no coordination or strength. All you had to do was step off. Because the cliff was so sheer, you didn't even have to jump out away from the wall. It was one step.

"I'll jump if you will," Pam volunteered. Having sat out the rest of the morning like me, I knew she was getting hot, too.

I looked over to the ladder. Knowing the rungs would be slippery and my hands would be shaking, that scared me almost more than the jump.

"You should do it, Stace," Tracy encouraged. "All you have to do is step off. The water feels great."

"What about the ladder? That terrifies me," I replied looking to him for advice then looking over at the silver extension ladder, which reached from the water's edge to the top of the cliff, a distance of at least 25 feet. He had seen me in action plenty of times on our eight foot ladder and knew how much trouble I had with heights.

"It's bolted into the rocks and very sturdy. Don't worry about it. You can definitely make it up. I'll climb up right behind you," he offered.

Although it was generous for Tracy to say he'd climb up behind me, the fact of the matter was that if I started to fall I knew he wouldn't be able to save me. I would end up taking him with me.

"Is it slippery?" I asked, remembering how hard it was to keep my balance on the rocks at the bottom of the stream.

"No, not really. Plus you'll have the water shoes on. That'll give you plenty of traction."

Momentarily convinced, I made my way to the flat protruding rock at the edge and looked down. From that angle, it didn't look so bad. The draw of the cool, clear water was enough to make me put aside my fears and for better of worse, take the plunge. I handed my glasses to Trace, who stood right behind me, ready to follow and looked over once again. Without my glasses on, everything changed. Blurred almost beyond recognition, everything in my sight was distorted and out of focus. Without my glasses, I was virtually blind for anything at a distance. It would be like jumping off into space blindfolded, knowing the bottom was out there somewhere, but not being able to see where it was. Without my glasses, I lost my nerve and backed away from the edge.

"It's too scary when it's out of focus," I explained.

Knowing how close I was to jumping, and knowing I would be terribly disappointed if I left without jumping, Tracy was ready to do anything to get me in the water.

"What if I jump off first and wait for you at the bottom?" he offered.

Even though I appreciated the offer, I still couldn't get past looking into a mass of unfocused, greenish/gray matter and free falling into space.

"I'm okay as long as I have my glasses on, but once I take them off it freaks me out," I explained. Knowing I couldn't jump with my glasses and risk losing them, I was convinced jumping was just not going to happen for me that day. Does a 48-year-old woman really need to jump off a 25-foot waterfall?

"Stace, you've got to do it," my brother Ted insisted. "It's so easy. You don't even have to jump, just step off. There's nothing down there that you're going to hit."

Desperate to win this challenge against my irrational fears, I came up with a plan.

"How about if you jump first, Trace, and wait for me at the bottom? Ted, you stand right behind me so I can take one last look over the edge with my glasses on. I'll hand my glasses back to you and jump right away before I have a chance to look again and lose my nerve."

"You got it," Ted responded.

"Sounds like a plan. Here I go..." and just like that Trace jumped off the rock.

Watching him float around in the relaxing, cool water below, I couldn't wait to join him.

"Okay, Ted, get really close," I instructed as I stepped up to the edge of the rock. Taking one last look down, I was nervous but ready. Knowing I had to strike quickly before I lost my nerve, I looked back at Ted and handed my glasses to him. Before the unfocused landscape in front of me was able to induce panic, I jumped. Having no idea where Tracy was at the bottom, I hoped he could get out of my way. As I soared through space, the scream that immerged from my throat I imagined could be heard for miles. I had no control over my arms and legs that swung wildly as I fell. At last, after several of the most frightening seconds of my life, I hit the water and plunged into its depths. Swimming my way back to the surface, I was glad the first part of the ordeal was over. As I immerged I could here claps and yells of congratulations from all around the pool. I had a bigger audience than I realized.

"Good job, Stace," Trace congratulated as he swam over to meet me. "I can't believe you actually did it!"

"Me either," I answered. "The water feels so good. Now we have to get Pam down here."

"Pam!" I yelled up. "It's real easy. The water feels great!"

"Okay, I'm coming!" she shouted back and within seconds she had joined us at the bottom. After sitting for so long on the black lava rock in the hot sun, the cool spring water was wonderfully refreshing. Listening to the water cascade down the falls while leisurely floating in the giant pool below was so relaxing…until I happened to glance over at my only way out. Even without my glasses on, the ladder looked impossibly high.

Anxious to get my climb up the dreaded ladder over with, I didn't linger too long in the water.

"Can you help me up the ladder, Trace?" I asked, knowing there was no way I could make it up the ladder without him behind me.

"Sure, let's go. It really isn't bad. Just don't look down."

We swam over to the side and I started the climb up. Just as Tracy had said, the ladder was anchored securely to the rocks and didn't wiggle, even under my shaking hands. I climbed rung after rung, keeping my eyes directly in front of me, careful to not look down. Tracy followed directly behind me and offered encouragement as we climbed. Finally I reached the top. That last step over the top of the ladder onto the rock wall was a tough one, but with Tracy behind me I managed. I stepped onto solid ground still shaking, but grateful that I had survived.

That morning if someone had told me I was going to jump off a cliff, I would've said they were crazy. With my history of acrophobia, jumping was insane. But life isn't always predictable—sometimes it catches us by surprise. Forever frozen in my mind, I'll never forget what it was like to jump blindly into the air and trust that everything was going to be okay. It took a lot for me to stare that demon down and make the leap. It was scary and probably a little bit dangerous, but the sense of satisfaction I felt was priceless.

While sipping a margarita on our lanai later that afternoon and watching the waves roll in, it dawned on me that living with alopecia meant taking leaps like that just about every day. Eyebrows could disappear; wigs could shift; even walking out the door could be risky if the wind was strong. Fearing that people will judge you if they find out the truth can become paralyzing. Social phobia, severe anxiety, low self esteem and depression are all recurring side effects for many with alopecia. If they could only see how accepting people have been of Stephanie. Playing basketball with a bandanna, boogie boarding bald, surfing with a swim cap—she has laid it all out there. Because she's okay with it, everyone else is too.

Twenty-eight

TATTOO?

O ur week on Kauai with the extended family was over all too quickly. Snorkeling and diving at Tunnels Beach, touring the Napali coast and enjoying an island luau were a handful of the ways we had enjoyed the week together. Although sad to see them leave, we were glad we had a few days left in Kauai before returning home to San Jose.

For the remaining four days on the island we checked out of our condo and moved down the road to the Sheraton. As soon as we stepped out of the car we were greeted with purple orchid leis that smelled heavenly. From the open air lobby we could see directly out to the ocean. I couldn't wait to get settled and walk out to the beach. It was going to be great not lugging all our gear to the beach—just towels, sunscreen and flip-flops.

After living for a week in a spacious 2 bedroom 2 bath unit with separate living and dining rooms, our small garden view room took some getting used to. With so little space, we felt like we were on top of each other. Stephanie especially wasn't happy, but the price was right and we could walk right out to the beach. That helped make up for the lack of space. Once we got unpacked and settled as best we could, Stephanie had one thing on her mind—her tattoo. Appropriating Tracy's laptop, she began scanning for local studios and designs.

"What do you think of this drawing?" she asked, turning the PC in my direction. Watching her lounging on the plush white cotton down comforter, I couldn't help admire her optimism. Did she really think I wanted to look at tattoos? Steph knew how I felt about the subject and I hadn't given her any reason to think I had changed my mind. Contrary to what she'd admit, I could tell that my opinion did matter to her. Unfortunately, my opinion on tattoos had not changed.

"I don't want to look at it, Steph, and I don't want you to get a tattoo. You know that."

"Fine! I just thought you might want to give me some advice, but I guess not. Dad will help," she replied, obviously bothered that I hadn't come around.

With Tracy backing her up, I was beginning to feel like I was fighting a losing battle. If Tracy felt that strongly about Stephanie tattooing her head, then I knew it was probably going to happen, but that didn't mean I had to play any part in it and I wasn't planning to.

Anxious to enjoy our new surroundings, Valerie and I wandered over to the hotel lobby to explore the hotel grounds while Trace and Stephanie stayed back in the room to surf the web. As usual we had another day of balmy weather, although according to the national weather forecast a tropical storm was headed our way. We had been lucky the previous week when Hurricane Felicia weakened to a tropical storm, turned north and completely missed Hawaii. But now Tropical Storm Maka was on its way and we were determined to make the most of the sunshine while it lasted. After checking out the pool area and grabbing beach towels from the pool hut, we found two unoccupied couches in the shade halfway up an outside staircase on the south side of the main building with a beautiful view of the ocean. Happy to sit and read a discarded newspaper, I watched while Valerie flitted up and down the beach taking pictures of the tiny sparrows she found so interesting. Before long, Tracy appeared.

"Looks like you found a great spot," he said, admiring the koa wood couch with generous sage green cushions.

"Nice suit," I commented sarcastically as I took in the new electric blue swim trunks he had on.

"What? I just bought these. I like them," he answered defensively.

"They're a little on the bright side and a little short," I commented. Preferring the elastic waistband and the mid-knee length, Trace opted for comfort over style. I much preferred the longer style suit he had that went well past his knees—it made him look twenty years younger.

"They're not short and I like the blue," Tracy answered, surprised that I had a problem with his choice of swimwear.

"Well, if *you* like them...don't count on Stephanie hanging around when you have them on, though."

"She never hangs around anyway so these won't make a difference," he observed with a laugh.

"Too true," I agreed. "Here, have a seat." I nodded toward the empty couch positioned perpendicular to mine.

"No thanks. I think I'm going to go work on my tan. Does Valerie have sunscreen on?" Tracy asked.

"Yep, I loaded her up before she went out on the sand."

With her red hair, blue eyes and fair complexion, Valerie burned easily and the tropical sun was ten times worse. Being a redhead myself, I spent most of my summers growing up dealing with sunburns. Wanting to spare her the painful inconvenience of a nasty burn, we were especially diligent with the sunscreen.

"I think Steph found a good place to get her tattoo," Tracy said before he stepped away.

"Hmm, so you're really going to let her go through with it?" I inquired.

"It's looking likely."

"Fine. Just don't ask me to take her. This is between you two and I don't want to have anything to do with it," I said, realizing at that moment that I was officially giving up. *Great,* I thought. *Steph's getting a tattoo and I have a feeling it won't be her last.* Visions of her with full sleeve art on her arms and creeping up her neck made me slightly nauseous.

"Don't worry. I'll take her," Tracy assured me.

"Good, cause I'm definitely NOT!"

"Okay, I got it. Want to sit out in the sun with me?"

I looked out at several empty lounge chairs not far away. "No, I think I'll just stay here in the shade. I've had enough sun in the past week. You go ahead. What do you want to do later today?"

"Well, it depends on what Steph finds out. She's trying to get in somewhere today; that way her scalp will have more time to heal before we head back to San Jose."

"Well, Valerie and I are happy to hang out here and enjoy the ocean. I'd really like to get back to Tunnels Beach to snorkel one more time before we leave, though."

"Yeah, I'd like to get one more dive in before we leave, too," Tracy added.

"What about the Sheraton Caverns dive?"

"I checked and they have one dive trip leaving tomorrow morning. After that, they're not scheduling any because of the storm that's coming."

"Shouldn't you sign up for that one, then?"

"Yeah, I guess I probably should. I'll do that on my way back to the room."

"Okay, enjoy the sun. Me and my skin cancer will hang out here in the shade," I joked, half teasing. During the previous winter I had a chunk cut out of my ear that had basal cell skin cancer on it. All those sunburns as a teenager were starting to catch up with me and I didn't want to temp fate further.

Almost an hour later, Stephanie came walking down the tiled staircase to the nook I occupied, bikini clad, towel in hand.

"Have you seen Dad?" she asked.

"Yep, he's right out there in the sun on that lounge chair. Do you see him?" I asked pointing down the beach in his direction.

"Ah…oh, yeah. With the bright blue swim trunks?" she asked, laughing.

"Yes, don't you love those?" I asked rolling my eyes.

"Well, he's easy to pick out."

"That's for sure. So, what did you find out?" I asked. Now that I knew the tattoo was inevitable, I figured I might as well be civil about it.

"You really want to know?" Steph asked a little surprised.

"Sure, why not?" Whether it was the easy going island lifestyle or the fresh ocean breeze that made me change my tune I'll never know, but at that moment principles just didn't seem so important any more.

"Well, the best place on the island to get a tattoo is this place in Hanapepe called 'Farsyde Tattoo'. I called there this morning and talked to one of the artists. He said that I wouldn't want just anyone tattooing my head—I guess it can be difficult. The owner of the shop, Jared, has done scalps before so this guy said I should talk to him. It sounds like Jared is legit, but he's booked out a month from now."

"That's too bad. Did you leave your number?" I asked.

"Yeah, Jared is supposed to call me back on my cell when he gets in. He has tattooed one of the Dixie Chicks and the actor that flies on *Heroes*."

"Wow, that's impressive." I'll have to admit, a part of me was glad this artist was booked, but I didn't let it show. Maybe we would leave the island without a tattoo after all.

"I'm going to join Dad for a little bit," Steph indicated as she started walking away, cell phone in hand.

"Okay. I hope you brought sunscreen," I called after her, joking. She hadn't worn sunscreen since our second day on the island. Blessed with her dad's olive skin, Steph virtually never burned.

"Right," she yelled back and waved.

Content to watch the ocean waves and the tourists walking along the beach, I lounged in the shade, enjoying the time to relax and not worry about a thing. About half an hour later both Tracy and Steph came walking off the beach.

"What's up?" I asked when they got within earshot.

"Jared called back and he wants to meet with me," Steph blurted out, her eyes alive with excitement.

"I thought he was booked." I said, wondering how she had secured an appointment with the exclusive artist.

"He is, but I ended up telling him my story—he wanted to know why I had chosen my scalp to tattoo—and when he heard about my alopecia he said we could come in this afternoon."

"No way," I shot back, utterly shocked. "I guess you can schedule your dive trip for tomorrow morning, Trace."

"Yeah, I'm going to do that on the way back to the room. I don't know how long we'll be gone, but you and Valerie are okay to hang out here, right?" he asked.

"Are you kidding?" I answered indicating the beautiful alcove I occupied with my outstretched hand. "I'd be fine here for months! Go ahead. Good luck, Steph. Don't get anything too 'out there'," I warned.

"We'll be back later," she answered with a devious smile and offered no promises.

An hour later, Valerie and I headed back to the hotel lobby for the bracelet making class that was scheduled that afternoon. By the end of the class, hunger was creeping into the picture, so we finished our wooden bead bracelets and made our way back to the room ready to chow down on whatever we could make out of the strange assortment of leftover food we had transported from the condo. Valerie was happy with peanut butter and jelly on a tortilla. I opted for an apple, some turkey and a smashed brownie for dessert. After finishing our eclectic lunch, Valerie turned the television on to catch a new episode of *Suite Life on Deck*. Stacking up the pillows on the bed, I got comfortable with a book and was ready to wait it out until Trace returned.

It wasn't long before we heard the familiar click of the electronic lock. I could hear them talking as the door slowly opened. Stephanie appeared first. I noticed she still had her wig on. Interesting.

"So, what happened?" I asked.

"Jared is going to open his shop two hours early to fit me in tomorrow."

"Really?" I asked. "So you didn't get anything done today?"

"No," Tracy answered. "We filled out all the paperwork and Steph talked to him about what kind of design she wants. He's seems like a nice normal guy—no weird piercings."

"Does he have tattoos all over?" I asked.

"Not an objectionable amount. He has some up his arm and the back of his neck, but none on his face. He said he born in California, then moved to Kauai when he was five, got his first tattoo when he was 11 and moved back to California when he was 17 to study tattooing."

"How much experience does he have?"

"He worked in California for ten years, and then came back to Kauai in 2007 to start his business here, so I would say he's pretty experienced," Tracy assured me.

"That's good. So what's his shop like?" I asked, knowing the reputation tattoo places had.

"It's clean. They just moved not long ago so things are kind of jumbled but it was nice enough."

"What did you think of him, Steph?"

"He's great—real friendly. I looked through his books and he's done some really cool designs. His head is tattooed, although his hair has grown back and covers it so you can't see it. He said tattooing my head is going to hurt like hell. I told him that was fine."

"I'm sure you can handle it. I never worry about you and pain. So what time tomorrow are you going in?" I asked.

"Nine o'clock."

"And when does your dive trip start, Trace?" I asked, knowing what was coming.

"Ah…I have to be there at seven in the morning and I'll be back around noon…"

Nice. Just what I didn't want.

"So I guess that means I'll have to take Steph," I announced more to myself than to anyone else in the room. I certainly didn't want Tracy to cancel his dive trip. Not only would we lose the money, but with the storm coming, he wouldn't get another chance at the dive before we had to leave for home. As adamant as I had been about not getting involved in the tattoo saga, it looked like fate had conspired against me.

"You're going to owe me big time, Steph," I informed her.

"I know, I know. Thanks, Mom."

"Don't thank me until it's done," I warned. "I guess Valerie and I will go hang out at the Kauai Coffee Company while you're getting your tattoo. I wanted to go there anyway and it's not too far from Hanapepe. We could go to the swinging bridge, too. How long did he say it would take?"

"About two hours."

"Ouch. That's a long time to have needles stuck into your head."

"Yeah," Steph agreed but that didn't appear to bother her.

"So I guess I'll drop you off in Koloa early, Trace, then come back and take the girls to Hanapepe. Hopefully we'll be back by the time you're done."

"If you aren't, I can just walk back to the hotel."

"With all your dive gear?" I asked, knowing that the mile and a half to the dive shop would seem much longer hauling his fins, mask, booties, gloves, etc. at noon in the tropical sun with the island humidity reaching its peak.

"Sure! It's not like I'll have tanks with me."

"True." On one of his dives in Monterey, I had helped carry the heavy steel tanks out to the ocean—it would be a Herculean feat to carry one of those monsters over a mile.

"Looks like we have a plan. I can't believe I'm taking you to get your tattoo," I said to Stephanie, a little annoyed, but mostly amused at how things had turned out. Sometimes you just have to go with the flow.

She smiled.

Twenty-nine

HIBISCUS AND PLUMERIA

Several times during the night I woke, startled by horrific nightmares. First in the series of dreams, Stephanie contracted a dreadful ulcerated skin rash from her tattoo and was never able to wear a wig again due to the damage on her scalp. In another, she became addicted, which was what I feared, and was clad head to toe in hideous tattoos—proud of each and every one. It was a gruesome night. Wakened by the vibrating alarm on my cell phone, I was glad to know the fitful night was finally at an end, and quietly made my way in the darkened room to the bathroom. Listening to the comical snores erupting from the other side of our bed, I knew I hadn't disturbed Tracy. After showering and getting dressed, I woke Tracy and wandered over to the hotel lobby to retrieve the morning paper. As we left for the dive shop just before seven the girls were still fast asleep—Steph sprawled over ninety percent of the bed she shared with Valerie, leaving Valerie clinging to the side.

Within half an hour, I was back in the room waking the girls.

"Steph, Valerie. It's time to get up!" I called. There was no response, which wasn't surprising. Neither of them were morning people so getting up early, especially on vacation, was definitely not a favorite thing to do.

"Girls, come on. Get up. Steph, it's tattoo day!"

Hearing "tattoo" got Stephanie moving and, after a little coaxing, Valerie rolled out of bed also.

"I'm getting in the shower," Steph announced as she rounded the bed towards the bathroom.

"Don't lock the door. I have to go!" Valerie yelled after her. Ah, the joys of sharing one room.

A short while later we were in the car, heading to Hanapepe, which is billed as the "biggest little town" on Kauai with a population of just over 2000. Originally founded by Chinese immigrants who worked in the sugar cane plantations, Hanapepe is well known for its art galleries, quaint shops and gourmet vegetarian cafes, most of which were not open at 9am when we drove through. Choosing not to mention or dwell on the awful nightmares I had had the night before, I motored through town, anxious to see what kind of place I would be dropping Steph off at. Tracy had assured me it was nice enough, but he wasn't looking through my skeptical eyes. At the far edge of town, I finally spied the hand painted "Farsyde Tattoo" sign and was pleasantly surprised as I pulled into the gravel parking lot and gazed at the quaint yellow building with large picture windows.

To the left of the entrance was a small cement patio in the shade of the front portico, complete with an inexpensive wrought iron table and two chairs. Other than a lone scrappy bougainvillea vine climbing up one column, there was no landscaping to speak of. On the outside of the building, the only points of interest were three colorful hand-painted retro Hawaiian signs announcing "Farsyde Tattoo"—one a topless hula dancer discretely covered with a lei, the second a large red fish splashing in ocean waves and lastly a portrait of hibiscus and butterflies—all reminiscent of the 60's. As we entered the shop, we were greeted by Jared and his young female assistant. Between the hanging macramé and the rattan couch covered with a batiked throw, the shop had a bohemian feel to it. I tried my best to hide my prejudices and misgivings about being there, but I'm afraid my body language betrayed me. I couldn't help it. I was completely out of my element and did not feel comfortable. As a conservative mother of three, I was somewhere that I just didn't belong.

Jared sensed my hesitance and did his best to put me at ease. I'm sure I wasn't the first cynical parent to enter his shop. After talking with him for several minutes, I felt Steph was in good hands. Tracy was right—he seemed like a normal kind of guy. Jared's wavy brown hair, Vans, black skinny jeans and simple black t-shirt helped dispel my image of the typical tattoo artist. I guess I was expecting tight leather pants, lace up boots, a wife-beater T complete with exposed chest hair, topped off with a bleached Mohawk, or something along those lines. Jared was much more conservative than I expected. The place seemed clean enough, although Jared apologized more than once for the clutter, explaining that the shop had recently relocated.

"So what were you thinking?" he asked Steph with tracing paper and pencil in hand.

"I'd like a big hibiscus in the middle with plumeria flowers on the sides," she answered.

Jared's pencil immediately was in motion and in seconds he had sketched a delicate hibiscus flower with two pinwheel shaped plumeria on the right and one on the left surrounded by a framework of elegant vines and leaves.

"Something like this?" Jared asked when the sketch was complete.

"That's perfect," Steph answered, the excitement in her eyes confirming her approval.

"Nice," I commented, trying not to sound reluctant, but not ready to give a rousing endorsement. Even though I was warming up to the idea, I still wished Steph would just forget the whole thing and we could leave.

"Show me exactly where you want it," Jared instructed.

Immediately she took off her wig and pointed out the right side of her scalp just above her right ear. "This area," she said as she indicated an area about the size of her hand that covered most of the right side of her skull.

Even though Steph had been bald for three years, it still shocked me on the rare occasion that she removed her wig in front of someone else. It didn't appear to bother her to be standing there with her head bare.

"So, you know this is going to hurt, right?" Jared asked. "For some reason the strip down the middle of your skull doesn't hurt too bad, but the sides are excruciating and that's exactly where you want it. You sure you're up for it?"

"Yeah, I can handle it," she answered, with no visible apprehension.

"That's one thing we never worry about with her," I added. "Pain has never been an issue."

"That's good, because she's definitely going to be feeling it today," he said. "Come on over here, Stephanie, and we'll get started." We followed him to his station where she sat on a black folding leather table—which to my relief was hygienically covered with a roll of white paper—while Jared got his equipment ready.

"So, is it okay if we leave for awhile and come back later?" I asked before the process began.

"Sure, no problem," Jared answered. "It'll probably be a couple of hours before I'm done."

"Great. I won't be far and I'll have my cell phone with me. Bye, Steph. Good luck!" I called as Valerie and I dashed out the door.

"Let's go check out the swinging bridge," I said to Valerie as she got into the back of our white Chevy Impala rental.

"Okay." A couple of years shy of being a teenager, Valerie was still happy to go along with just about anything I had planned.

Yes, I was nervous about what I would find on Stephanie's head when we returned to the shop, but I knew the ball was in her court. I might as well make the best of my time and not waste it worrying about something I had no control over.

About a quarter of a mile down the road we spied the wooden sign, "Hanapepe Swinging Bridge," and pulled into the gravel parking lot. With just three twelve-inch boards across its base, the bridge was only wide enough for foot traffic. Composed almost completely of wood, the bridge spanned the slowly moving Hanapepe River. Originally built in 1911, the bridge had been rebuilt after Hurricane Iniki hit the island in 1992.

"I'm going all the way across this time!" Valerie shouted as she mounted the wooden steps and started running across the bridge. As she approached the middle, she grabbed onto both sides. With generous help from me, the bridge came alive. I jumped up and down on my end and heard Valerie shriek with each swell. With the bridge bucking and swooping, she had a hard time keeping her balance, but finally made it all the way across. On previous attempts when she was younger and smaller, her nerves got the best of her and she baled halfway. Not this time. When she returned from the other side, I gave her a high-five.

"Let's go find something for breakfast," I suggested.

"Good. I'm hungry!" Valerie answered, grinning from ear to ear.

Situated across the street was the Hanapepe Café. Never having been to Hanapepe to eat I was curious as we walked in the door. An interesting selection of baked goods displayed in a glass case looked appealing but nothing really stood out. Vegan cuisine appeared to be their specialty. While the cashier was busy with another customer, I took the opportunity to glance at their menu and decided that we wouldn't stay.

"Let's just go to the coffee place," I whispered to Valerie.

Just a few miles up the road in Eleele, we pulled into the parking lot of the Kauai Coffee Company Visitors Center. Composed of a gift shop, museum, outdoor tasting room and bake shop/deli, the small but adequate center was located on the edge of thousands of acres of coffee trees. If the colorful, beautifully crafted coffee sign wasn't enough to draw you in from the road, the exquisitely manicured lawn and landscaping surrounding the quaint green cottage was sure to. One of my must-see spots when visiting Kauai; I was typically rushed when touring the coffee center. That day we had time to kill and I relished the fact.

Passing through the retail shop, Valerie and I high-tailed it to the tasting room and bakery where we hoped to have a delicious breakfast. Valerie ordered a malasada—traditional Hawaiian donut with no hole— and I chose a scrumptious looking bear claw. With breakfast in hand, we picked a table on the covered lanai with a gorgeous view of the ocean and sampled several blends of coffee. With the breeze blowing through the covered porch and an unlimited amount of free gourmet coffee, I was in heaven. Valerie decided that even with three packets of sugar in the tiny little cups and lots of creamer, coffee just wasn't for her.

After I had had my fill of coffee, we took the self-guided walking tour around the building, which documented the entire coffee-making process from tree to cup. Although the coffee cherries didn't typically ripen until September, we did find some red berries on the trees and took pictures. The walking tour was very informative. From plant to steaming mug, I was amazed by all that went into producing a good cup of coffee

Finally we hit the retail store. Although the store was packed with unique Kauai gifts and merchandise, I managed to resist temptation and left with just one bag of coffee beans. Back outside, Valerie and I took more pictures by the fragrant blooming plumeria trees. With scrapbooking in mind, I had to get a shot of her sitting in front of the sign by the road. No trip is complete without one. Satisfied with the shot, I glanced at my watch and realized it was time to head back to Hanapepe.

I was certainly curious about what we would find when we saw Stephanie again. Rationalizing that my cell phone hadn't rung, I knew Stephanie was handling things physically, but what would her head look like when we returned? Maybe the skin would be so red and chewed that the design would be unrecognizable at first. Was it going to be one big scab or a field of blood? I knew virtually nothing about tattoos so I had no idea what to expect. Having just spent a relaxing couple of hours with Val, the closer we got to Hanapepe the more tense I became.

Finally, we arrived back at the studio. As I opened the door, the brass entry bell clanged. Once I passed through the front tiled hallway, I could see that Steph was still lying on the leather table. Jared was busy adjusting his equipment. Steph looked up, alerted by the bell.

"Hey, Steph. How's everything going?" I asked as I approached.

"Great!" she answered, as she sat up, grinning. If she had experienced much discomfort, she was doing a great job hiding it.

"How bad has the pain been?" I asked.

"Not bad at all," she answered. I could tell by how relaxed her face was that she was telling the truth.

"Really?" I asked in disbelief. Having pictured the whole process as one big torture session, I couldn't believe how relaxed she looked—like I had dropped her off for a massage.

"Yeah, it really hasn't hurt that much."

"Women put us guys to shame," Jared chimed in. "She's a tough one."

"Can I take a look at it?" Steph asked Jared.

"Sure. Here's a mirror," Jared said as he handed her a large mirror.

All the black detailing and shading was complete—the bones of the tattoo were there. As I inspected the 4" by 7" spot on her scalp that now had permanent pigment, I was pleasantly surprised by the simplistic beauty. Two hours ago, Steph's head was a blank canvas—which still had a tendency to evoke sadness in me. Even though after three years I was accustomed to seeing her without a wig, at times I continued to grieve for the loss of her long blond hair. Looking at her scalp now, I watched as an exquisite piece of artwork took shape. Jared had managed to capture the essence of her in this one image—his drawing was soft and feminine, but edgy and fun at the same time—almost like he knew her.

Jared was busy preparing new inks, so I took the opportunity to look more closely at the design. Besides the black detailing, the only other color he had used at that point was green. The leaves and vines were filled in and shaded. Marveling at the level of detail he used with shading, I saw leaves run the gamut from deep emerald to bright lime. The scrolling vines were highlighted in various shades of pine. Upon closer inspection I noticed little pools of blood forming on the areas he had most recently worked—this was not a painless process.

"Can I take a picture?" I asked Jared, not sure if he allowed cameras in the studio or not.

"Sure, go ahead."

With Jared's permission, I took a picture first of Steph lying on the table, smiling, enjoying the whole process. Then I took a close-up of the tattoo. Her skin was in good shape—just a little red with a few dots of blood here and there.

"All right, on to the flowers," Jared announced. Immediately I heard the sharp vibrating buzz of the electric machine and watched as his hand guided the tool over the flesh colored spots on her scalp, transforming the skin with a vibrant array of colors. Repeatedly driving needles in and out of the skin, the oscillating tool delivered ink at a rapid rate. The flowers sprang to life. Having been impressed by the shading in the leaves, I was blown away by the detail Jared put into each flower. Mixing varying shades of scarlet, orange and yellow, the hibiscus flower evolved into a seemingly three dimensional object as he worked. Each hibiscus petal became lifelike, appearing to dance in the breeze. As the needle passed over the same patch of skin for the second and third time, infusing color, I could see more puddles of blood form, which Jared was quick to wipe away with his gloved hands and sterile cloth. At that point, Steph had stopped speaking. By the way she was squeezing the pillow, I knew the pain was intense. The surface area of skin affected when coloring in the flowers was much greater than the skin under the black outline. Also, numerous passes were necessary to color each area. She was definitely in pain.

"We'll be waiting right out front," I announced. For the time being I had seen enough. There was nothing I could do to ease Steph's pain—she was going to have to stick it out, so I might as well get comfortable outside and enjoy the fresh air.

Valerie and I sat outside, where I enjoyed the breeze in the shade while Valerie amused herself by spinning in circles with her eyes closed—ah, to be eleven again. Both happy to be out of the studio for the moment, we relaxed and waited. With camera in hand, I used the opportunity to scroll through the pictures of our trip and delete any duplicates or unflattering shots. Being on the outskirts of Hanapepe, an occasional car drove by, but in general we weren't bothered by much traffic even though we were on the main drag.

About twenty minutes later I glanced in the big picture window and watched Steph get up off the leather table. Assuming Jared was done, both Valerie and I walked back into the shop, anxious to see the final product.

"Are you finished?" I asked when I caught Steph's eye.

"Yup. Will you take a picture so I can see it?" she asked. I could tell she was relieved that Jared was done.

"Sure," I said.

"She was a real trooper," Jared added. "Didn't complain once, and I know it was hurting. What do you think?"

Examining the new piece of artwork that now rested where Stephanie's bare scalp had been I was nearly moved to tears. Almost half of her scalp was covered with a colorful visual reminder of paradise. Sitting directly above her ear, the 3" orange and yellow hibiscus was the center of attention. Three smaller pink and yellow plumeria surrounded the hibiscus. The flowers were framed by swirling vines that ran from just above her right eye down to the base of her scalp. The design was young, fresh and beautiful.

How could I have been so wrong? Now without her wig, Steph's tattoo spoke for her, making a bold yet feminine statement. Jared's design was youthful, but timeless. Even in her later years I knew Steph wouldn't regret her design choice.

"It's amazing. You did a wonderful job," I answered, noticeably moved.

"Will you take a picture with your phone so I can send it to Lindsay?" Steph asked, anxious to share it with her older sister who was thousands of miles away in New Jersey.

"Sure. How do I work this, Val?" As usual, my kids were much better with the latest technology than I, so I waited while Valerie got the camera on my phone ready.

After taking his own photos, Jared placed two padded black drylock bandages on top of Steph's tattoo and reviewed after-care instructions with her. We were to remove the bandages in an hour and Steph was to stay out of the sun for the rest of the day. Once payment was made, we said our thank yous and goodbyes, got back in the car and headed for the Sheraton.

"Steph, it looks incredible. Do you like it?" I asked, astounded by how happy I was about the whole thing.

"I absolutely love it," she answered.

"How does it feel now? Does it hurt?" I asked, curious about any lingering pain.

"Not bad. I'm just glad it's over.

"It looked like it started hurting pretty bad when he was filling in the flowers," I said.

"It killed! When he was going over the same skin for the third time in a row it felt like my head was on fire."

"Yeah, I kind of thought so. He was wiping up a lot of blood."

"That was blood? I thought he was wiping away extra ink."

"Ah, no. That was definitely your blood."

"Ew! Well, at least it's over. I'm not planning on getting another one."

That was music to my ears.

"What about you, Valerie? Are you going to get a tattoo?" I teased.

"NO!" she roared. Seeing the blood and hearing the buzzing needle, not to mention seeing her sister in so much pain, was enough to discourage Valerie—at least for a few years.

Safe in the confines of the car for the first fifteen minutes of the drive, I began to worry as we approached the hotel. Sitting inside a car without her wig on was one thing, but walking from the car to the hotel was another. Poipu Beach was a pretty populated area. To get from our car to the hotel room, there was no telling how many people Steph would have to walk by. Racking my brain for a way around this dilemma, I was drawing a blank. I saw no alternative but to park in the lot and walk in.

"Do you want me to grab a towel out of the trunk to put over your head?" I asked as I pulled into the parking lot adjacent to our room.

"No, I'll be fine. Just give me a key," Steph answered. The confidence in her voice was encouraging.

"Sure," I said as I fished a key out of my straw bag.

Valerie and I followed as Steph got out of the car and walked ahead to the room with the black bandage on her bare head. It didn't seem to bother her—with her shoulders back and head up, she wasn't rushing. Thankfully our room wasn't too far from the car and although there were a few hotel guests wandering around, none of them openly stared at Stephanie.

"What do you girls want for lunch?" I asked as we settled in the room.

"I think I'll make a PB & J," Steph answered.

"Me too," Valerie said.

"Okay, you girls fix yourself lunch while I go pick up Dad. You sure you're okay, Steph?"

"I'm fine! Go ahead."

Not long after I passed the slightly dilapidated but always busy "Garlic Shrimp" truck on Lawai road, I spied Tracy with his scuba bag in tow trudging down the copper colored sidewalk. Ubiquitous on Kauai, the red dirt stained everything it came in contact with, especially cement. Happy to get out of the sun and humidity, Tracy hopped in the passenger side.

"How was the dive?" I asked.

"Great. We saw some cool fish and lava tubes. So, how does the tattoo look?" He was more anxious about what had happened in Hanapepe than in recounting his dive.

"I can't believe I'm saying this, but I love it," I admitted.

Hearing that welcomed piece of information, Tracy smiled, knowing he had been right to push for the tattoo even without my backing.

"Wow, really?"

"There's a picture on my phone if you want to look at it before we get back. Right now it's covered by a black bandage, but that's due to come off soon."

"Great. Let's see…" he said as he grabbed my phone and pulled up the picture.

A few minutes later, we returned to our room and found Valerie watching TV and Steph texting her friends—no doubt informing them of her morning activity. Disappointed about the bandage, Tracy couldn't wait to see Stephanie's tattoo up close. He wouldn't have to wait long.

"Valerie, it's just about time for that bracelet class in the lobby. Do you want to go?" I asked after I placed my purse on the dresser between the half empty wine bottles and nearly depleted boxes of crackers.

"Um, okay. When do we have to leave?"

"We should get going in a couple minutes," I said as I checked the time on my watch. "Hey, Steph, it's time to take the bandage off." I was eager to see the image again and see how her skin was doing.

All four of us crowded in the small bathroom alcove to watch her peel the bandage away.

"Hey, I want to see!" cried Val as we all squeezed in to get a closer look.

"Okay, here goes," she said as she carefully peeled back the black plastic. Thankfully, the gauze lifted away from her skin easily. Once again I was amazed at the beauty and precision of the design as I stared at the floral image above her ear. Fortunately the bleeding had stopped and her skin looked remarkably well--considering.

"Really cool, Steph," Tracy remarked after seeing the tattoo for the first time.

"Thanks," she answered, twisting her torso and trying to get a good look at the side of her head in the mirrored wall above the sink. "Mom, do you have a mirror?"

"I might in my make-up bag," I answered and grabbed my travel case off the counter. After rummaging through, I pulled out my blush which had a small mirror attached. Although the mirror was small, I hoped it was big enough to give her a better view.

"Guess this is the best I can do," I said as I handed her the compact. By angling the mirror into the light and reflecting the image off the vanity mirror Steph was able to get a pretty good idea of what her tattoo looked like from the side. The look of satisfaction that settled on her face was reassuring. After all, there was no going back.

"Steph, it looks incredible and I'm glad you got it. As much as I hate to admit it, I was wrong to fight you and Dad about it," I said as I hugged her from the side. I could see by her smile that it meant a lot for me to admit my error in judgment and be on board with her decision.

"You really like it?" she asked.

"Yes, it's beautiful. He did a great job. Just don't get any ideas about another one…"

Thirty

BALD AND BOLD

A re you ready, Valerie?" I asked as I grabbed some money from my purse to cover the cost of the jewelry class Valerie and I were headed to. Exhausted from his dive trip that morning, Tracy was looking forward to a relaxing nap. Knowing that her head was pretty sore, I assumed Stephanie would kick back in the hotel room for the rest of the afternoon since she was unable to wear her wig, but on a hunch I offered up an alternative.

"Steph, why don't you join Valerie and me and come to the class? I saw the beads they're using when I was in the lobby earlier and they're really nice. It looks just like something you would wear. I'll pay for it."

Knowing full well it wasn't the $5 fee that would keep her from the event, I waited as she thought about it. Not only would this involve sitting in the middle of the hotel walkway, bald, during the entire class, but to get there she would have to cross the gardens on our side of the complex, then the road that divided the property, and enter the main lobby and registration area. I wasn't sure I'd be up for it had I been in her shoes, but knowing her I thought there was a chance.

"Um…" she said as she considered the idea, knowing full well the exposure it involved. "Okay, I'll go. Just let me change first."

Wow, part of me honestly thought she'd never do it. Wrong again.

Never one to be subtle, Steph came out of the bathroom in a low cut, yellow tank top and short white shorts. If her head wasn't going to attract attention, her hourglass figure and island tan were sure to. I took another five dollar bill from my wallet, stuffed it in my pocket and we headed out. Let me just say, if you've never walked next to a bald woman, you've missed an inspiring moment. The path we followed through the hotel grounds wound around several beautifully landscaped gardens. Surrounded by a wide variety of tropical plants, from the deep velvety purple of Persian shield, to the red leaves of the tall croton plant, richly detailed with dark green and vibrant yellow highlights, we made our way across the complex. Lilies, hibiscus, anthuriums and orchids were all in bloom. For me, none of the vibrant flowers held a candle to the beauty of my daughter walking across the garden path with every inch of her bare head exposed. As I followed, I kept thinking she could be back in the room waiting for her head to heal instead of risking ridicule going out in such a public venue. That's where I would be. Determined that life wasn't going to pass her by for even one afternoon, she'd thrown caution to the wind and walked out the door. I wanted to clap and cheer for her and shout all kinds of proud mushy things that only a mother would say like, "Steph, you're my hero!" but instead I walked alongside her, trying to appear as relaxed and nonchalant as possible. She got nothing but admiring glances.

Finally we stood in front of the Hawaiian Culture Center tables in the courtyard just outside the front lobby. In various forms of Hawaiian dress, three women were stationed at the tables.

"Can I help you?" inquired a friendly woman who appeared to be in her mid forties. Her blond hair, blue eyes and freckles made it immediately apparent that she wasn't an island native, but judging by her inventory of jewelry, she knew a thing or two about beading.

"Yes, we'd like to make the seed bracelets," I answered, grateful that she didn't seem distracted by Stephanie's head.

"All three of you?" she asked.

"Yes. These are my daughters, Valerie and Stephanie."

"Great. I'm Mary. It's nice to meet you. Go ahead and have a seat and I'll get your materials ready."

Seated at the massive wood table, we waited while Mary prepared the items we needed. Looking at Stephanie as we sat enjoying the warm tropical breeze blowing through the expansive courtyard I knew this event was not about the bracelet for either of us. It was a test—how would the public react to a bald female? The first fifteen minutes had gone extremely well. I prayed that vibe would continue.

"We'll be working with these seeds," Mary explained as she spread a container full of variegated gray, white and cocoa colored seeds on the table.

"They're called 'Job's Tears'". I harvest them from a grass plant that you see growing along the roadside all over the island."

Smooth and cool to the touch, it was easy to see where the seeds got their name. Each bead was shaped like a teardrop ready to burst, with a pointed top and a full, rounded bottom. Fairly uniform in size, the seeds were about 1/4" in diameter across the widest portion and about that long. Mary handed each of us a double coil of silver wire with a small crimped loop on one end and demonstrated how to thread the beads onto the wire. Interestingly, when harvested and dried the seeds have a natural hole that runs through the middle all the way from the bottom to the top, making them perfect natural beads—no drilling necessary. Valerie, Stephanie and I got busy turning our plain coil of wire into wearable art that would remind us of our trip to Kauai for years to come.

"How long have you had your tattoo?" asked Mary once she saw we needed no further instructions.

"I just got it this morning," Steph answered with a smile as she maneuvered bead after bead onto the wire.

"Wow, it's beautiful. I love the hibiscus. Where did you have it done?"

"In Hanapepe at a place called Farsyde Tattoo."

"Oh sure, I've heard of it. They have a good reputation," she said as leaned over the table for a closer look. "I'll bet that hurt."

"Yeah, it definitely did," Stephanie answered.

"So, will your hair grow back?" Mary asked, most likely under the assumption that Stephanie had either shaved her head for the tattoo or had undergone chemo.

"No, I have a skin disease called alopecia that causes the body to attack the hair follicles, so my hair won't grow back. I usually wear a wig, but my head is too sore right now."

It was great to hear Steph be so frank about her situation.

"Wow, you look beautiful and that tattoo is amazing. I can see why you got it," Mary said, her new found respect for Stephanie evident. "When did you lose your hair?"

Instead of ignoring the elephant in the room it was refreshing to have someone unafraid to ask questions. Overhearing our conversation, the other two craftswomen came over and joined in. Stephanie didn't seem to mind the attention. Having lived in Hawaii for years, all three of the women had many tattoo tales, although none of them had any visible tattoos themselves. Stephanie told them an abridged version of her story. They were all impressed.

Soon our bracelets were finished and after thanking Mary for the opportunity we left the courtyard and headed back to our room. Relieved that things had gone so well, I was hoping that maybe Steph would come with Tracy, Valerie and me when we headed to Tunnels Beach later that afternoon.

"Aren't these bracelets cool? The seeds are so smooth," I said as we made our way through the lobby and out to the dead end road that divided the property.

"Yeah, I'm really glad I went," Steph answered as we walked.

Just as we crossed the road and headed up the stairs to the pavilion on the opposite side of the road, a young dad with his grade school son approached. Knowing how brutally honest kids could be I was apprehensive. Busy looking up talking to his dad, the boy finally caught sight of Stephanie's head as our paths crossed. *Uh oh, here it comes,* I thought.

"Whoa!" yelled the boy as loud as he could while stopping in his tracks and staring directly at Stephanie. You could hear him a hundred yards in every direction.

Being in the middle of the road there was nowhere to hide. I flashed a nervous glance in Stephanie's direction as we continued walking and wondered if this was when everything would fall apart. To my relief, as soon as the father and son were out of ear shot she looked at me and laughed as we continued along our way. Grateful that she wasn't embarrassed, I joined in the laughter.

"I'm sure that dad and his son are going to have quite the conversation," I whispered, knowing the dad was probably mortified. As parents, you do your best to teach your kids appropriate behavior, but sometimes situations come up that you aren't prepared for. Kids will be kids. Thankfully Stephanie realized that and wasn't upset.

Later that day, Steph once again didn't want to miss out, so all four of us packed in the car for the hour and a half drive up to Tunnels Beach. I don't know what I like about Tunnels more—the two mile stretch of beach, the huge half moon shaped reef full of tropical fish or the shade from the ironwood and palm trees—but the combination makes for a great place to spend the afternoon. With the sun setting to your back there is no shortage of shade bordering the sand, and with the extensive beachfront, it's never too crowded.

The previous week, we had spent a memorable day at Tunnels with the extended family. Tracy dove along the outside of the reef with my brother Ted, brother-in-law John, and their kids Matthew, Andy, Emily and Michael while the rest of us snorkeled and puttered along the beach. Tracy's sister Pam, my sister Terri and I enjoyed snorkeling on the reef together while all our kids were otherwise occupied. Following the schools of fish through the endless channels and tunnels we explored the crevices and cavities, amazed at the variety of fish and coral we saw.

Once we had seen about all there was to see, we made our way back to the shallow water. As the waves gently crashed, it was nice to have the flippers off and feel the smooth sandy bottom being drawn out from under my feet with the current. Pam joined her husband, Dick and their kids Sarah, Scott and Amy along with Sarah's boyfriend Ben up on the beach. Terri and I stood on the shore for awhile reminiscing about the last family reunion we had in Kauai while our mom was still alive. The highlight of that trip was an all day scavenger hunt—we had a picture of Mom "climbing" a coconut tree in an attempt to win. As we leisurely walked down the sand recalling how surprisingly competitive our loving, easygoing, unassuming mom got during our friendly family games, we stopped abruptly as a small white sand crab, about the size of my hand, sped sideways in front of us, motoring swiftly on the sandy surface.

"I've never seen a crab crawl sideways!" Terri exclaimed.

Although having seen many crabs myself, I had to admit it never failed to amuse me to see a creature scamper so fast sideways—like watching an animated cartoon. Skittering across the sand, the crab eventually ended up in the shallow ocean water. Floating in the mild surf, the white crab was nearly invisible, at least to the human eye. Within seconds I noticed a large triggerfish come swimming by. I was shocked to see the big black and yellow fish swimming so close to shore. Normally fish stayed out of the shallow water where the break in the reef was. With a wide channel of open sand under the water it was a perfect spot for snorkelers and divers to enter the water, but for fish there was no protection, so the fish generally stayed next to the reef. Occasionally a rogue fish would venture away from the rocks, but not too often.

On a mission, the triggerfish swam right up in the ankle deep water directly at the unsuspecting crab. Sensing danger, the small crab immediately raised its pincer claws above its head. Outweighing the sand crab by at least three times, the triggerfish made its first swipe at the crab. The crab dodged the attack with a quick sideways jerk, all the time keeping its claws raised, snapping them for protection. At that point I expected the tiny crab to make a hasty retreat in an attempt to save its life, but instead, the crab valiantly stood its ground, shifting quickly left to right, opening and closing its claws, ready for action. Like watching David defy Goliath, I couldn't help but root for the brave little crab, who against all odds was putting up a good fight. With each pass, the carnivorous fish dove in trying to catch part of the crab with its powerful teeth. Using its only defense, the crab continued to deflect the fish with its raised claws, knocking away the strong jaw that could so easily crush its shell with a strategic blow. Unfortunately, the crab was no match for the large fish and soon the triggerfish had severed one of the crab's legs. The crab was a fighter and continued the battle despite being severely wounded. With fresh blood in the water, in a flash the triggerfish was joined by several of his buddies and a feeding frenzy ensued. Within seconds it was over. The crab was torn limb from limb—obliterated. The fish returned to the reef. The only remaining trace of the crab was a small piece of leg that floated by. I stood frozen in place, shocked at the brutal attack I had witnessed. The water was now crystal clear, calm and devoid of fish, with no sign of the savage event that had taken place just seconds before.

When we rolled into the dirt lot at Ha'ena Beach Park around the corner from Tunnels about three that afternoon, I thought about that brave little crab. Excited to snorkel again, I was hoping I wouldn't witness another brutal attack like that, but one never knows. Out in the ocean it was survival of the fittest.

As was typical we had come through several downpours on our way through Hanalei, but the weather seemed to be clearing for the moment. Because of the rustic but functional bathrooms and fresh water hose, we always parked at the Ha'ena Beach lot and walked down the sand to Tunnels proper. Taking advantages of these amenities meant at least a five minute walk schlepping our beach gear down the sand, but it was worth it in the long run. Riding home with sand everywhere was never pleasant. As we unloaded, I was keenly aware of how long that walk would be for Stephanie without her hair. Although the beach was spacious, it was also very popular and there was no shortage of tourists that day. Steph got out of the car, grabbed the towels, a grass mat and headed down the beach. Valerie skipped ahead and Tracy and I followed with the snorkel gear and boogie boards.

Jared had instructed Stephanie to keep her tattoo out of the sun for a few days, so she parked herself in the sand under the palms and continued reading a vampire novel she had started the previous evening. Happy with her choice to join us at the beach instead of staying back in the room alone, I put on the snorkel gear and waded out into the ocean. Knowing that this would be my last snorkel excursion I hoped that the reef wouldn't disappoint. At first the water felt shockingly cold, but once my entire body was wet I acclimated quickly. Just as I was putting my face in the water about to enjoy the diverse underwater world, what I thought was a rock next to me began to move. To my complete surprise, I was nose to nose with a giant green sea turtle. Frightened by the large creature, I inhaled a mouth full of salt water through my snorkel and gasped for air. Panicked by the proximity of the giant turtle and the unpredictable swells that threatened to send me crashing into him, I stumbled backwards trying to get away with the unwieldy snorkel fins on. I didn't want to get anywhere near that giant frowning mouth and menacing looking eyes. Fins were great for swimming, not so much for walking. On my right I was blocked by the jagged coral reef complete with sea urchins and moray eels so I didn't have much room to maneuver. Just at the moment when I felt completely trapped in the shallow water, face to face with the turtle and nowhere to go, the turtle swam away. I breathed a sigh of relief, stood up and pulled my mask off. Observing from the sand on the edge of the water, Tracy had watched the whole encounter and found it quite hilarious.

"Did you see that?" I asked, breathless, standing in the waist deep water as the waves rolled in and the sea water poured off my body.

"Yes," he said, grinning. "You know they won't hurt you."

"Yeah, well, they certainly look like they can do some damage. Where did it go?"

"Over in that direction," Tracy answered as he pointed farther north up the reef.

"Okay, I guess it's safe. I'm going back in."

While I snorkeled, Valerie busied herself making a survivor shack out of the dried palm fronds on the beach. Carrying the heavy dried branches that were at least twice as tall as she was, she made an impressive shade structure by anchoring them in the sand and slanting the tops against a nearby tree trunk. Tracy had seen enough of the reef diving the previous week so he stayed out of the water. Steph was happy to sit under the trees in the shade and read. Fortunately the sun made a brief appearance. From the morning forecast we knew that might be the last we saw of the sun on the island. Satisfied with the amount of fish I saw, it wasn't long before I was ready to get out of the water and head back. Once again, words can't describe how proud I was of Steph as she walked past the various tourists and surfers on our long walk back to the car.

"Are you up for stopping at the Olympic Café for an early dinner?" I asked Steph as we traveled down route 560 towards

Princeville. One of our favorite stops, the Olympic Café, is a second story open-air restaurant that has great food, a cool island vibe and nice views of the ocean in historic downtown Kapa'a. At about the halfway point between Tunnels and Poipu, Kapa'a was a great place to stop, especially if we were hungry after spending a day on the beach. The Olympic Café had the perfect casual atmosphere for salty ocean hair and semi-wet clothes.

"Ah...sure. I guess so," she answered. Being bald on a beach several yards from probing glances was one thing; hanging out in a restaurant close to fellow diners was an entirely different matter.

"We don't have to," I assured her. "We can pick something up and take it back to our room."

"No, it's fine. I'm getting kind of hungry anyway."

"Okay, great. It's only five so the wait shouldn't be too long," Tracy added.

Before long we had reached Kapa'a and parked across the street from the restaurant. The downtown was bustling with traffic and activity. Catching a break in the traffic, we jaywalked across the Kuhio Highway to the restaurant entrance and climbed the stairs to the café. I breathed a sigh of relief that no one had honked at the sight of Steph's head while we crossed. Fortunately there was an ocean-side booth available when the hostess greeted us and we were seated immediately.

Soon our waitress came over—attractive, late twenties, hair in a messy bun. "Can I get you something to drink to start?"

"What's the coldest light beer you have?" I asked.

"We have these new Coors Light aluminum bottles that have a liner inside that keeps the beer extra cold. We keep them in a separate frig that's set very low. That's what we all drink when we get off work."

"Sounds great. I'll take one."

"Make that two," Tracy added.

"And what would you two ladies like?" she asked the girls sitting on the other side of the booth.

"Diet Coke, please," Steph answered.

"A Coke, please," Val said.

"That's an amazing tattoo," she commented after jotting down our orders. "Looks like a hibiscus…and…"

"Plumerias," Steph was quick to add.

The waitress was not shy about examining the tattoo, which I know made Stephanie feel more comfortable, although she didn't appear to be affected by being the only bald person in the restaurant.

"Very cool. How long have you had it?"

Even without knowing Stephanie's situation, it was evident that the waitress admired Stephanie's courage…if she only knew.

"I just got it this morning," Steph answered. From her smile I could tell Stephanie appreciated the inquiry.

"I'll bet it hurt."

"Yeah, it did. A lot. Especially where all the shading is."

"Well, it looks like it was worth it cause it's awesome," the waitress commented.

"Thanks!"

"I'll be right back with your drinks," the waitress said.

Trying not to stare at Stephanie sitting across the table with her deep blue eyes, expertly penciled brows, shiny beige lip gloss and beautiful shining scalp I was so proud of her I felt like I was going to cry but I managed to keep myself together.

As twilight approached we enjoyed our food and the ocean view. Just as the waitress said, the beer in the new aluminum bottles stayed nice and cold and went down easily in the warm humid breeze. Good food, great service, spectacular views and cold beer—what more could you ask for?

Stephanie sat through the whole meal, relaxed and completely at peace with herself, enjoying the moment. There was no indication in her body language that she was uncomfortable. An integral part of our conversation and laughter, Steph carried on as if it was nothing out of the ordinary to be sitting in a restaurant without her wig.

Driving home that evening watching the sun set in front of us we were all unusually quiet. Reflecting on the events of the day as I watched the last slips of light disappear behind the distant palms as we sped down the highway I marveled at Stephanie's new found freedom. No longer a pariah without her wig, she became the object of admiration with her new tattoo. I learned many things that day; most notably that even after 48 years I had the ability to be very wrong. I still had a lot to learn about life and vowed to be more open-minded in the future. However, most importantly, I knew at the end of the day that whatever the future held for Stephanie, that tattoo would help ease the way.

Thirty-one

SENIOR YEAR

My tattoo healed quickly and I was back in the pool in no time, looking forward to another water polo season. Unlike the previous year, which was a crash course in the basics, this season I was able to concentrate on speed and technique. With a lot of hard work I managed to earn my way into a starting position and became one of the leading scorers on the team. Between AP Calculus and Honors Physics, it was tough keeping up with my classes and polo, but I managed.

The girls on the team loved my tattoo—they thought it was really cool. Other than my family, they were the only ones who saw it on a regular basis. In the locker room I felt more comfortable taking my wig off now that I had something interesting to look at on my head. After games at the pool had always been an awkward time for me— everyone took off their caps and let their hair fall free. If possible, I would head to the locker room with my bag, change into my wig in privacy, and reappear with dry hair. Many times parents wanted to take a team picture after a game, which created a dilemma. Did I run to the bathroom and change into my wig, hoping that I could make it back for the picture, or did I stay and pose as the only one with a cap on? No one wanted a picture with caps—even wet messed up hair was better than that.

Now, with my tattoo, I felt comfortable putting my wig on poolside. So what if people saw my head? Instead of looking sickly, my head now was fashionably cool. Why not let everyone get a glimpse of the hibiscus above my ear? Sometimes the smallest thing can mean so much. Feeling free to take off my cap in public was liberating. It was great to have one less thing to stress about. It's funny how Mom fought me so hard about the tattoo. After seeing how it changed things, she now says if she lost her hair, she'd get her head tattooed. Go figure.

By the end of polo season I had athletic scholarship offers from Sonoma State University and Cal State Monterey Bay. Both schools were Division II, fairly small and close to home. They had decent programs and I liked the coaches, but my dream was to play for a DI school and maybe go out of state. I knew at some point I had a big decision to make about college, but in the meantime, basketball had started at Mitty, and Dad was insisting that I play my senior year.

"We think you'll really regret not playing basketball this last year, Steph, so I'm saying you have to," Dad announced at dinner, ruining a great slice of lasagna.

"That's so unfair!" I protested, slamming my fork down on my plate. "You don't know what it's like at practice. Coach is a maniac— we barely have a chance to breath the whole two and a half hours we're in the gym. It's so stressful. If you mess up on one of the plays, the whole team gets punished. All day I dread going to practice. I can't take it another year. Coach takes every minute too seriously—it's not fun. I can't believe you're going to make me do this."

"Steph, don't you remember how your season ended last year? How can you quit after that? Sue gave you the "Most Inspirational Player" award and now you want to leave? You finally worked your way into a valuable spot on the team. After all that hard work, how could you walk away?" Dad asked. He just didn't understand.

"Easy. It's too much stress and I just don't want to. I want my senior year to be fun."

"Sorry, Steph, but I'm not budging on this. We're paying a lot for you to go to Mitty and you're going to finish out the basketball season," he answered.

"I'm not hungry anymore," I said as I pushed my plate away and stood up from the table. "Can I be excused?" I asked Dad, glaring at him.

"No, you…"

"Let her go, Trace. She's not going to eat anymore," Mom said, trying to keep the peace between the two of us.

"Fine," Dad agreed and I raced up the stairs trying to put as much distance as I could between me and the man who was trying to ruin my life.

"Want to see my tattoo?" I asked Coach when I walked into basketball practice the first day, resigned to that fact that I had to join the team even if I didn't want to.

"Sure, Weed. Let's see it," Coach answered. Visible tattoos were forbidden at Mitty. I knew she probably expected me to take my sock off and show her something hidden on my ankle—that's what most kids did at Mitty to get around dress code if they really wanted a tattoo. Instead, I whipped my wig off in front of her and the team.

"Whoa, that is awesome!" Coach answered, shocked to see my bare head. It wasn't easy to surprise her, but I definitely caught her off guard. I knew she'd like my tattoo. Any teacher who regularly rode a motorcycle to school had to appreciate artwork like that.

"Nice, Steph!" Liz said. "Love the colors."

All my teammates came over to get a closer look. Predictably, they liked it, or at least they said they did. After a minute or two, show-and-tell was over and I stashed my wig in my bag, pulled out a bandanna and got ready to sweat.

Dad was right. I would've regretted not playing basketball my senior year, big time. We took home the league title, were CCS champions and made it all the way to the Nor Cal Finals in Arco Arena. A starter in every game, I was a valuable contributor all season.

During the season Cal-High Sports did a follow-up feature on me. This time around, I felt more relaxed during the interview and had no trouble expressing myself.

"I have a lot of fun with it. I get to switch my hair color up whenever I want and if we're going out on the weekend I can be brunette. I see it as a blessing in disguise. Showers are shorter..."

On Sunday, when the three-minute feature aired I got to hear what Coach Phillips had to say.

"She has a great disposition about her condition and I think she's a role model for anyone who is having to deal with adversity of all types…She's been an unbelievable blessing to this community on and off the court. She's such a pleasure to coach. Her energy is absolutely infectious to the group and inspiring to both her teammates and coaching staff alike."

Hearing such high praise from Coach was music to my ears. They included some footage of me playing as a freshman at Leigh with my hair almost gone. So much had happened since then—I didn't even feel like the same person.

Towards the end of the season I was awarded Scholar Athlete of the Year at Mitty for 2009/2010. With all the stellar athletes attending our school, I was extremely honored. That put me in the running for the CIF/Central Coast Section Scholar/Athlete Award. For the CCS award, I would be competing against athletes from 138 other schools in California for six scholarships—and there was money involved. After reviewing my essay, I was chosen as a finalist and interviewed by a panel of judges. A week later I received a letter from CIF/CCS:

> *"You join the five other fine student/athletes listed below*
> *as CCS Scholar-Athlete Award winners. We are extremely*
> *pleased and proud to present this award to you in*
> *recognition of all your accomplishments – in the competitive*

arena, in the classroom and in the school community.
As with all the fine candidates this year, you are indeed a
positive role model for your peers."

I couldn't believe I had made the cut. That meant $500 in the bank for college.

Coach Phillips also nominated me for the REACH Youth Scholarship. Sponsored by the San Jose Sports Authority, the REACH program "recognizes student-athletes who have overcome adversity in their lives to excel both in the classroom and on the playing field." I submitted the required essay and subsequently my parents and I were invited to an awards breakfast hosted by former 49er Ronnie Lott at the San Jose Marriott. As I walked into the Grand Ballroom I noticed the beautifully set tables with fresh white orchids and red Gerber daisies filling the expansive space. Orange juice in stem glasses sat waiting at each table along with a raised tray of delicious looking pastries and muffins. I couldn't wait to dig in. Along with Ronnie Lott, several other famous athletes were there, notably Brandi Chastain (Olympic Gold Medalist, women's soccer), Joe Cannon (San Jose Earthquakes), Bret Hedican (retired NHL player), Joshua Morgan (San Francisco 49er), Mike Ricci (San Jose Sharks) and my favorite, Ronny Turiaf (Golden State Warrior). Being in the same room with so many amazing athletes was awesome.

A brief synopsis of nineteen high school athletes' stories along with my own—our various struggles and successes—was noted in the folded color program at each place setting. After reading about some of the other nominees, I felt my life had been a relatively easy road. One basketball player lost both of her parents that year. Several athletes had battled cancer. In my case, all I had lost was my hair. My parents were still around and I was healthy. Wearing a bandanna was nothing compared to going through chemo and fighting for your life.

During the presentation, I was shocked when Brandi Chastain read a few paragraphs about me losing my wig on the basketball court and called me up to receive one of the eight awards they gave out that morning. I was given a $1500 scholarship for tuition at the college of my choice. By the end of the presentation, all eight of us stood on stage in front of the crowd of athletes, family members, administrators and friends, holding our certificates as the cameras flashed. I felt honored to be standing with my fellow athletes who hadn't given up when life got tough. Like me, I'm sure they all felt a little unworthy of the praise— athletes compete, that's just what they do. Sure we had more challenges than most, but give up? Never.

Whether deserved or not, I enjoyed the applause and had fun afterwards talking to the celebrities in the room. It meant so much for them to take time out of their lives to recognize our achievements. I knew if Dad hadn't pushed me into playing basketball that year, I wouldn't be at the Convention Center having breakfast with Brandi Chastain, Ronny Turiaf and the rest, and I was grateful.

In May I got a chance to pay it forward. Every spring for the past three years Mom had coached an after school girl's running club— Girls on the Run—at our neighborhood elementary school. With over thirty girls, the club was popular. For girls from grades three to five, the program was designed to teach them the benefits of exercise. In addition, they learned valuable life skills, like how to handle bullies, why gossip hurts, and how to stand up for themselves. Freshman year, while I was still at Leigh High School, I was able to help out with the club after school. With over thirty girls, Mom needed the extra hands. I loved running around the track and talking to the girls, encouraging them. Once I transferred to Mitty, because of my basketball schedule, I couldn't make it home in time to help with the club. When basketball ended, Mom asked if I would consider being a guest speaker and talk to her group about my experiences with alopecia.

"I think it would mean a lot to them to hear your story," she said. "I've been telling them to believe in themselves, think positive, and stand up for themselves. To hear what you've done would make it all seem more real, and convince them that a positive attitude really works. You'd only have to talk about ten minutes—I know they all would be interested. I'm sure you'd have their full attention."

"You really think they'd want to hear my story?" I asked, thinking all they wanted to do after school was run around and play games.

"I'm sure they would. Let me know which Tuesday or Thursday you can make it over to Guadalupe and I'll work you into the schedule."

"Okay, I'll do it," I agreed.

The next week I found myself standing in front of 36 antsy, energetic little girls in shorts and running shoes, all sitting on the blacktop waiting to hear my story.

"Hi, everyone," I said while giving a little wave after Mom introduced me to the group. There I was on the blacktop at my old elementary school giving a speech to kids half my age. It seemed like yesterday that I was running around on that very blacktop during recess, playing four-square, pounding the tether ball, shooting hoops. Although the playground was new, everything else looked pretty much the same. Offering welcome shade, the giant maple trees bordering the track were still standing tall. I had put a lot of miles in myself on the track around the upper grass field in the four years I was at Guadalupe. A lot had changed since fifth grade.

"When I was twelve, part of my eyebrow started to fall out..." I began.

One by one the girls lost interest in the person sitting next to them and turned their attention to me. It wasn't long before all eyes were looking in my direction and everyone was quiet. They listened intently while I told them about losing my hair and how hard that process had been. When I got to the part about my wig coming off in the game, you could've heard a pin drop. Throughout my whole story their attention never wavered. I concluded with:

"...the hardest part for me was when my hair was falling out. Now that it's gone, I'm okay with it. Showers are shorter. I can change my hair color any time I want. In some ways it makes my life easier. But I want you all to know that the biggest thing that helped me get through the toughest days was having good friends that supported me and had my back at school. Having their support made me strong enough to get through even the worst times. Without them it would've been so much harder. So, if you have a friend who's going through something really tough, you can help just by being there for them. The littlest thing, like saying something nice, might make a huge difference. You never know. Being a good friend is very important."

"Does anyone have any questions?" I asked signaling the end.

A few hands went up. I pointed to a little girl in front with red hair and freckles.

"Yes?"

"How many wigs do you have?" she asked.

"I have a lot of old ones in my closet, but I only wear about three right now. I have a dark brown one, this blond one and an old blond one I wear to work out in."

"How about you?" I pointed to a girl with dark curly hair in pigtails towards the back.

"Will you take off your wig?"

Mom had warned me about this. I had thought long and hard about what I would do if this question came up. At that moment, there was no hesitation. Even though I was out in the open, surrounded by my old classrooms and teachers, with parents still milling around, I pulled off my wig. They all kind of froze.

"Wow," I heard from a few of them.

"You can come up and see if you want," I offered, holding the wig in my hand.

With that, the floodgates opened and all the girls crowded around to look at the wig and my tattoo. They were fascinated by the webbing on the inside of the wig and how the acrylic hair felt. Some couldn't stop staring at my tattoo. Strangely, I didn't feel exposed. The girls were looking at me with adoration. I could see it in their faces. At that moment I felt like a true role model, and was glad I had taken the time to tell my story. These girls were so young and had so much of life left to live. If my story could help even one of them someday in the future, it was worth it.

Thirty-two

COLORADO STATE

Stephanie finished out her senior year with all the typical festivities: prom, senior cruise, senior dinner, graduation, and other celebrations. May was overloaded with one event after another. As I watched her receive her diploma I couldn't help but wonder, *where did all the years go?* This little girl who wore her Jasmine costume until it was in shreds, saw every rock she stumbled upon as a rare and special treasure, studied in fascination at the tiniest bug, had grown into a woman overnight. No more tricycles, Barbie dolls, or play kitchens. No more rides on Dad's shoulders when her legs got tired. No more falling asleep in my lap when she needed to recharge. Steph was eighteen and, whether I was ready for it or not, she was an adult.

Back in 2007 when Stephanie first lost her hair, there were two major concerns I saw for her future. First, I wondered if she'd feel comfortable enough to attend college away from home. Every time she walked in the door to our house, her wig was off within seconds. Although the wig wasn't that uncomfortable, after all day it got hot and made her scalp itch, so she loved having it off—like taking off your shoes at the end of a long day. Even with the tattoo, she still was selective about whom she hung out with bare-headed—just the family and a couple of girl friends—so living on campus somewhere would be challenging. There were several great schools nearby that she could commute to (Stanford, San Jose State, Santa Clara University), but I hoped she wouldn't miss out on living in the dorms.

Once Stephanie started considering colleges, I was happy to see having alopecia wasn't holding her back. In fact, living away from home was a priority. She looked at schools in Boston, Rhode Island, Maryland, Michigan, and Colorado, as well as schools scattered around California. Pretty much any school with a DI water polo team was of interest, with Colorado State being at the top of the list. With a 4.3 GPA and a 2040 on the SAT, she wasn't limited.

What made Colorado so attractive to Stephanie I wasn't sure, but after visiting Colorado State University in Fort Collins in the spring, her heart was set on attending CSU. She was accepted into the Honors Program there with an accompanying scholarship. That money, along with a Western Undergraduate Exchange (WUE) Scholarship, helped ease the cost of attending out of state. After spending a couple of hours with the water polo coach during our visit, she planned to walk on the team and hopefully earn her way into an athletic scholarship.

On August 18, 2010, Steph boarded a plane with her dad and three suitcases and flew to Denver to begin her academic career at CSU as a biomedical science major. The first couple of days were a little tough, but by the end of the week, she was loving life. Her roommate,

Lauren, was also a freshman on the water polo team and they got along well. Via Facebook I kept up with her college life. It was encouraging to see pictures of her surrounded by so many new friends, doing fun stuff—decked out in orange for the homecoming game, hiking in Estes Park, tanning at Horsetooth Reservoir, and just being goofy in the dorms.

"Are you nervous about someone coming into your room when you have your wig off?" I asked one weekend while we were chatting on the phone.

"No. The door automatically locks when it shuts, so no one can come in without a key," she answered. That was a blessing. Also, the fact that they had an ensuite bathroom helped.

"So, you're liking Corbett Hall?"

"Yeah, it's fun…get's a little crazy at night, which sucks when we have to get up at five for morning practice, but it's good."

"How's the food?"

"It's great. I love having a big breakfast after practice—you should see how much we eat."

From her reports, the water polo workouts were insanely tough, but she was hanging in there. It was official. She was a CSU Ram and had her nameplate on a locker to prove it: "S. Weed Water Polo". In late October they got their team sweats—with the arrival of the cold weather, those would come in handy.

"You won't believe it…they do our laundry for us!" Steph reported.

"What?" I asked. I knew athletes got perks like free tutoring, early registration for classes and access to the Academic and Training Center, but I had no idea someone did their laundry.

"Yeah, it's just our workout gear, but with practice everyday, that's pretty much all I wear. You put your clothes on a loop, send them in and they come back folded and clean."

"That's like having a mom at school."

"I know. It's great!"

As the semester progressed, I missed having Stephanie at home, but was pleased things were going so well. She was able to keep up with her classes on top of all the workouts and seemed genuinely happy. For Thanksgiving, she got seven days off. I couldn't wait for her to come home.

"I think I have my ride to the airport figured out," Steph let me know the day before she was due to fly out.

"That's good. Are you sure you don't want me to reserve the shuttle?" Fort Collins was an hour ride from Denver International Airport and for a reasonable fee there were shuttles that ran hourly from campus to the airport.

"No, I've got it covered. Oh, guess what happened to me last night?" Steph asked.

"What?" I couldn't tell by her tone if it was good or bad.

"Someone pulled my wig off at the Ludacris concert."

I couldn't believe it. "How did that happen?"

"Well, it was really crowded in Moby—the concert was sold out. Lauren, two other girls and I from our hall handed over our tickets at the door and went inside. I saw Amber and Caroline—they're members of the polo team—standing down in front next to the barriers by the stage. The concert hadn't started, so with the lights still bright they spotted us and waved us over to come join them. The floor was already packed, but we decided to try making our way over to them."

"It must've been pretty hard getting through the crowd," I said.

"It was. People were packed in tight. We got pretty far over, then we ran into this obnoxious group of girls, and things started getting intense. There was a lot of pushing and shoving going on."

"That doesn't sound good," I said.

"Yeah, I thought Lauren was going to slug this one girl who seemed to be looking for a fight, so I switched places with Lauren and put my back to the girl, separating the two of them."

"Uh oh."

"Yeah, as I was talking to Lauren, I felt a sharp tug on my head, and I looked down and saw my wig on the ground."

"No way! In front of everyone?" I asked. Having been inside the arena when we visited in the spring, I could just picture the standing room only crowd, wild with excitement, filling the massive venue to capacity.

"Yup, about 10,000 people."

"Wow! What did you do?"

"I picked it up and put it back on."

That didn't surprise me. "I'll bet you didn't even blush."

"Nope."

"What about the girl that pulled it off?" With my protective instincts roaring, I was hoping she had at least pushed the girl to the ground.

"She ran."

"I'll bet she got the shock of her life."

"Probably. The person she was with all of a sudden got all nice and concerned about me and asked what happened."

"One of the ones that had just been pushing you?"

"Yup."

"What did you say?"

"I told her I had cancer."

"You didn't…"

"Yes, I was pissed, but she caught me off guard and asked me 'what kind?'"

"Oh no. What did you say?"

"Well, the only thing I could think of was skin cancer, so that's what I said."

I couldn't help but laugh. Steph joined me.

"What? With all the diseases you're learning about in your human diseases class, that's all you could come up with?" She loved to talk with me about all the interesting sicknesses she was learning about that semester.

"Yeah, I know. Pretty lame, but it worked. She felt really bad that her friend had pulled off my wig and finally left us alone."

"I'll bet that girl never pulls anyone's hair again. That's going to stay with her for the rest of her life."

"Maybe."

"You probably weren't embarrassed at all."

"Not really. I just wanted the concert to start. Having my wig come off in public once every four years is more than enough."

"Was it really four years ago..."

"Yup."

I don't know what I would've done in Stephanie's shoes, but I'm glad she stayed for the concert and had a good time. Wishing I could get my hands on that girl and give her a piece of my mind, I had nowhere to go with my anger. Colorado was far away, the girl was long gone and the incident was in the past. The more I thought about it, though, the more I was convinced that the guilt the girl undoubtedly felt would be punishment enough. Maybe she'd become a better person. One never knows how far-reaching the consequences from one thoughtless act can be.

Thirty-three

AMORE

My first concern about Stephanie's future with alopecia had been put to rest the day she checked into the dorms in Colorado. A hard day for every parent when you have to let go, I was sad when she left our home but excited that she was ready to be off on her own. Without me there to run interference for her when her wig was off, she was doing just fine.

My second and perhaps biggest concern with her future: could she find a man to love her, baldness and all? She had dated in high school—gone to proms, homecoming, and parties. None of the guys at Mitty seemed put off by her alopecia, but she hadn't been in a long term relationship yet. That was a different story.

Every parent longs for their child to find a soul mate—someone who loves them for who they are, who's in their corner no matter what, who loves them through the good and the bad, who'll protect them whatever the cost. For Stephanie, this was going to take a special kind of man. Hair plays such a dominant role in our society's view of beauty and she has none. Of course I saw perfection when I looked at her. The smooth golden head and delicate ears were magnificent in my eyes, but was there a man out there who could see beauty in her baldness?

December 17th Stephanie came home for Christmas. She got ten days off. Classes were not in session for an entire month, but for athletes in training, vacations were cut short. Winter Training Camp at the Olympic Training Center in Colorado Springs started on December 28th, so she had to be back sometime on the 27th. It would've been great to have her at home for the whole month, but at least we had her for Christmas.

After being gone for several months, she had really changed. By the time she was a senior in high school, family gatherings had become an inconvenient annoyance that she tolerated to keep Tracy and me happy. Now, she looked forward to any event that involved the extended family. Wonderfully complimentary of my home cooking, she enjoyed dinners at the kitchen table and squeezed her friends in afterwards. Such a short time away on her own put things in perspective and made her appreciate all the little things we had done for her over the years. It was nice to feel wanted and appreciated.

All too soon, the ten days were over and she was headed back to the snow in Colorado and three weeks of three-a-days in the pool before classes began. Sometime in January I got a text from Stephanie after eleven one night.

"Check my Facebook status."

Already on my way up the stairs to bed, I reluctantly turned around and walked back out to the family room. Thinking it must be important—she didn't make a habit of texting so late—I sat down and rebooted the computer.

"I thought you went to bed," Tracy said from the recliner where he sat watching the news.

"I did. Steph wanted me to see something on Facebook."

"Ah."

Just then the screen came alive and I logged into my Facebook account.

After typing Stephanie's name into the search engine, nothing came up except the same pictures I had seen a couple of days before of her with her friends dressed up for Halloween.

"I don't see anything," I texted back.

"Check my relationship status."

I looked at the profile information under her name and saw the words "In a relationship with Luciano Trevor Holzmer".

"Nice! We'll talk tomorrow," I texted back.

"Okay. Love you."

"Love you too =)"

"Steph's seeing someone," I informed Tracy.

"Really?"

"Looks like it. Now I'm definitely going to bed," I announced as I turned off the computer for the second time that night. I was dying to know if this new guy was aware of her alopecia. If he was, that was monumental, but maybe it hadn't come up yet. The guys she dated at

Mitty knew she was bald because she wore a bandanna at basketball games. I wasn't sure how many people in Colorado knew other than her teammates, but I was guessing it wasn't very many. Regardless, I went to sleep feeling happy for her.

"So this Luciano, is he a nice guy?" I asked the next day when we spoke on the phone.

"Everyone calls him Trevor."

"Ah, okay. So I assume Trevor is a nice guy?"

"He is. A real gentleman. He's also really funny. We have so much fun together. I feel like I can be myself around him, you know."

"That's great! Does he know about your tattoo?" I asked, hoping she wouldn't think I was being too nosey.

"Yes. He thinks it's cool."

That was a relief. I had no idea how she broached the subject with him, but she had and he was still around. I liked him already.

On the bottom of the totem pole again, Steph's first season on the water polo team in Colorado was frustrating. Although she played occasionally, her minutes were limited. It was hard sitting on the sidelines knowing she could help. But she was willing to work hard, pay her dues and hoped it would pay off sophomore year.

She didn't have to wait that long.

In need of some fresh basil and cilantro for the pasta dish Valerie was preparing for dinner, I grabbed a shopping cart at the local grocery store and walked through the automatic doors, hoping to get in and out quickly. As I turned to the left in front of the lettuce, I heard a familiar sound coming from my purse. Having stashed my phone in my bag when I got out of the car, I frantically dug through my assorted paraphernalia, hoping I could locate the phone before whoever it was hung up. Finally, I found my cell—it was Steph.

"Hello," I answered. Although we texted just about every day, it was unusual for her to call.

"Guess what?" Steph asked, sounding kind of excited.

"What?" I asked as I continued on through the produce section heading to the herbs. I had a feeling whatever she had to tell me was going to be good.

"I just signed for a 50% scholarship for next year," she announced with pride.

"For water polo?" I asked.

"Yup. I signed the NCAA form today."

"Really? That's great!" The coach had hinted during the season that she was working her way into a scholarship, but you never knew. "So, all that hard work was worth it."

"I know. They're going to cover my books and fees too."

"Wow, that's even better! I'm so proud of what you did this year, Steph. I know it was hard working out and keeping up with those tough classes—especially since you weren't playing much. I'm glad you stuck with it and didn't give up."

"Me too," Steph answered. "It was tough, but I know next year's going to be better."

By the end of the second semester, Steph had found off campus housing and roommates for the following year. With a 3.5 GPA as a freshman, she earned an All-Academic award from the ACWPC.

"Trevor wants to come visit the end of May. He's going to stay for a week. That's okay, right?" Steph asked as the second semester was winding down.

"Of course," I answered, eager to meet this new person in Stephanie's life.

Plans were easy to make, but following through was something else entirely. I wasn't going to count on the visit until the ticket was bought.

"Can't wait to have you home," I said. With her being gone all year, I was looking forward to having her home for the summer.

"I can't wait to *be* home, and to make some money. I've already talked to my manager at Hot Dog on a Stick. She's going to give me some hours."

"Terrific! See you at the airport tomorrow."

"Okay. Love you."

"Love you too!"

By the end of the first week Steph was home, Trevor had purchased a ticket from Denver to San Jose. Although I had spoken with Trevor briefly while skyping with Steph, I still knew very little about him. All I knew was what Steph had told us. So far he sounded like a good guy, but I decided to reserve judgment until I could see for myself the kind of man he was.

"Hi Trevor," I said as Trevor walked into our kitchen.

"Hi, Mrs. Weed," Trevor said as he extended his hand.

"Welcome to California."

"I'm excited to be here."

"Well, I'm glad you made it. If you're hungry, Steph can make you something to eat. We're going bed, but make yourself at home. We'll have pancakes for breakfast." I gave Steph a hug goodnight. It was already one o'clock in the morning and we were all tired.

"Love you, Mom," Steph said.

"Good night," Trevor said.

"See you in the morning."

Over the next few days, it was great seeing Steph and Trevor together. They had fun up in San Francisco walking on the Golden Gate Bridge, driving down Lombard Street and shopping at Pier 39. Besides spending a day at the beach in Capitola, they were able to squeeze a trip into San Luis Obispo to see her newlywed sister, Lindsay, and Lindsay's husband Nathan.

Towards the end of Trevor's visit, I went on my daily run in the hills by our house. The hour that I spent running each day was time I used to clear my head and organize my life. Without the distractions of laundry, dishes, computers or phone calls my mind was free of the obligations of home and free to wander wherever I wanted it to go. Sometimes I simply enjoyed the beautiful area we lived in. Sometimes I prayed for friends and family. Sometimes I made elaborate plans for coming events that got more elaborate as the miles went by. That day I thought about Trevor. Although I had only known him for a week, I felt like I had a pretty good idea of what kind of man he was. He treated Stephanie with respect—seemed to always be looking out for her. You have no control when Cupid's arrow strikes your child's heart and can only hope that with the years you spent raising them, they make a good choice. Trevor was a good choice.

As I came in the front door when I returned from my run and walked down the stairs into the kitchen, I saw Stephanie, Trevor and Valerie all sitting together on the couch, huddled under one of my quilts watching TV. They were smushed together and enjoying the lazy morning. I stopped suddenly, overcome with emotion, as I saw Stephanie there without her wig. Trevor was gently massaging her bare head. I backed out of the kitchen quickly and stood out of sight while a tear ran down my face. She had found someone to love her without her wig or false eyelashes. He loved her as she was. It wasn't long ago that I wondered if she'd ever find a man like that and now one was sitting on our couch.

Alopecia hasn't held Stephanie back in any way; in fact, she stated in a high school essay, "It's arguably the best thing that has ever happened to me, transforming me into the fearless person that I am today." Whether she's brunette today, blond tomorrow or a redhead the next, I'm confident that Stephanie will handle whatever life throws her way. For those facing similar situations, she would challenge you to have the courage to be yourself. Courage is beautiful.

About the Author

STACY WEED was born in San Jose, California, and spent her childhood and young adult years in Northern California. She graduated with a degree in chemistry from the University of California, Riverside, where she met her husband, Tracy. An exercise enthusiast, she runs everyday, and enjoys encouraging others in her blog "You Can Run by Stacy".   www.youcanrunbystacy.blogspot.com